'A Time of Unhappy Commotion'

'A Time of Unhappy Commotion':

the Church of England and the people

in central Nottinghamshire

1820–1870

Michael Austin

MERTON

First published 2010

Published by
Merton Priory Press Ltd
9 Owen Falls Avenue
Chesterfield S41 0FR

© Michael Austin 2010

ISBN 978-1-898937-75-3

Printed by
Dinefwr Press
Rawlings Road, Llandybie
Carmarthenshire SA18 3YD

Contents

For David Leaning

and in memory of

John Murray Irvine

Preface

This is a social history of the Church of England in and near to Southwell in Nottinghamshire in the middle years of the nineteenth century. It tells of the Church as the notional religious defensive bulwark of a composite of political and social values and relationships which found its identity and its sanctification in the notion of 'Church and King'. It is the Church of England as by law established with its bishops as the Lords Spiritual being the First Estate of the realm, and with the parish church and the parson as its local embodiment. Inevitably it focuses on the clergy as a professional group in parishes, rural deanery, archdeaconry and diocese, representing and exemplifying these values and relationships both in the social roles that they played and in the religious ministry that they exercised. Early in Victoria's reign the Church of England offered the nobility and the gentry their religious justification as the enforcers of social control and the defenders of the integrity of the state.[1] The Church of England today is, sociologically, no more than one religious voluntary organisation among others, and, moreover, one of decreasing public interest and perceived value. This local and regional study offers some clues as to the origins of the social revolution which, in the space of much less than one hundred years, brought the Church of England from being the pre-eminent national embodiment of religious values and certainties to seeming, to very many, to be of little more than peripheral interest as one leisure activity among others. The consequences of its recent history for today's Church of England, the ways in which it is perceived and should perceive itself, and therefore for its mission, are as important as they should be obvious, but to explore them would require another book.

This book had its origin in the discovery in Southwell Minster's Historic Library of a notebook which records the visitation in 1855 by

---

[1] Much has been written which engages with aspects of this topic. There is no space to consider this literature here. Publications up to 1995 are comprehensively reviewed in the first chapter of Frances Knight's *The Nineteenth Century Church and English Society* (Cambridge, 1998). For the clergy as a professional caste in the early years of the period covered in this present book, see particularly W.M. Jacob, *The Clerical Profession in the Long Eighteenth Century, 1680–1840* (Oxford, 2007).

the rural dean, John Murray Wilkins, of the 23 parishes in his newly revived and reconstituted deanery of Southwell. This was a formal visitation, almost certainly in preparation for the primary visitation by the bishop of Lincoln, John Jackson, who had been appointed two years earlier. Wilkins visited each parish a few years later and amended his earlier record. An edited transcription of the text of the original manuscript, with Wilkins's amendments, is reproduced in the final chapter of this book.

The significance of this visitation lies partly in its date. Four years earlier the first and last official census of religious worship had been taken. The results had been published in 1854. They showed that the nation was not as church-going, or the Church of England as dominant a religious force, as very many churchmen had supposed. A growing, increasingly confident, and politically conscious evangelical nonconformity was justifiably seen as a threat to Anglican supremacy. In 1850 Pius IX established a regular diocesan hierarchy in England to replace the previous pattern of apostolic vicariates. This politically calculated move, following the secession to Rome of a number of well-known Anglican clergymen, further undermined the self-confidence of many in the Church of England.

The parishes in the deeply conservative rural deanery of Southwell were communities which, with two exceptions, had been largely untouched by industrialisation and social change. The pattern of social relationships, largely created and certainly dominated by the economic influence and legal and religious authority of the chapter of Southwell collegiate church and which were enshrined in its peculiar jurisdiction,[1]

---

[1] A peculiar jurisdiction was a parish or number of parishes exempt from the jurisdiction of the bishop of the diocese. There were several classes of peculiars: individual monastic peculiars, peculiars belonging to whole monastic orders, episcopal peculiars, archiepiscopal peculiars, cathedral peculiars, donatives, and royal peculiars. Southwell was a peculiar of the archbishop of York. That is, the right of the chapter of Southwell collegiate church, invested in the vicar-general, to exercise episcopal authority (except for consecrations of buildings or land, confirmation and ordination) in the 28 parishes within the peculiar arose from Southwell Minster having been the seat of the archbishop of York in Nottinghamshire since before the Conquest. Although the 28 parishes in the Southwell peculiar were in the diocese of York, until the peculiar jurisdiction was abolished in 1841 the archdeacon of Nottingham had no role in them. For example the vicar-general of Southwell and not the archdeacon of Nottingham conducted formal parochial visitations. In addition the vicar-general granted probate and issued marriage licences and exercised other significant civil responsibilities. The only authority that the archbishop reserved to himself, other than consecration, confirmation and ordination, was the appointment of the prebendaries and the right formally to 'visit', or inspect, the collegiate church to ensure that the chapter obeyed its statutes. Other than the still existing royal peculiars, peculiar jurisdiction was gradually abolished in the second half of the nineteenth century.

had lasted for many generations. Enclosures had had little direct effect on this pattern of relationships. Although the archbishop of York and the Southwell prebendal estates had been beneficiaries of the enclosure of wastes and common land, the incomes of the prebendaries, and of the benefices in their patronage, remained low. But what economic change could not effect, the law did. In 1841, under the provisions of the Ecclesiastical Commissioners Act of 1840, the collegiate church was disendowed and its peculiar jurisdiction abolished. Its prebendal estates were gradually transferred to the Ecclesiastical Commissioners principally to endow the newly created sees of Manchester and Ripon. As prebendaries resigned or died, no new appointments were made. Both locally and nationally these years were indeed a time of 'unhappy commotion' as George Wilkins, archdeacon of Nottingham, described them. This book tells of the impact of these radical changes on the parishes of central Nottinghamshire.

I am indebted to Brian Whitehouse, librarian of Southwell Minster Historic Library, to the Dean and Chapter of Southwell, to my former colleagues on the Southwell chapter, to Charles Leggatt, to the committee of Southwell and District Local History Society for a grant towards editorial costs, to Professor Stanley Chapman, to Garth Turner, to the staffs of the British Library, the National Archives, the Borthwick Institute for Archives, the Nottinghamshire and Lincolnshire county archive offices, the local studies library of Nottingham Central Library and of Newark library. I am very grateful to the trustees of the Aurelius Charitable Trust without whose generous grant the publication of this book would not have been possible. I have drawn on contributions I made to *Minster People* (Southwell 2009), edited by Stanley Chapman and Derek Walker. Any errors of fact or lapses of judgment are, of course, entirely my responsibility.

Michael Austin
Southwell
March 2010

Abbreviations
used in the Footnotes

BI	Borthwick Institute for Archives
CCEd	The Clergy of the Church of England Database, 1540–1835
d.	Deacon
LAO	Lincoln Archives Office
NAO	Nottinghamshire Archives Office
QAB	Queen Anne's Bounty
p.	Priest
SMHL	Southwell Minster Historic Library

Introduction
Truth and Transformation

Throughout the period from the end of the wars with the French to the 1870s many, perhaps most, Church of England clergy believed their church to be under threat.In 1832, in his first charge as archdeacon of Nottingham, George Wilkins claimed that in no period in the Church's history had it been 'beset by enemies more numerous, or more inveterate, than those who now on every side assail it.' In his opinion 'the judgments of God' had 'visibly commenced', for 'in our own, once happy country, cities, towns, and villages have suffered from the mad violence of the people, and our dwellings have been visited by calamity and disease'. It might well be, he believed, that 'the time of fiery trial' was near at hand.[1] This was not the first time that Wilkins had voiced this fear. In 1820 he had devoted a series of 14 lectures in Nottingham St Mary, of which he was the vicar, to the 'Refutation of Infidelity'. These were subsequently published in a volume of 299 pages printed 'in conspicuous type' by George Stretton, one of Wilkins's parishioners, 'upon such favourable terms as have enabled a considerable impression to be sold and disseminated among the lower classes throughout the Town.'[2]

Wilkins addressed the 'lower classes' because he believed that

> never, perhaps, was our Country nearer the dreadful precipice of revolution than at the commencement of the year;[3] never was it exposed to more inveterate or more profligate enemies – enemies who, aiming at the downfall of our Civil and Ecclesiastical Polity,

---

[1]   George Wilkins, *A Charge delivered to the Clergy of the Archdeaconry of Nottingham … at his Primary Visitation, in May, 1832* (1832), 5–6.

[2]   The lectures refuted infidelity in religion by reference to the entire Bible (incidentally, dating the creation, as was then generally accepted, at 4000 BC). Three of the lectures were prepared and delivered by his then curate William Shepherd.

[3]   Probably a reference to 23 Jan. 1820 when the Cato Street 'conspiracy' to murder Cabinet ministers was discovered and its leaders subsequently tried and executed.

> struck at the very root of all religious faith ... [These] wicked and
> factious spirits have united all their energies, not merely to excite
> distrust in the sacred cause of truth, but to hold it out to the lowly
> and uninformed as the engine of their oppression, and as the
> means adopted by their designing superiors, to bring them to a
> state of slavish subjection ... [1]

Wilkins was by no means alone in his fear that revolution was a present
threat. A few years later, on 15 July 1826, a young clergyman in
neighbouring Derbyshire, George Paulin Lowther, rector of Barton
Blount and curate[2] of Longford, had been even more pessimistic about
the future of the nation and the church, though for him the threat lay in
a different direction. On that day he wrote a letter describing the
alterations recently undertaken in Longford parish church, placed it is a
bottle and buried it beneath the new pulpit. He ended his letter:

> I feel strongly assured that when these papers see the light it will
> be under the hierarchy of the Roman Catholic Church which will
> doubtless gain the ascendancy in proportion as ignorance prevails:
> and I cannot help predicting the downfall of the English nation, as
> I fancy I behold in it all the signs of a declining state.[3]

In 1843 George Wilkins's son, John Murray Wilkins, preaching before
his bishop and fellow clergy, broadened the threat by asking whether the
Church of England was not in worse danger from within its own ranks:

> Is not our holy Zion not only attacked by open enemies and

---

[1]   George Wilkins, *A Course of Lectures in Refutation of Infidelity, delivered in the
Church of St Mary's, Nottingham* (G. Stretton, Nottingham, 1820), vii, ix.

[2]   Generally at this time the word 'curate' meant either (1) a stipendiary 'sole' curate, that
is, one appointed to serve a parish by its non-resident incumbent, (2) a deputy or assistant
to a resident incumbent (rector, vicar or perpetual curate, the latter being the designation
of the incumbent of a benefice augmented by the governors of Queen Anne's Bounty), (3)
a 'donative curate', that is a priest appointed by the patron of a benefice which lay outside
the jurisdiction of the bishop, or (4) a priest licensed by the bishop to serve a benefice to
which no incumbent had been appointed. However, in addition to the general, non-technical
sense in which the word is employed in the rubrics of the *Book of Common Prayer* (that
is one having the cure of souls of a parish), there were, in the nineteenth century, a number
of other technical meanings of the word 'curate'. These are set out in Felix Makower,
Constitutional History and Constitution of the Church of England (1895), 335ff. In this
book the word 'curate' usually carries the meaning in (1) above.

[3]   Quoted and cited in M.R. Austin (ed.) *The Church in Derbyshire in 1823–4: The
parochial visitation of the Rev. Samuel Butler, archdeacon of Derby in the diocese of
Lichfield and Coventry* (Derbyshire Archaeological Society Record Series, v, 1974), 3.

insidious foes from without, but by false and luke-warm friends within her pale, but is she not also in, perhaps, greater danger from 'those of her own household,' from our unhappy divisions among ourselves? – torn by dissensions and party spirit, harassed with ceaseless agitation, distracted with controversy.[1]

George Wilkins was no less alarmed about the future of church and nation when he delivered his visitation charge in 1859. He began:

> We live in a time of trouble – a time of unhappy commotion, unsettling to all that outwardly appeared to lead to the consummation of general peace; but now changed to a cloudy prospect, threatening heavy storms and direful conflicts. Wars and rumours of wars abroad, and religious dissensions at home, excite general agitation and perplexity; and it seems that our patience, wisdom and faith are about to undergo a trial of such difficulty, that nothing but a firm reliance on the grace and mercy of God can enable us to meet and overcome.[2]

Wilkins acknowledged that change was inevitable, but held firmly to the view that in threatening times the authority of Bible and church must never be undermined:

> In many instances we must admit that reformation duly and calmly considered has been attended with manifest improvement; for, undoubtedly, everything worldly and of the world being liable to change may, and does, from time to time, require readjustment. But not with regard to Christianity. Holy Scripture admits of no addition nor abridgement, for it knows 'no variableness nor [sic] shadow of changing'; and the doctrines which our branch of the Church Catholic has derived from this Volume of Inspiration, from the earliest ages, are those which are, and which always will be, one and the same.[3]

Much had happened in the forty years between the first and last of Wilkins's gloomy predictions. In many spheres of public and private life

---

[1]   J.M. Wilkins, *Unity and love essential to the making increase of the body of Christ: a sermon preached in the Collegiate Church, Southwell, Nottinghamshire, at the visitation of the Right Reverend John, Lord Bishop of Lincoln, on Saturday, 5 July 1843* (1843), 12.

[2]   *Newark Advertiser*, 1 June 1859.

[3]   Ibid.

the England of 1859 was very different to that of 1820. By the 1860s the Church of England was generally more efficiently managed than it had been a generation earlier; its clergy more conscious of their pastoral responsibilities; non-residence and pluralism had been significantly reduced; more benefices had parsonage houses; the clergy in many parishes were better paid; and the restoration of churches previously in poor condition had begun ('churchwardens' restorations' may be criticised, but they saved many neglected churches from demolition). New parishes had been created and churches built. This modest revolution was due to a number of factors: the energy of evangelicals and the sacramental discipline of the Tractarians within the Church of England and of a zealous and politically aware nonconformity outside it; an increasingly critical press; the rise of new professions which challenged the complacency and lack of professionalism of many of the clergy; awareness of the existence and expansion of the industrial slums; the challenge to faith posed by both radical theology and new scientific theories; and, by no means least, the attempts by Whig governments to bring a measure of reform to this seemingly obdurate institution. Neither Wilkins's nor Lowther's gloomy forecasts were fulfilled, but, despite this modest revolution, each correctly anticipated a loss of authority by the Church of England in national affairs and therefore of the loss of morale of its clergy.

Wilkins and Lowther undoubtedly spoke for the majority of Anglican clergy serving at a time when the old social patterns of rural economy were rapidly giving way to the new configurations of the first industrial nation. Critically, both believed that England was a Christian nation; that, by law established, the Church of England was the conscience of the state; that it alone held fast to the eternal truths, and that where the Church of England led the nation should follow. This almost theocratic (or at least theocentric) notion had never possessed much validity. Quite the contrary. Although Wilkins might wish that where the church led so society should follow, by the 1860s England was a burgeoning enterprise economy, and where enterprise led, the church eventually, and perhaps inevitably, followed. Peter Mathias argues that

> many theologies, Christian and non-Christian, have become associated with value systems favourable to enterprise, when the economic context has been favourable and the communal context of the group with the particular religious faith has nurtured such an economic role. This fact alone casts doubt on the importance of any single theology as the prime initiating factor in the constella-

tion of related variables.[1]

As we will see, the enterprise of local entrepreneurs influenced the
church profoundly. In and around Southwell families whose wealth had
been generated from commerce and trade were the public face of the
church – the Wyldes, the Bechers, the Lowes and the Barrows among
them. These were families who had made their money in banking,
business, industry and land. From them came a number of locally
powerful clergy. But it was in just this dependence of these families on
recent entrepreneurial fortune that the ambivalent relation between the
old traditional social patterns and the emerging new configurations can
be seen. Speaking of the new forces of capitalism that emerged after the
Civil War Tony Novak notes that

> Puritanism and the Protestant ethic were to be the cutting-edge of
> capitalist ideology – with their emphasis on hard work, abstinence
> and the view that individuals alone were responsible for their own
> destinies. But in this the new ideology had to take battle with
> established religion and morality, and its view of a static society
> in which people's position in the social structure was fixed by
> divine order, and in which property had obligations towards the
> poor.[2]

What we see in Southwell and its surrounding villages are a few leading
families that had made their money from the new capitalism and who
were driven by the conviction that people were responsible for their own
destines joining (or seeking to join) a traditional land-owning gentry
class with very different social assumptions. The clergy who came from
these entrepreneurial families were driven by the same protestant and
puritan ethic as their fathers but they clearly wished to enjoy, and to
reinforce, the traditional patterns of society. But the idea that property
brought with it obligations towards the poor sat uneasily with the notion
that men and women were responsible for their own destinies. This
'battle' between the new capitalist ideology and established traditions is
fought out just beneath the surface of the story that follows.

George Wilkins and his clergy, whether or not they were sympathetic
to the poor, saw the presence of Christ embodied in the old patterns of

---

[1]   Peter Mathias, *The First Industrial Nation: an Economic History of Britain 1700–1914*
(1969, 1978), 164.
[2]   Tony Novak, *Poverty and the State* (1988), 13.

social authority, and the voice of the multitude as necessarily antithetical to it. Ultimately it was a question of where the truth lay, and for them it was to be found in scripture as interpreted by religious authority, and in the social traditions in which that authority was embedded. In his 1859 visitation charge, Wilkins quoted the previous bishop of Lincoln, John Kaye[1] who had argued that

> Truth in matters of human science is elicited by the labours of successive enquiries – each adds something to the stock of facts which have been previously accumulated; and as new discoveries are continually made, the crude notions of those who first engaged in the pursuit are disregarded for more matured and more enlarged views, and in this case the most recent opinions are those most likely to be correct. But, in the case of divine revelation, this sort of process can have no place. Those to whom is committed the trust of communicating it to others are thoroughly instructed in its nature and its objects, and possess a knowledge which no enquirers of successive ages can improve.

Most church people, clerical and lay, accepted as self-evident that traditional social patterns had been determined by 'divine revelation', the communicating of which was entrusted to the clergy as those 'thoroughly instructed in its nature and objects.' They alone 'possessed [the] knowledge', and they possessed it as much by virtue of their social position as by their ordination. The clergy, in their catechising of the children of the parish before their confirmation, taught them to order themselves 'lowly and reverently' to their betters, and to do their duty 'in that state of life, unto which it shall please God to call me'. God did indeed 'order their estate.' Except, of course, it was only the children of the poor that were instructed to keep to their God-appointed and lowly place. The children of the wealthy were not. Thomas Mozley noted that in nearby Derby in 1820, his mother's friends 'laughed at the idea of children of respectable people being examined for Confirmation. They applied for tickets, and received them as a matter of course.'[2]

---

[1]   Bishop of Lincoln 1827–53.

[2]   Thomas Mozley, *Reminiscences chiefly of Towns, Villages and Schools* (1885), ii. 86. Mozley's evidence must be treated with some caution. Meriol Trevor says that Mozley's two volumes of reminiscences are 'full of tall stories, inaccuracies and nonsense', though this is a harsh judgment (*Newman: Light in Winter* (1962), 615). The practice of confirmation with or without a ticket seems to have persisted in Nottinghamshire for many years: notices in the local newspapers regularly gave readers a few days warning of where and when services of confirmation were to held.

Wherever one looks we see a Church only slowly coming to terms with a world the social and economic contours of which were rapidly changing. What this book attempts to do is to set an account of the Church of England in the parishes in mid Nottinghamshire in the mid nineteenth century in this wider cultural, economic and political setting, and to show that it struggled then (as it still does) to develop a theology radical enough to free it to find its role in a new world.

1

'They expect to be esteemed': the state of the Church in the 1830s

Contemporary opinions

There is little doubt that on the eve of the passing of the 1832 Reform Bill the Church of England was what was even then believed to be unprincipled by candid friend as well as foe. The state of the church in Southwell and the surrounding villages measured by the value of its benefices, the residence or non-residence of the clergy, the existence and condition of glebe houses, and the structural condition of the churches was significantly worse than in the county as a whole. The presence and authority of the collegiate church in Southwell was the major factor in the shaping not only of the Church of England in the area but also the economy and social relationships of this part of Nottinghamshire. The pervasive influence of the collegiate church made the perceived venality of the Church of England evident to contemporaries. In 1832 the admittedly hostile John Wade in his *The Extraordinary Black Book* described the Church in Southwell thus:

> The small collegiate church of Southwell has attached to, in the gift of the chapter and prebendaries, twenty-seven livings, amongst them several large and populous parishes: of these there are four resident incumbents, very few of them have any resident officiating minister, and almost all, if not all, of the parsonage houses have been allowed to fall into decay. The following particulars will exemplify the state of ecclesiastical discipline.
>
> In the gift of the Chapter:–
> 7 Rectories . . . . None resident
> 4 Vicarages . . . . One resident
> 3 Perpetual Curacies . . . . One resident
> 1 Chapelry . . . . Not resident

In the gift of Prebendaries:–

    11 Vicarages .... Three resident

    4 Ditto .... Believe none resident

> Many of these are held by clergymen living in Southwell, who are pluralists, and several of the curates also live in Southwell, so that the people of the parishes never see their ministers except on a Sunday in the pulpit. That they find Southwell more agreeable than living in a retired village is possible; but ought they not to remember that their duty is to visit the sick and afflicted, and to go about doing good. They are thus suffered to neglect their duty, and to let fall down their houses, because they are in the gift of the church, and yet they expect to be esteemed and their delinquencies overlooked.[1]

John Wade's criticisms were to the point, and in fact the situation was somewhat worse than his figures suggest. The residence or non-residence of the clergy was dependent on several factors: whether the incumbent was a pluralist and living in another of his benefices, whether he employed a curate in the parishes in which he was not resident, and whether there was a parsonage or glebe house fit for residence. In 1836 Robert Simpson, in his *The State of the Church in the County of Nottingham*[2] listed the 21 benefices in the patronage[3] of the chapter and 16 in that of the prebendaries. Of these 37 parishes, 30 were in the county. Ten of the 30 had no glebe house at all. Thirteen had a house that was described by Simpson as 'unfit for residence'. There was a house fit for residence (or at least held to be fit for the residence of a clergyman) in only seven of the 30 parishes. Therefore at least three-quarters of these parishes had no house for a non-resident incumbent or a resident assistant curate. Admittedly very many of the chapter and prebendal livings had small populations, but four had substantial numbers (as considered at the time) served by incumbents with low benefice incomes. The incumbent of the industrial village of Calverton, with a

---

[1] John Wade (ed.), *The Extraordinary Black Book. An Exposition of Abuses in Church and State, courts of Law, Representation, Municipal and Corporate Bodies with a Précis of the House of Commons Past, Present and to Come* (1832), 99–100.

[2] *The State of the Church in the County of Nottingham and Diocese of York compiled from authentic sources, with Hints for its Improvement*, published in London by Hamilton, Adams and Co., Paternoster Row, and in Nottingham by W. Deardon. Robert Simpson was to become vicar of Basford St Leodagarius in 1840. He is not to be confused with the Robert Simpson who was perpetual curate of Newark Christ Church at this time.

[3] For a note on the patronage of local benefices in 1855 see p. 66, n. 3.

population of 1,160 in 1831, received £127 gross a year and had a 'fit' house to live in, but the non-resident vicar of Farnsfield, with a population of 1,010, who received £165, had a glebe house which was described in the 1830s as 'a mere hut'. There was no glebe house in the village in 1855 though the population had increased. The glebe houses of what were rapidly becoming the industrial villages of Blidworth and Oxton, both held by the same non-resident incumbent, were regarded as unfit in the 1830s, and in 1855 were described as 'bad'. And this despite the passing of the Pluralities Act of 1838 which, if rigorously enforced, should have effected radical change.

Evidently, what classed as a parsonage fit for the residence of a clergyman was a house that suited the social status to which the clergy had only comparatively recently aspired. The archdeacon of Derby, Samuel Butler, during his visitation of Derbyshire in 1823 and 1824, would describe a glebe house as 'good' if, as for example at Brampton, it possessed 'two or three sittings rooms' and 'bedrooms and offices in proportion', with 'stable, coach and cow house.'[1]

Many glebe houses, built at an earlier time when the social status of the parson was not as high as it was to become, were of far lower quality. So, in his returns made to the Ecclesiastical Revenues Commission in 1832, George Wilkins described the glebe house or parsonage of his Lowdham benefice as 'a mere hovel ... let to a Labourer – for superintending the Sunday School', and of the glebe house of another of his benefices, Farnsfield, as 'a mere hut, consisting of two very small rooms and let to some Occupier for £3 10s. pr. ann. with a small garden.' Samuel Butler was Wilkins's contemporary. He demanded equally high standards. Of the glebe house of the wealthy benefice of Weston-on-Trent in Derbyshire, he noted that it was 'a bad, old rambling house', was 'in very bad repair', and 'occupied by a farmer: will not do for a clergyman'. Neither the incumbent (who was insane) nor the curate were resident in the parish.[2]

There were many similar examples in Derbyshire and Nottinghamshire. Although it is unlikely that in many cases incumbents (who were responsible for the maintenance of the parsonage house) had deliberately 'let fall down their houses' it is clear that in the majority of the parishes in the gift of the chapter and the prebendaries of Southwell in the early 1830s there was no resident clergyman exercising his duty 'to visit the

---

[1] M.R. Austin, *The Church in Derbyshire in 1823–4* (Derbyshire Archaeological Record Series, 1972), 53.

[2] Ibid., 177.

sick and afflicted and go about doing good.' The pastoral situation was little better in the county as a whole. Simpson lists the 251 benefices and curacies in the county recorded in the returns to the Ecclesiastical Duties and Revenues Commission which reported in 1835.[1] This number includes parishes in united benefices and those where the church was derelict or where there was no church at all.[2]

Simpson notes that there were in the county 152 glebe houses of which 106 were fit and 46 unfit for residence. There were no glebe houses in 67 benefices. Assuming the accuracy of these figures it seems that, as there were no houses for them to live in, there were no resident clergy in 45 per cent of the communities in the county. In practice the situation may not have been as bad as this. The law allowed that where there was no benefice house any house could be the legal residence of a clergyman provided that it was within the parish and less than two miles from the church. In fact, with the agreement of the bishop, a clergyman could be held to be resident if he lived outside the parish but sufficiently near to perform his duties, and that he lived in a house purchased by the governors of Queen Anne's Bounty.[3]

But it seems that these concessions were rarities in Nottinghamshire. Simpson lists 38 parishes where the benefice income was £300 a year and with populations of more than 300, and a further 41 where the population exceeded 1,000. In the first list three parishes had glebe houses that were unfit for residence (Lambley, West Bridgford and Weston-in-the-Clay), but in the latter list eight had no glebe house at all (Basford, Lenton, Mansfield Woodhouse, Misterton, Radford, Rudding-ton, Sneinton, and Sutton-in-Ashfield), and nine had houses that were unfit (Attenborough, Eastwood, Farnsfield, Hucknall Torkard, Lowdham, Selston, Stapleford, Sutton-on-Trent and Nottingham St Peter). Simpson noted that in all but one parish, Sneinton, where there was no glebe house, the incumbent was a pluralist, as were six in parishes with unfit

[1] This Commission, which was established in June 1832 to 'make a full and correct Inquiry' into the revenues and patronage of all Church of England sees and benefices 'with or without Cure of Souls', made its report on 16 June 1835. The Commissioners compiled returns of income based on an average of the three years up to 31 December 1831. Material in this report was used in the reports of the Ecclesiastical Commission, first appointed in February 1835, the remit of which was to inquire into the distribution of episcopal revenues and duties and to consider how cathedrals and collegiate churches (such as Southwell) could be made more efficient. This Commission eventually became the Ecclesiastical Commissioners for England, the present Church Commissioners.

[2] The archdeacon of Nottingham, George Wilkins, worked to a figure of 192 benefices in the county, including 44 united benefices.

[3] Simpson, *State of the Church*, 74.

glebe houses. Yet 12 of these benefices had received grants from the Queen Anne's Bounty commissioners to augment benefice income. Six of these 12 had also received parliamentary grants, and five had been augmented by private benefactions. The incumbents of benefices with unfit glebe houses were also entitled to payments for dilapidations. There was legislation in place in 1777, confirmed and amended by subsequent Acts, to provide parsonage houses, but, Simpson noted 'we have no one to put [these laws] into force.' If enforced, the legislation would have provided parsonage houses 'for a vast proportion of those places in this county which are now either utterly destitute, or have habitations returned as unfit for residence', yet

> in some instances, where *the Glebe house* has been unfit for residence, it has been taken down, and *one built in its place little above the rank of a barn!!!* so unwilling are *non-resident pluralists* to deprive themselves of a plea for absence. In other cases, the *Glebe house is illegally let to a layman, neither Incumbent nor Curate residing in the parish.*[1]

Pluralism, for Simpson, was indeed 'the ABOMINATION THAT MAKETH DESOLATE'. Of the Nottinghamshire incumbents, Simpson tells us,

> 80 clergymen hold amongst them 229 Churches and Chapels, in this and other counties; there [is] *one* Clergyman holding *seven* churches; *six* holding *five*; *fifteen* holding *four*; *sixteen* holding *three*; and *forty-two* holding *two* churches, besides *prebendal* stalls, and other *dignities*. These *eighty* clergymen have also *one hundred and forty-eight Glebe houses*.

And this despite repeated statutes since Henry VIII's reign[2] designed to curb non-residence. Though, as Wilkins and others[3] argued, some pluralism was inevitable given the low level of many benefice incomes, clerical pluralism had been prevalent since at least the thirteenth century with benefices collected and held in plurality by unscrupulous clergy. But the holding of sinecures was by no means confined to the Church. As

---

[1]   Ibid., 82.

[2]   Beginning with 21 Henry VIII c. 13.

[3]   For example, at his visitation in Derby All Saints in 1832, Henry Ryder, bishop of Lichfield and Coventry, regretted that the poverty of the clergy necessitated the continuing evil of pluralism. His successor, Samuel Butler, himself a pluralist when archdeacon of Derby, also accepted the necessity of the practice.

one example of many, in the eighteenth century the registrarship of the Commissioners of Excise carried a stipend of £450 but the work was carried out by a deputy who received a mere £30.[1]

What was good for the secular goose was evidently good for the clerical gander. If a gentleman, a layman, could obtain a substantial income for work that he could pay another a meagre salary to perform, an ordained gentleman might think it reasonable to do the same.

The radical press was quick to seize on this supposed evidence of corruption. When the Clergy Residence Act was passed in 1814 the *Nottingham Review* noted that the nation's 10,501 benefices were served by 9,703 incumbents of which 3,856 (40 per cent) were non-resident.[2] In 1823, in a detailed article on the extent of pluralism, the *Review* reported that 2,936 clergy held more than one benefice, and that 'one man, it seems, has thirty-four livings.'[3] Exaggerated or not, such reports increased public suspicion of the venality of the clergy. In 1831 the far from radical *Nottingham and Newark Mercury* published a letter from 'A Constant Reader'[4] who noted that the parish of Sutton-on-Trent, with a population of nearly 1,200, had no resident clergyman. The benefice was worth £400 a year with the non-resident curate receiving £50 – £60. 'The incumbent', the author said, 'has enjoyed the benefice 25 years … [but] has never visited the place.' The same correspondent noted that the parish of Weston, near Tuxford, 'has been held for many years by an overgrown Pluralist whose pastoral visits, happily for the parish, have been "few and far between"'. His curate lived within two miles of the parish. Thomas Hulse was the incumbent of Sutton-on-Trent, a parish in the gift of Sir Charles Hulse. He had been instituted in 1809 and, in 1831, held no other benefice.[5] In that year he returned his average annual gross benefice income to the Ecclesiastical Duties and Revenues Commissioners as £200, and paid his curate £65. In the same year the incumbent of Weston was John Cleaver who was also vicar of Edwinst-

[1] David Lindsey Keir, *The Constitutional History of Modern Britain since 1485* (1964), 327.

[2] *Nottingham Review*, 9 Sept. 1814.

[3] Ibid., 11 April 1823.

[4] *Nottingham and Newark Mercury*, 26 Nov. 1831. See also a letter from 'XYZ' in the same edition making similar comments about the parishes of East Stoke, Coddington and Newark.

[5] Thomas Hulse: Merton College, Oxford; d. 1805 (Oxford), p. 1806; BCL 1807; fellow of All Souls' until 1837; vicar of Sutton-on-Trent 1807–33; rector of Buckland until his death in 1853 (CCEd Record ID 34210; Joseph Foster, *Alumni Oxonienses*; Joseph Foster, *Index Ecclesiasticus 1800–1840*). Edmund Herring was his curate at Sutton-on-Trent in 1832.

owe and of South Leverton. Again, although the report exaggerates it illustrates popular perceptions of pluralism.

Robert Simpson was well aware of the 'sin' of pluralism. He quoted George Wilkins's letter to Earl Grey. On the subject of beer-shops Wilkins had argued that:

> It is impossible that any sacrifice too great can be made to arrest this growing evil, THIS *soul-destructive* plague, – THIS *pestilence*, – THIS *deadly curse*, which blights our atmosphere and spreads its baneful influence far and wide, turning a land flowing with milk and honey *into a wilderness of sin*.[1]

Simpson held that the sin of pluralism was ten times worse than that of beer shops.

The worst excesses of the practice were gradually removed by the Pluralities Act of 1838. George Wilkins was caught by its provisions when, in 1839, he resigned one chapter benefice, Farnsfield, for another, Hatcliffe in Lincolnshire. His reason for doing so are clear: Farnsfield was worth £165 gross, Hatcliffe was valued at £280, and, unlike Farnsfield, it had a 'fit' glebe house. This exchange infringed the provisions of the 1838 Act. In April 1839 Wilkins wrote to Joseph Buckle, the archbishop of York's registrar:

> I send you a duplicate Copy of the Declaration which is required by the Act 1 & 2 Vict: ch: 106. You will have the kindness to file the same in your Registry and to return to me a Certificate of the same – or I may forfeit my Stall at Southwell. Some *Clerical* Reformers and *Informers* have detected my omission to be re-instituted at St Mary's [Nottingham] after taking the little Living of Hatcliffe – by which St Mary's has lapsed to the Crown. The Chancellor is about to re-institute me to it, but at the expense of Hatcliffe, Lowdham and Wing!! That is more than half of my entire income is cut away by this very good-natured act of my reverend Brethren![2]

Wilkins remained a prebendary and retained all his benefices.

---

[1]   Simpson, *State of the Church*, 90, quoting Wilkins's letter to the Whig reformist prime minister Earl Grey, *A Letter to Earl Grey in the Subject of Ecclesiastical Reform* (Nottingham 1832), 31.

[2]   B.I., letter in Ord.P. 1839 John Murray Wilkins (Deacon).

Pluralism, patronage and privilege

Simpson's bitter criticism would have not endeared him to George Wilkins who, at the time, held six ecclesiastical benefices and to whose pluralism Simpson drew attention when he noted that the archdeacon could not possibly fulfil all these responsibilities, for 'if the *Archdeaconry* be properly attended to, the *parochial* duties must be omitted; and if the *parochial* duties be faithfully discharged, the duties of the *Archdeaconry* can never be fulfilled.'[1] Most of the 16 Southwell prebendaries in post in 1831 were not blatant pluralists by the standards of the day. In addition to their prebendal stalls, five held but one benefice, five held two benefices, four more held three, and one prebendary held four benefices. One prebendary seems to have had no other ecclesiastical preferment. Being appointed a prebendary of Southwell by the archbishop of York was regarded either as a token of favour, or, as George Wilkins believed of himself, a mark of merit.[2]

The income from prebendary assets was modest. The wealthiest prebend, Oxton the first part (or *prima pars*), had an average gross annual income for the three years to 1831 of £74. The poorest were Eaton, Halloughton, North Leverton and Sacrista, each worth £10 gross.[3] But what prebendaries gained, apart from status, were not only rights of presentation (each prebendary had at least one benefice in his gift, the prebendary of North Muskham had three and the two prebendaries of Oxton had four) but also options on the benefices in the chapter's gift. Collectively as a chapter the prebendaries had 21 benefices in its gift. This patronage enabled the prebendaries to bestow favours, not least on each other. As we will see, the two most powerful prebendaries in the middle years of the nineteenth century benefited greatly from the patronage of the chapter to which they both belonged. John Thomas Becher was appointed by the chapter to its richest benefice, Barnborough in Yorkshire, in 1830, and George Wilkins to the second richest, Beelsby in 1843. Objections were raised when Becher was selected for Barnborough. The senior canon felt that he should have been appointed, and complained to the archbishop of York, Edward Venables Vernon, as

---

[1]   Simpson, *State of the Church*, 53.

[2]   Wilkins's appointment as a prebendary was, he said, 'a feather of distinction conferred upon me as a reward, of what my Diocesan was pleased to call, merit' (George Wilkins, *A Letter to Earl Grey on the Subject of Ecclesiastical Reform* (1832), 18).

[3]   The total average gross income for the 16 prebends was £561. In the 1535 King's Books the total returned was just under £280.

Visitor of the collegiate church. Vernon instructed the chapter to determine 'what rule shall be observed henceforth in the disposal of preferments.' Fourteen members of the chapter met, established a rule, and all of them confirmed Becher's appointment.[1]

That prebendaries should have privileged access to the chapter benefices as they fell vacant was given legal force through the chapter's decrees: the chapter created the rules under which its members benefited. Despite Vernon's instruction in 1830, rules governing privileged preferment had been long in use. For example, in 1785 the chapter decreed that 'if any Prebendary should happen to be prevented by sickness or any other unavoidable Impediment from being present at a Chapter when a Living shall be disposed of, and that sufficiently proved, that such Prebendary shall not lose his option to such Living.'[2]

By 1800 it had become clear that this privilege was being abused. In that year the chapter resolved that

> No Prebendary having one Living in the Gift of the Chapter shall be presented by the Chapter to another Living until it has been offered to all such Prebendaries as are not in possession of any Chapter Living and been refused by them – But if any Prebendary is in possession of one or more Livings given to him by any other Patron, He shall not be debarred on this account from taking any Chapter Living.[3]

Five years later the chapter rescinded this rule, 'it appearing that it is contrary to the established custom of the Church, and that it was only intended to prevent one Prebendary from holding two Chapter Livings until all other Prebendaries had the option of accepting a vacant one.'[4]

George Wilkins, archdeacon of Nottingham, John Thomas Becher, the chapter's vicar-general, and Richard Barrow, a vicar choral, were significant pluralists. Wilkins had six preferments, including his arch-deaconry.[5] He was vicar of Nottingham St Mary 1817–43, prebendary of Normanton in Southwell collegiate church 1823–65, rector of Wing,

---

[1]   Richard Beaumont, *The Chapter of Southwell Minster: a Story of 1,000 Years* (Southwell 1994), 29–30.

[2]   NAO, SC/01/13, Southwell Chapter Decree Book, 1784–1814, 20 Jan. 1785.

[3]   Ibid., 17 April 1800.

[4]   Ibid., 18 July 1805.

[5]   His income from the archdeaconry was modest. The average gross yearly income in 1831 was £65, but the average yearly payments were £50, giving George a mere £15 a year from this source.

Rutland (a Crown benefice) 1827–39, archdeacon of Nottingham 1832–65, vicar of Lowdham 1815–39, and vicar of Farnsfield 1831–34 (exchanging this benefice for the rectory of Hatcliffe in Lincolnshire, both chapter livings). Wilkins had been vicar of Laxton 1813–15, having been presented to both Lowdham and Laxton by the first Earl Manvers. The second earl presented him to the wealthy benefice of Nottingham St Mary in 1817. In 1843, having resigned Nottingham St Mary, Wilkins was immediately made rector of the wealthy chapter living of Beelsby. Such patronage and pluralism were by no means unusual, and they made George a comparatively wealthy man. The total net value of the benefices held by him in 1865 (the year of his death) as returned by him and published in *Crockford's Clerical Directory* for that year[1] was £1,225 together with The Residence, the house used by the resident prebendary, that he occupied in Southwell. The average gross income for the three years to 1831 (as returned the Ecclesiastical Revenues Commissioners) of the archdeaconry and the five other benefices he held when the report was published in 1835 was £1,658. His gross income as vicar of Nottingham St Mary with St Paul was £755, or about 45 per cent of the total.[2]

The report of the Ecclesiastical Revenues commissioners in 1835 gives net benefice income (gross income less 'permanent yearly payments' such as land tax) and payments made to curates. Wilkins paid his curates between £70 (at Farnsfield) and over £100 (at Nottingham St Mary, where he paid his two curates £210 between them). An example of the income that a non-resident, pluralist, incumbent could receive was George Wilkins's benefice of Wing in Rutland, some 40 miles from Nottingham. His gross income from the benefice was £350, or £340 net after permanent yearly payments. His curate lived in the glebe house and was paid £80. This gave George some £260 a year from this benefice alone.[3] His total average net ecclesiastical income was £1,128, a

---

[1]   Note that in *Crockford* benefice values were notoriously undervalued by incumbents.

[2]   The report of the Ecclesiastical Duties and Revenues Commissioners gives only average gross figures for the three years to 1831. The report of the Ecclesiastical Revenues and Patronage Commission in its 1835 report gives gross and net income returns. These suggest that net benefice incomes, excluding payments of curates' stipends (by far the biggest outgoing for incumbents who employed curates), were, on average, about 3.75 per cent below the gross figure.

[3]   In the commissioners' report average gross benefice income figures include 'Arrears, if any', and the net income is arrived at after 'not deducting Arrears, if any'. It is difficult to interpret what this means in individual cases, and so these figures must be treated with some caution, but they at least provide a general idea of the sums of money that a non-resident incumbent could receive at the beginning of the 1830s.

reduction of 32 per cent from the gross figure. Little wonder that, in the late 1830s, he was described as 'a venerable pluralist and panter after prebends.'[1]

Given the very poor average net income received by archdeacons (£87 gross in 1835) many had no option but to be pluralists. Because of this an archdeacon had some relief from the provisions of the Pluralities Act 1838[2] relating to residence 'while upon his visitation, or otherwise engaged in the exercise of his archidiaconal functions' — not that George, with his several freehold benefices, needed this concession. This did not inhibit him from complaining in his letter in 1832 to the prime minister, Earl Grey, that 'as an Archdeacon, a Prebendary of Southwell, a Rector, and as holding *three* Vicarages, I am remunerated from all these, with a less clear income than that which arises from each of three Rectories in my Archdeaconry with populations under 400, or than that of each of two others with a joint population of 2000.'[3]

George Wilkins's benefices of Lowdham, Laxton and Nottingham St Mary had been presented to him by successive Earls Manvers. Wilkins's father, William Wilkins, had been estate architect to the head of the Pierrepont family, who since 1806 had been styled Earl Manvers. George therefore benefited from personal patronage, and he was to exercise it himself when, as prebendary of Normanton, in whose gift lay the appointment of the parish vicar, and subsequently the first rector, of Southwell, he appointed his brother-in-law, Morgan Watkins, a vicar

---

[1]   See pp. 161–2.

[2]   The scandal of pluralism caused the passing of this Act (1 & 2 Vict. c. 106). Under it no clergyman, other than those already with freehold benefices, was allowed to hold more than two benefices, and these were to be within ten miles of each other. Non-residence required a licence from the bishop, but exceptions were granted to prebendaries, vicars choral etc. of cathedrals and collegiate churches. When doing duty they were regarded as resident. Under this Act, too, the bishop could insist that two 'full services' should be conducted in parish churches each week. By the Pluralities Act 1850, the restriction on pluralities was tightened, so that no clergyman could hold two benefices except where the churches of these two were within three miles of each other by the nearest road, and the annual value of one of them did not exceed £100.

[3]   George Wilkins, *A Letter to Earl Grey on the Subject of Ecclesiastical Reform* (1832), 24. The 1831 returns do not bear out Wilkins fully, but the five benefices he may have been referring to were Averham (population 183, gross income £1,467), Bingham (1,738, £1,600), Gedling (2,343, £1,150), Plumtree (605, £1,113) and Warsop (1,280, £1041). Wilkins was urging reform of a system under which benefice income had no correlation to the size of parish. He himself, as vicar of Nottingham St Mary, was faced with a population exceeding 41,000, 'with two very large Churches'. He received £755 gross, half that of the vicar of Averham who had a population of 183. Of the five incumbents, only the vicar of Averham, the pluralist Robert Chaplin, employed a curate (at £82 a year).

choral,[1] to the post of vicar of Southwell in 1831, and his own son, John Murray Wilkins, to be the first rector of Southwell in 1840. He undoubtedly influenced the appointment of Morgan Watkins to the chapter living of Bleasby in 1837, and, as permanent residentiary canon, he appointed his nephew Henry Wilkins to the chapter living of Farnsfield in 1849, and Frederick Drummond Hay as vicar of Rolleston in 1865 — and Frederick Drummond Hay was a kinsman of George Wilkins's wife Amelia Auriol, neé Drummond Hay.[2]

John Thomas Becher (1770–1848) was not as unashamed an acquirer of benefices as George Wilkins. In 1799 he was presented to the perpetual curacies of Thurgarton and of Hoveringham, both of which he held until his death. He was also vicar of Rampton 1801–04, and vicar of Midsomer Norton in Somerset 1802–27. In 1818 he was appointed prebendary of South Muskham in the collegiate church of Southwell, and from 1827 to 1830 he was also vicar of Farnsfield (where he was succeeded by George Wilkins). As we have noted, Becher was presented to the chapter living of Barnborough in Yorkshire in 1830. In 1831 his then five preferments, including his prebendal revenues, produced £801 a year gross (with £640 coming from his benefice income as vicar of Barnborough in Yorkshire.[3] In 1830 he was appointed vicar-general of Southwell.

These examples show how rife nepotism and favouritism were locally. Yet, in his first visitation charge as archdeacon George Wilkins had inveighed against blatant partiality. Speaking of the giving of titles[4] to candidates for ordination 'where there is no need of them, and, what is

---

[1] Originally, each of the sixteen prebendaries employed a vicar choral to exercise his choir duties for him. By 1818 there were six vicars choral at the Minster. After the dissolution of the collegiate church the vicars choral became minor canons. In 1853, according to *White's Directory*, there were two minor canons. As noted in the 1855 rural deanery visitation return for Southwell St Mary, their duties were to conduct daily services in the Minster: morning and afternoon on weekdays, and in the afternoons on Sundays.

[2] Frederick Drummond Hay was the grandson of Amelia Wilkins's step-brother, Edward William Auriol Drummond Hay, and son of (Sir) Edward Hay Drummond Hay, successively President of the British Virgin Islands 1839–50, Lieutenant Governor of St Kitts 1850–55, and Governor of St Helena 1856–63. Frederick was born on Tortola Island, British Virgin Islands, on 6 July 1839, and married Elizabeth Ann Johnson (who had been born on St Helena) in Southwell in 1868.

[3] As to residence, on census day 1841 Becher, then aged 71, was living with Mary Becher (35) and Michael Becher (22) and six servants in Hill House in the Burgage in Southwell, while George Wilkins lived on High Pavement in his parish in Nottingham in a household of 14. George had moved into the Residence in Southwell by the time that the 1851 census was taken, having resigned Nottingham St Mary in 1843.

[4] A 'title' was appointment to a parish or other sphere of ministerial work, with an income, as a condition of ordination.

worse, where there is no intention of any permanent engagement', he said that this 'direct fraud' arose from the 'culpable wish to confer favours upon friends at the expense of the establishment.' Wilkins restricted his condemnation to that practice alone, but there is no doubt that he, and the chapter generally, did 'confer favours upon friends' when they exercised their patronage – a practice which was no less culpable.

As there were more clergy than there were benefices such direct nepotism, patronage of the clergy scions of favoured families, and the preferment of the Minster's vicars choral to benefices in the chapter's gift, would have been expected at the time. The family names and connections of prebendaries and of the incumbents of parishes in the gift of the chapter and of prebendaries provide further examples. Edward Garrard Marsh was prebendary of Woodborough from 1821 until his death in 1862. In 1848 his son John William Marsh was given the chapter benefice of Bleasby. William Becher (1741–1821) was E. G. Marsh's predecessor as prebendary of Woodborough from 1778 and vicar-general from 1795. He was also incumbent of the prebendal or chapter benefices of Calverton (1766–71), Cropwell Bishop (1766–71), Hatcliffe, Lincolnshire (1778–85), Farnsfield (1785–1821) and Waltham in Lincolnshire (1815–21), as well as being rector of Whissendine, Rutland (1771–8), rector of Cole Orton in Leicestershire (1778–1815), and rector of Whittington, Derbyshire (1796–8). He was succeeded there by his son Sherard (until 1811), who was a vicar choral in 1802, and also vicar of East Markham and rector of West Drayton (1811–52). When William's son-in-law John Thomas Becher, prebendary of Southwell and vicar-general, was appointed to the wealthy chapter benefice of Barnborough in 1830, he succeeded Henry Watkins (1743–1829), who had been rector of Barnborough since 1815, a prebendary both of Southwell (1774–1829) and of York (1773–1829), vicar of the chapter benefice of Waltham (1800–15), as well as vicar of Birstall (1774–1800), and of Conisborough (1770–1829) where he lived. Henry's son, also Henry (1775–1844), was vicar of Silkstone (1835–44) and of the prebendal benefice of Beckingham (1802–44) to which he had been appointed by his father who was prebendary of Beckingham in the collegiate church.

John Thomas Becher, vicar of the chapter benefice of Farnsfield in 1827, was succeeded there by George Wilkins in 1831, who was followed by his nephew Henry Wilkins in 1849. Michael Henry Becher, John Thomas Becher's nephew, became rector of the chapter benefice of Barnoldby-le-Beck in 1846, where, in 1861, he was succeeded by Morgan George Watkins. John Drake Becher (1806–64) was vicar of the prebendal benefice of South Muskham (1835–64) to which he had been appointed by his father, John Thomas Becher, prebendary of South Muskam. In 1858 John Ash Gaussen, within months of his marriage to John Drake Becher's daughter Mary Ann, was presented to the chapter benefice of Rolleston, where, when Gaussen moved in 1865 to Waltham in Lincolnshire (another chapter benefice) he was succeeded by Frederic Drummond Hay, kinsman of Amelia Wilkins. In 1837 Morgan Watkins, vicar choral and vicar of Southwell, became also vicar of the chapter benefice of Bleasby. His first wife, Henrietta (she died in 1832) had been the half-sister of George Wilkins's wife Amelia. Morgan George Watkins was his son by his second marriage.

A scion of another notable local family, Robert Henry Wylde, was to succeed Morgan Watkins as vicar of Bleasby in 1841, and was to follow his father William as head of the family bank in Southwell. His ordination papers illustrate the mutual loyalties of the local families. Wylde was made deacon by the archbishop of York on 3 August 1834 to a title at Rolleston where he was curate to the vicar Charles Fowler. He was paid £60 a year 'for his maintenance in the same' together with surplice fees[1] (which Fowler estimated at £2 a year on average), though Wylde continued to live in Southwell. Before his ordination he was formally examined by George Wilkins. On 31 July, just three days before the ordination, Wilkins wrote to the archbishop to say that, though Wylde 'only heard of your Grace's Ordination from me a few days hence', he had examined him as a candidate for deacon's orders. Wilkins certified that Wylde 'has answered the various questions in writing which I have put to him satisfactorily [and] has translated the Greek of the four Gospels where I have required and has written and translated Latin fairly.' At the head of the letter Wilkins added what was clearly the clinching argument in Wylde's favour: 'Mr Wylde is a steady young man the son of the wealthiest Gentleman in the County of Nottinghamshire, Mr Wylde the Banker of Southwell.'[2]

Wylde's local letters testimonial[3] were signed by Morgan Watkins, John Thomas Becher and Charles Fowler. Robert's great-uncle Charles Wylde (1747–1825) had been curate of Attenborough with Bramcote (1770–73) before becoming vicar of Nottingham St Nicholas

---

[1] The fees from marriages, funerals and, in some parishes, baptisms.

[2] BI, Ord. P. 1834, Robert Henry Wylde (Deacon).

[3] Canon 34 of 1604 required that before a candidate for holy orders could be ordained he must present to the ordaining bishop a certificate signed either under the seal of his Oxford or Cambridge college or one signed by 'three or four grave ministers together with the subscription and testimony of other credible persons'.

(1773–1825), and the pluralist incumbent of the chapter benefices of Rolleston (1802–25), Barnby in the Willows (1802–21) and of Waltham (1821–5). He was also prebendary of Sacrista in Southwell collegiate church (1798–1825) and a county magistrate. In 1783 he had been appointed deputy Official to the archdeacon of Nottingham, and became the Official (that is, the surrogate) to the archdeacon, Thomas Bevers, in 1791.

Robert Lowe, related by marriage to John Thomas Becher, was appointed curate of Oxton (where his family had substantial landholdings) in 1803, and became rector of Bingham (the richest benefice in Nottinghamshire) and also prebendary of Halloughton.

Ordained members of the local Clay and the Cane families were appointed to chapter benefices. Benjamin Clay (1763–1851) became absentee rector of Hockerton (1787–1851) where Richard Barrow served as his curate 1817–22. Clay was also rector of East Worlington in Devon (1796–1851). Possibly of this family, or of a collateral branch, was John Hall Clay, vicar of Blidworth (1794–1824), of Cropwell Bishop (1795–1824) and of Oxton (1806–24) all in the gift of the prebendaries of Oxton. He was married to Anna, a sister of Henry Watkins. Robert Cane (c. 1754–1802) was vicar of Bishop's Norton, Lincolnshire (1779–1802), rector of chapter benefice of Brigsley (1788–98), vicar of Barnby in the Willows (1798–1802), also in the chapter's gift, and a vicar choral of Southwell, where he died in 1802. His son, Thomas Coats Cane (1801–87), who had been curate of the chapter benefice of Woodborough, became non-resident perpetual curate of the prebendal benefice of Halloughton (1840–67) and vicar of the chapter benefice of Kirklington (1836–87), living at Brackenhurst. In 1831 he was also donative curate of Winkburn,[1] and, in 1838, J.T. Becher's surrogate as vicar-general. Further examples of this restricted but intricate interrelationship of church, family, fortune and patronage will be considered later.

The influence of these families extended into every area of social life and civil administration locally. For example, in 1818 William Hodgson Barrow was coroner of the soke or liberty of Southwell cum Scrooby, George Hodgkinson (whose family was connected to the Barrows by marriage and business ties) was steward of the archbishop's copyhold court, and the justices of the peace for the liberty consisted of four clergy, William Becher, John Thomas Becher, William Barrow LLD and

---

[1]   Variously spelled 'Winkburn' or 'Winkbourne'. The current spelling is the former, but both will be used here as in the sources.

William Clay, together with two lay magistrates, William Wylde (whose daughter Elizabeth was married to George Hodgkinson's son, also George) and Thomas Wright. In the same year George Hodgkinson Barrow (son of the vicar choral and pluralist Richard Barrow) was the chapter's registrar, receiver and clerk. He was also the clerk of the peace. For more than half a century the Becher and Barrow families in particular virtually controlled the affairs of the Minster, the chapter, and therefore the ecclesiastical and civil administration of the parishes in the Southwell liberty and peculiar jurisdiction.[1]

William Barrow (1753–1836) was vicar-general from 1821 to 1829 succeeding William Becher. He had been made prebendary of Eaton in 1814, and was non-resident rector of the chapter benefice of Beelsby in Lincolnshire (the second wealthiest benefice in the chapter's gift), and archdeacon of Nottingham (1830–32).[2] On taking the oaths as vicar-general he immediately appointed John Thomas Becher as his surrogate, empowered to act for him as circumstances demanded.[3] Thus, on occasion, Becher conducted the annual visitation of the benefices in the peculiar. In 1830, on William Barrow's appointment as archdeacon of Nottingham he was succeeded as vicar-general by J. T. Becher who appointed as his surrogates his son, John Drake Becher, and William Barrow's brother Richard Barrow, the long serving vicar choral and pluralist.[4]

Richard Barrow (1747–1838) was master of the Minster grammar school in Southwell (1774–1785), vicar choral of the collegiate church (1776–1838), and was, in 1831, pluralist incumbent of five benefices in the gift of the chapter or of prebendaries. He held at least eleven curacies or incumbencies in their gift throughout the 62 years that he was a vicar

---

[1] The liberty and the peculiar were not coterminous.

[2] William Barrow wrote *An Essay on Education; in which are particularly considered the merits and the defects of the discipline and instruction in our academies* while at Queen's College, Oxford. This was enlarged for its first publication in two volumes in 1802. The questions of the use of corporal punishment, the role of religious instruction, early education, the desirability of teaching the classics, and the merits of public schools as opposed to education at home are discussed. In the second edition in 1804 two additional chapters consider drama in schools (imprudent and likely to lead to adverse results, according to Barrow) and the state of English universities. Education, for Barrow, was a defence against the influences of the French Revolution which had 'done an essential injury to the sentiments and principles of the populace of Britain, by propagating … notions … incompatible … with the stability and permanence of all social order' (p. 372). Barrow was to be master of an academy in Soho Square in London.

[3] NAO, SC/01/29/A, Southwell Chapter Visitation and Correction Book, oaths taken 17 Sept. 1821.

[4] Ibid., oaths taken 7 May 1830.

choral.[1] On Richard Barrow's death in 1838 Becher appointed Thomas Coats Cane as a surrogate. In 1836 George Hodgkinson Barrow was succeeded as the chapter's registrar, receiver and clerk by his son, the 26 year-old Richard Bridgman Barrow.[2] In 1847 Wilkins complained to his bishop that 'Barrow' (evidently Richard Bridgman Barrow) aided and abetted the vicar-general, John Thomas Becher, in the management of the chapter's affairs[3] as, undoubtedly, had George Hodgkinson Barrow before him.[4]

These were the families the members of which had been archbishops' stewards, magistrates, clerks of the peace, overseers of the poor, bankers, solicitors, landowners, merchants, ironmasters, industrialists and members of parliament. Their names appear together on subscription lists for worthy causes, in the names of officers of the local militia, poor law guardians, justices of the peace, and in reports of those who attended balls, archery shoots and other social occasions.[5] Their unity was forged and their inheritances protected by business partnerships and by marrying into each other's families. These few 'Families of Independent Fortune'[6] comprised what Stanley Chapman has called 'Southwell's hereditary ruling class' and they lived in mansions as their status befitted them. In 1818, of the ten remaining (and, with one exception, 'improved' and 'embellished') prebendal houses in Southwell, mostly by then alienated from the church and among the best residences in the town, eight were owned or occupied by members of the Barrow, Becher, Wylde and Clay families.[7]

---

[1]   CCEd record ID: 43120.

[2]   When Richard Bridgman Barrow married Avice Elizabeth May in Southwell Minster on 2 Aug. 1836 the marriage was solemnized by his great-uncle, Richard Barrow.

[3]   LAO, Cor.B. 5/8/8/1, Wilkins to Kaye, 23 April 1847.

[4]   The mutual loyalty of the Becher and Barrow families was occasionally tested. In February 1851 John Drake Becher wrote to the Poor Law Board complaining that the master of Southwell Union workhouse had flown the flag of a Mr Barrow, one of the candidates at a local election. The master refused to take down the flag. Becher noted that the master and the children in the workhouse had been wearing ribbons in the same party colours. Such behaviour, Becher said, was inappropriate in a public workhouse 'supported by persons professing different opinions' (TNA, Poor Law Board, ff. 239–40).

[5]   For example, in 1841 the *Newark and Mansfield Times* noted that the Royal Sherwood Archers' third target shoot of the season had been held at the cricket ground in Southwell. It was attended by 117 people, including seven members of the Barrow family, four Bechers, and several members of the Wilkins and Foottit families. Thirteen clergy were named in the report (11 Aug. 1841).

[6]   *Nottingham Journal*, 30 Nov. 1776: from an advertisement for the collegiate church's grammar school by its master, Richard Barrow.

[7]   Richard P. Shilton, *History of Southwell* (Newark, 1818), 89ff.

Together these families formed 'a coterie, an inner circle whose dynasties were prolonged for several generations by the insularity of Southwell.'[1] They controlled the civil and ecclesiastical institutions of much of central Nottinghamshire, and, through their administration of the church's extensive estates, they determined the economy of the area. For these families there was no practical distinction between their civil and their religious rights and responsibilities. They exercised their patronage and reinforced their connections as much in the granting and renewing of leases as in their disposal of benefices. It was this overarching pattern of social assumptions which wholly determined the relationship of church and people.

Chapter patronage and the vicars choral

The preferment of vicars choral to chapter benefices was systemic. It was argued that the practice was less an indication of favouritism and more one of economic necessity. Pluralism and protection by patronage had been forced on the chapter due to the very low stipends paid to vicars choral, the very low benefice incomes of many of the livings in its gift, and their lack of parsonage houses. Each of the 16 prebendaries originally had his own vicar choral to fulfil his liturgical duties for him, but by at least the mid eighteenth century the number of vicars choral had been reduced to five or six. In 1764 the archbishop of York, Thomas Herring, held his primary visitation. He sent articles of enquiry to every incumbent or assistant curate in his vast diocese. Of the parishes in the chapter's gift, the incumbents of four (Farnsfield, Upton, Rolleston and, as its parish vicar, Southwell) were vicars choral. A further four (Edingley, Halam, Kirklington and Morton) together with the donative of Winkburn were served by curates who were vicars choral. But five vicars choral served all these parishes in that year: thus John Laverack, vicar choral (1742–79) and parish priest of Southwell, was also curate of Edingley (1752–68) and vicar of Rolleston (1759–68).[2]

Charles Fowler was vicar of the chapter benefice of Farnsfield (1760–75). William Leybourne was curate of both Halam (1760–78) and of Morton (1760–68). John Holmes was curate of Kirklington (1760–85)

---

[1] Stanley Chapman and Derek Walker (eds.), *Southwell, the Town and its People*, II (Southwell, 2006), 18, 33.

[2] He had also been rector of the chapter benefice of Brigsley in Lincolnshire 1744–59.

and of Winkburn.[1]

Edmund Crofts was vicar of the chapter benefices of Upton (1746–73), of Hawerby with Beelsby in Lincolnshire (1760–73), was perpetual curate of West Ravendale (1764–91), and was also curate of Halloughton (from 1761).[2]

What pastoral care these men could offer to the parishes they served is questionable. The case of William Leybourne suggests that they offered little. Leybourne was ordained deacon in 1748 and became curate of Bulmer in the North Riding of Yorkshire. In 1760 he was appointed a vicar choral of Southwell and was also licensed as sole curate of three parishes in the gift of the chapter: Kirklington, Morton and Halam. He resigned Kirklington in the same year and was instituted as vicar of the chapter benefice of Barnby in the Willows, some 15 miles from Southwell. Replying to the archbishop of York's primary visitation in 1764 Leybourne said that he could with 'great ease' exercise his ministry in Halam, and also in Morton, that village being only '2 small miles from Southwell' where he resided as a vicar choral. Leybourne resigned Barnby in the Willows in 1767 when he became sole curate of Wood-borough and, in 1768, also of Edingley. In that year Leybourne resigned his curacy of Morton. In 1773 he resigned the Edingley curacy and became vicar of Upton and also rector of Bulmer. In 1776 he became vicar of North Wheatley. In 1778 he again became curate of Edingley. In 1779 he was appointed parish vicar of Southwell. In 1780 he resigned Upton and was made vicar of Rolleston.[3]

Apart from Bulmer and North Wheatley each one of these benefices was in the gift either of the Southwell chapter or of individual preben-daries. Leybourne died in 1784 having remained sole curate of Wood-borough since 1767. His neglect of Woodborough led the churchwardens formally to present him (make complaint about him) to the Southwell chapter and to the archbishop of York, and, as a consequence, Richard Oldacres, the master of the endowed school in the village, was ordained and, in 1774, made stipendiary assistant curate at Leybourne's expense.[4]

---

[1] He was to be vicar of Rolleston (1768–76), vicar of Farnsfield (1775–85) and rector of Beelsby in Lincolnshire (1779–85). He had been curate of Rampton (1759–61). It is of interest that the donative curate of Winkburn, Samuel Abson (also vicar of Eakring and residing there) felt obliged to make a return to the archbishop. He paid John Holmes £15 a year.

[2] He had been rector of the chapter benefice of Hatcliffe (1755–60).

[3] CCEd, Person ID 88689.

[4] CCEd, Record ID 301603; Walter Edward Buckland, *The History of Woodborough and the Prebendal Church of Woodborough in the Peculiar of Southwell* (1897), ch. 8.

Vicars choral had been following each other as incumbents or curates of each of these parishes, and others, for centuries, serving simultaneously as incumbents of some parishes and as curates of others. Yet without them the small parishes near to Southwell would not have had even minimal pastoral care and opportunities for worship. These benefices were among the poorest in the county: in 1831 Edingley was worth £51, Halam £85, Bleasby £107, Kirklington £49, Morton £81, Upton £91, and Woodborough £93. Halloughton, the poorest of the 16 benefices, produced £46 a year for its incumbent. In 1831 only five of the 21 chapter benefices had glebe houses, and none of its local parishes could house a resident parson. The wealthiest of the local benefices in the chapter's gift, Rolleston, worth £246 a year, had no glebe house but was clearly a prize. In 1764 John Laverack, the vicar choral who was also the parish vicar of Southwell, had secured it. Vicars choral, whose duties required their daily attendance in Southwell Minster, seem rarely to have been appointed to the more distant, wealthier, chapter benefices. The exception was, inevitably, the well-connected Richard Barrow.

Richard Shilton gives us the names of the vicars choral in 1818. They were: Richard Barrow (from 1774 until his death in 1838), William Bristoe or Bristowe (from 1779 until his death in 1818), James Foottit, also schoolmaster (1812), Charles Fowler (1780 until his death in 1840), Henry Houson (1782, and parish vicar from 1784 until his death in 1831), and Houson's son, also Henry (1813).[1]

In 1831 the vicars choral were: Thomas Still Basnett, Richard Barrow, James Foottit, Charles Fowler, Robert Hodgson Fowler and Morgan Watkins. Except for Morgan Watkins, the vicar choral appointed to be vicar of the parish and who was paid £144, each received £25 a year from the chapter, a stipend that had remained unchanged for many years.[2] This was about a third of the average salary paid to a curate in the county. Evidently the chapter could not recruit vicars choral unless it could augment their meagre incomes from other sources. As had been reported to Thomas Herring nearly a century earlier this was easily provided by appointing them as non-resident incumbents to parishes in the chapter's gift. In 1831 all six vicars choral held, or were to hold,

---

[1]   Richard Shilton, *History of Southwell* (1818), 109–10; death notices etc.

[2]   Robert Simpson, *The State of the Church in the County of Nottingham* (1836), 18. Several vicars choral served for very many years in addition to holding benefices. This was because, for £25 a year, recruiting vicars choral was very difficult. In consequence, in 1776 it was decreed by the chapter that, on appointment, vicars choral were to enter into a bond of £500 to be forfeited if they resigned while retaining other preferments. (cited in R. M. Beaumont, *The Chapter of Southwell Minster: a Story of 1000 years* (Southwell, revised ed. 1994), 27).

benefices in the county and beyond. Richard Barrow was then rector of Barnoldby le Beck in Lincolnshire, perpetual curate of Halloughton, rector of South Wheatley, vicar of Rampton and vicar of South Muskham, all in the gift of the chapter or of individual prebendaries.[1] James Foottit was vicar of Barnby in the Willows and vicar of Upton and was to become vicar of Farnsfield, Charles Fowler the younger was perpetual curate both of Morton and of Woodborough and vicar of Bleasby and of Rolleston, and Robert Hodgson Fowler was perpetual curate of Edingley and also of Kirklington, rector of Brigsley in Lincolnshire and was to become vicar of Rolleston. In the early nineteenth century vicars choral succeeded each other at Rolleston: Richard Barrow became its incumbent in 1784, Charles Fowler sen. in 1785, Thomas Still Basnett in 1840, and Robert Hodgson Fowler in 1841.[2]

Sons frequently followed their fathers as vicars choral. The father of Charles Fowler (c. 1758–1840), also Charles (1729–78), was the son of Francis, a Nottingham mercer. He was born in Southwell, educated at the collegiate school and at St John's College, Cambridge. Having been the curate of East Stoke with Syerston (1750) and of Hockerton (1752) he was appointed a vicar choral in 1753, curate of Kirklington (1755–60), vicar of Farnsfield (1760–75), rector of Hatcliffe (1760–78), curate of Morton (1768–73), curate of Edingley (1773–78), and rector of South Wheatley (1775–78), all of them chapter benefices, and rector of Claypole for two months before his death in 1778.[3]

His grandson, son of Charles, was Robert Hodgson Fowler. Robert and his father were vicars choral together, as were the Henry Housons, father and son. Earlier, Henry Bugg was a vicar choral 1730–36, and his son Whalley 1773–82. Father and son were each appointed vicar of the chapter benefice of Bleasby.

[1] When Richard Barrow died in 1838, aged 91, *The Gentleman's Magazine* (1838, 441), noting his plurality of benefices and the length of time that he had held them, commented somewhat wryly that 'all of these livings, most of them of small value, are in the patronage of Southwell Collegiate Church'. But a number of small livings could produce a reasonable sum. In 1831 Barrow's gross income from his five Nottinghamshire benefices alone came to £452.

[2] Notwithstanding that as vicar choral Robert Hodgson Fowler was reprimanded by the chapter in 1835 for using violent and intemperate language in the school 'producing an affray to the great scandal of Church and Clergy' (R.M. Beaumont, *The Chapter of Southwell Minster: a story of 1000 years* (Southwell, 4th edn, 1994), 27).

[3] CCEd Personal ID: 60569.

'A lamentable WANT of CHURCHES, and MINISTERS'

Quite apart from the fact that parochial duties could not be performed by absentee pluralists, and that non-resident sole curates, often serving more than one parish, could provide only minimal pastoral care, there were at least two consequences for a county beset by what Simpson in 1836 called the 'abomination' of pluralism. The first was a 'lamentable WANT of CHURCHES, and MINISTERS.' Simpson lists 43 parishes in the county with populations of more than a thousand and having seats in their churches for only 19 per cent of the population, 50 with populations between 500 and 1,000 (with seats for 44 per cent), and 54 parishes each having between 300 and 500 (with seats for 62 per cent). A typical parish in the first list was Basford St Leodegarius of which Simpson was to become vicar in 1840. His predecessor, the non-resident pluralist Thomas Hosking,[1] scarcely ever visited his benefice. He was sharply rebuked by George Wilkins because 'the parish is in a most deplorable state and the spiritual concerns there have been grossly neglected.' He asked Hosking to place 'a clergyman of zeal and activity in the parish.'[2] The parish had a rapidly growing population of 6,325 in 1831 (10,093 by 1851), but no parsonage house. In the 1841 census, Simpson, then aged 55, and his wife Ann (45), with two domestic servants, were living in the parish in their own house. It was in just such a parish as this, that (quoting the Ecclesiastical Revenues Commissioners) Simpson had noted that 'the mass of the ADULT manufacturing population, is, in fact, WITHOUT RELIGIOUS INSTRUCTION OF ANY KIND.'[3]

With its many framework knitting and bobbin net machines Basford had become a lace and hosiery manufacturing centre well before 1840, and Simpson had framework knitters among his neighbours in Basford Lane. It was also a hub of Chartist agitation. It was the kind of parish that Thomas Chalmers had in mind when he observed that

> The truth is, that in our large cities, and more especially in their suburbs, as well as in those manufacturing districts which so teem with recent villages, and where every establishment has its clusters of families, it may with all safety be affirmed, that *greatly more*

---

[1] Also rector of Rempstone, Nottinghamshire. In 1831 the benefice of Rempstone was valued at £482 a year and had a population of 398. The value of Basford was £260 (less £90 for an assistant curate) with a population 16 times larger. Hosking's gross income from his two benefices was £742.

[2] Quoted in southwellchurches.nottingham.ac.uk/list, for Basford St Leodegarius.

[3] Simpson, *State of the Church*, 69–70.

than ONE HALF *of the people of sufficient age for church-going*
ATTEND NO WHERE; *and that they neither own nor occupy seats in
any place of worship whatever.*[1]

And this in a county, in which, Simpson observed, ' *there are several
Churches closed every Sunday,* where, of course, no duty whatever is
performed!!!' and in fact '*many places ... where there was once a*
CHURCH, *there is now no place of worship whatever*', even though there
was provision, under 57 George III. c. 99 and 58 George III, c. 45, for
parsonage houses, clerical residence, a second and even a third service,
with a sermon, on Sundays, and salaries for assistant curates. But
Simpson complained that because it could not be enforced this legislation
was 'almost a dead letter'.

Chalmers's observation greatly underestimated the extent of non-
attendance in the towns and cities. It was also somewhat naive. Twenty
years later, the findings of the 1851 census of religious worship were to
shock the Established Church by showing how remote from the poor it
was. That the 'mass of the adult population', the urban (or, for that
matter, the rural) labouring poor, should have neither the money nor the
inclination to own or rent seats in church, or even to sit in the few free
pews of those churches which had them, shows how far the well-
intentioned commissioners were from appreciating the extent of the
alienation of the poor from the Church of England.

The other consequence of pluralism in a county as large as Nottinghamshire, Simpson pointed out, was that as a pluralist its archdeacon
could not adequately oversee the parishes, and

> a variety of evils ensues – the canons and rubrics are violated,
> *catechising* is omitted, clergymen officiate *without licenses, pews*
> in parish churches are bought and sold, the second service is not
> performed, the book of Homilies, which ought to be in every
> church, is scarcely to be found in one, the Sacraments are not duly
> administered, the occasional services are abridged, &c. &c. &c.

Simpson urged that the Church of England should be in practice what it
was in theory (and here he quoted George Wilkins in his letter to Earl
Grey), namely to 'support the national faith, and to extend its blessings

---

[1] Thomas Chalmers, *Literary and Ecclesiastical Endowments* (1827), 112, quoted ibid.,
70.

over every portion' of the county.[1]

It was assumed by many that the rapid spread of nonconformity was due to the lack of Anglican churches and clergy. In 1839, a petition to the House of Lords urged that the largely defunct legislation which provided that public worship must be conducted only in licensed buildings be enforced, and that no church be built or clergyman be appointed to it, unless, as the *Nottingham and Newark Mercury* reported, that church were endowed 'under the Ecclesiastical Establishment as a place of worship.' The *Mercury* noted that the archbishop of Canterbury, William Howley, 'seems to have a natural horror of dissent, and the very apprehension of its spread prevents him from seeing the advantages which would and must arise to real religion from the building of unendowed Chapels.' It continued: 'There are two things that are mainly instrumental to the spread of dissent; the first is the want of ... places of worship ... and the second, and greatest, is not the paucity of Clergymen, but their utter incapacity to fulfil the onerous duties devolving upon Ministers of the Gospel.'[2]

But three years earlier, Robert Simpson, quoting Thomas Chambers, had denied that 'if the people are not in the established churches, they are in dissenting chapels, and are not therefore destitute of religious instruction' for 'the truth is not so.' In the cities 'and more especially in their suburbs' what Chambers described as the 'impenetrable mass' of the people was untouched by religion, even that of the 'sectarians, with all their activity and zeal' and 'notwithstanding the fullest toleration of their efforts' — a toleration that George Wilkins, together with his archbishop and orthodox high-churchmen, was never able to extend. Simpson argued that while it cost no more than half-a-crown to license a dissenting chapel, 'appoint their minister and collect a flock', it took a thousand pounds to endow a Church of England church, so 'let *Churchmen* have the same facilities for building which the *Dissenters* enjoy.'[3]

Simpson did not directly address what the *Nottingham and Newark Mercury* was to identify as the primary reason for the spread of dissent – the 'utter incapacity' of clergy to exercise their ministry – but it is implicit in his impassioned criticism of non-residence, pluralism, and the pursuit of preferment. He cited Shakespeare's angry Queen Mab:

[1]   Simpson, *State of the Church*, 54–5.

[2]   *Nottingham and Newark Mercury*, 16 Aug. 1839.

[3]   Simpson, *State of the Church*, 69–70.

Sometimes comes she with a tithe-pig's tail,
Tickling the parson as he lies asleep;
Then dreams he of ANOTHER BENEfiCE.[1]

Having published his *State of the Church in The County of Nottingham*
Simpson could not expect that he would be popular with his archdeacon,
a notable pluralist. He alludes to this possibility when, having quoted
George Wilkins telling of the onerous nature of his duties, Simpson
writes: 'Whatever treatment the observations of the writer of this
pamphlet may receive, surely the *declaration of the Archdeacon* is
worthy of regard.'[2]

Nevertheless, he was appointed to Basford St Leodegarius, a Crown
living, in 1840.

---

[1] Ibid., 80; *Romeo and Juliet*, iv. 80 (Simpson's italics and capitals).

[2] Ibid., 63, quoting Wilkins's *Letter to Earl Grey*, 22.

2

The Established Church

'A collection of independent congregational churches': the archdeaconry of Nottingham

When Simpson published his recommendations in 1836 the archdeaconry of Nottingham, which comprised the whole county geographically, was in the diocese of York. It consisted of 192 parishes, including 44 parishes said to be 'united'. There were, as listed in the report of the Ecclesiastical Duties and Revenues Commissioners presented in 1835, four donative curacies: Winkbourne, Cotham, Sibthorpe and Ossington, but only Winkbourne was listed as 'Not returned to Parl. Ret'. Several parishes were said to be under the peculiar jurisdiction of lords of the manor or of a manorial court, but those within Southwell's peculiar jurisdiction are not so indicated. Nine parishes or chapelries were reported as having no church, one had a 'dilapidated' church, and four had had their church 'destroyed'. There is no indication of the large number of churches that must have been in poor repair.

Measured in terms of benefice income, the parishes in the archdeaconry were relatively poor. In his letter to Earl Grey in December 1832, George Wilkins noted that 76 (almost 40 per cent) of the benefices were valued at less than £200 a year, and that the remaining 116 varied between £200 and £1,300. Of these, 77 were valued at £400 or less.[1]

In their 1835 report the Ecclesiastical Duties and Revenues commissioners proposed that Nottinghamshire be transferred to the diocese of Lincoln. The far-sighted Robert Simpson criticised this proposal, for, he said, it would make the diocese of Lincoln 'FAR TOO LARGE for any one man *efficiently* to superintend.' Simpson noted that the addition of Nottinghamshire to the diocese of Lincoln would create a diocese of 780 benefices, five times the size of the dioceses of Durham and Ripon. If the bishop were to visit a different parish on most Sundays in the year it would take him many years to visit them all. He continued:

[1] George Wilkins, *A Letter to Earl Grey on the Subject of Ecclesiastical Reform* (Nottingham, 1832), 28.

43

The *people* know nothing of their Bishop under existing circumstances, and the *clergy,* almost as little; the Church in this county, at present, presents but a collection of independent congregational churches, in which little more than the *name* of Episcopacy is preserved. It can hardly be supposed that an episcopal visitation once *in about sixteen years* can effect any very great good.[1]

When, in 1837, Nottinghamshire was transferred to the diocese of Lincoln, Simpson's fears proved to be well founded. Bishops of Lincoln soon discovered how unwieldy the diocese was. It was not until 1884 that the diocese of Southwell was created. It was to comprise virtually the whole of Nottinghamshire (from the diocese of Lincoln) and Derbyshire (from the diocese of Lichfield). It was a reform, but, with some 500 parishes by 1911 (following a major church building initiative by the first bishop of Southwell, George Ridding) it did little more than redistribute the episcopal load. It took over four years for the then bishop of Southwell, Edwyn Hoskyns, to conduct a personal formal visitation of every parish in his diocese.

'A variety of evils'

As we have seen, in 1836 the archdeaconry was, in Simpson's opinion, so poorly supervised that the independent congregationalism of the parishes had led to 'a variety of evils'. George Wilkins, the archdeacon, was well aware of the problems that the clergy faced, but, inevitably, he exercised his duties more by correspondence than by personal visitation (although he did visit parishes where problems had been brought to his attention) and more by lengthy public admonition than through personal pastoral care. Each year he conducted visitations in four centres in his archdeaconry: Nottingham St Mary, Southwell St Mary, Newark St Mary Magdalene and Retford. These visitations took place within a service in church. The clergy were required to attend, together with newly elected (or otherwise appointed) churchwardens who had to make their formal declarations. On each occasion George Wilkins read his charge during which he expatiated at length on a variety of national issues as they affected the Church of England. Robert Simpson attended on these

---

[1] Simpson, *State of the Church,* 49. In 1869 the bishop of Lincoln calculated that it would take him 15 years to 'make the circuit' of his diocese, which then included Nottinghamshire.

occasions. He describes them thus:

> The visitations, as at present conducted, are of the least possible benefit to the Church, for the good that might be obtained from the sermons usually preached, and the charges delivered on these occasions, is almost entirely lost by reason of the constant influx of Churchwardens, so that the house of God, during the whole time of divine service, presents more the appearance and bustle of the Exchange, than an assemblage of the clergy and others for the purposes of divine worship. This evil has not been overlooked by our present venerable Archdeacon, who, in his 'Directions to Churchwardens,' has specially enjoined them 'to use all practicable despatch with the Registrar, so as to be in readiness to attend divine service,' but hitherto without effect.[1]

To overcome the problem of managing 'the vast extent of this Archdeaconry' Simpson recommended that two 'active' archdeacons be appointed, one for the northern and one for the southern division of the county, the archdeaconries of Southwell and Nottingham respectively, with funding provided from the revenues of the sinecure mastership of St Leonard's Hospital in Newark. It was not until 1912 that a second archdeaconry, that of Newark, was established in the county (and within a new diocese) — almost exactly as Simpson had proposed 76 years earlier. By 1860 the conduct of visitations had not improved, and clergy and churchwardens stayed away when they could. In that year George Wilkins's son John Murray Wilkins, acting as his father's Official or surrogate, held a visitation in Nottingham to hear churchwardens make the formal declarations without which they could not hold office. The *Nottingham Journal* reported that when the churchwardens of Nottingham Holy Trinity were called to make their declarations 'no one answered', that only the vicar's warden from Calverton attended, that the wardens from Sutton Bonington St Michael were not in attendance, and those for

---

[1] Ibid., 54. In 1846, for example, the spring visitations were held on 27 April (Nottingham), 28 April (Southwell), 30 April (Retford) and 1 May (Newark). Occasionally Wilkins's registrar would act on his behalf and merely 'call over' the names of churchwardens. At the archdeacon's visitation in Newark on 28 November 1856, Wilkins's son and registrar, John Murray Wilkins, did no more than this (*Nottingham Journal*, 5 Dec. 1856). J.M. Wilkins was his father's registrar from 1849 to 1853, and thereafter held the more senior post of Official from 1849 to 1879. The archdeacon's registrar was responsible for maintaining the archdeaconry records, and collecting fees and fines. The Official was the archdeacon's surrogate and could fulfil all his administrative and judicial roles. The work of each of these officers could be undertaken by deputies.

Cossall 'also neglected to attend.'[1]

But churchwardens could evidently be a law unto themselves: at his visitation in June George Wilkins noted the 'manifestly improper' practice of churchwardens calling vestry meetings without informing the clergy![2]

George Wilkins: archdeacon, prebendary, and polemicist

There is no space here for a critical memoir of George Wilkins (1785-1865) but, because he is a key figure in this period, note should be made of his personal life, early career and theological and political opinions. George Wilkins was educated at Gonville and Caius College, Cambridge, graduating BA in 1807, MA in 1810, and DD in 1824. He was made deacon in 1808, ordained priest in 1809 and was successively assistant curate of Great Plumstead in 1808 and then of Hadleigh 1808–15. On 3 September 1811, in Cambridge St Giles, George Wilkins was married to Amelia Auriol Hay, daughter of Edward Auriol Hay-Drummond, incumbent of Hadleigh, Suffolk, whose assistant curate Wilkins was. They were married by Herbert Marsh DD, Lady Margaret professor of divinity in the university of Cambridge.[3] On George Wilkins's death in

---

[1] *Nottingham Journal*, 30 Nov. 1860.

[2] Ibid. 8 June 1860.

[3] The brief, incomplete and uncritical account of Wilkins in the *DNB* was originally written by M.G. Watkins (revised for the *Oxford DNB* in 2004 by M.C. Curthoys). Morgan George Watkins was in 1861 presented to the rectory of Barnoldby le Beck by the chapter of Southwell collegiate church. Both the original and the revised entries claim that George and Amelia eloped to Gretna Green in 1811. They may have done, but the implication is that they married there for no mention is made in the *ODNB* entry of their marriage in Cambridge in the same year or that there is no record of a marriage of George Wilkins and Amelia in the index of Gretna Green marriages. Evidently the story of the elopement was passed to M.G. Watkins by his father Morgan Watkins, perhaps out of pique for not (as he was already vicar of Southwell) being appointed by Wilkins to the far better paid and more prestigious post of rector of Southwell at the time of the 1837–41 reforms. However, as Amelia was only 16 or 17 when she married, it may be that she did elope with George to Gretna, yet they married in Cambridge and not Gretna. It seems clear that the couple did not elope to Cambridge. Though no member of Amelia's family witnessed the marriage, a Lady Margaret professor (and later bishop of Llandaff and of Peterborough) would not have been party to a questionable marriage. In 1845 George Wilkins remonstrated with the vicar of Radford St Peter, Samuel Creswell, for not being strict in requiring evidence of residence in the parish from those making applications for banns. Wilkins said that Radford was being made the Gretna Green of Nottinghamshire. When vicar of Nottingham St Mary, Wilkins had been assiduous in demanding evidence of residence of everyone making an application for banns. It is unlikely that he would have made this remark if he himself had been married in Gretna Green or had even eloped there.

1865 the *Daily Record* and the *Guardian* published obituaries. His will was proved at some £9,000.

George Wilkins was politically a Tory because theologically he was a high churchman in the sense in which the latter term had been employed since at least the late seventeenth century. It denoted an orthodox 'Church and King' man, one who held firmly to a doctrine of the church as a divine institution, to the divine right of kings, and, as appointed by the king, to the authority of bishops as the Lords Spiritual, the first estate of the realm. In 1832, writing to the prime minister, Earl Grey, about proposals to reform the Church (the general thrust of which Wilkins supported), he expressed his position in these terms:

> The King, as supreme Head of the Church, and bound by the strongest ties, divine and human, to support it — Parliament, bound by considerations religious, moral, and political, to uphold the monarchy — and the Clergy, bound by the solemn obligations of conscience, feeling, and duty, to discountenance vice and to promote, with the increase of religion, the spiritual welfare of the state, are all, in their separate stations, imperiously called upon, at the present juncture, to unite their influence to set this high matter upon a secure, wise, and proper basis, and to cooperate with Providence in the support of the national faith, and to extend its blessings over every portion of the kingdom.[1]

This standard assertion of the unique responsibility of the Church of England and robust defence of its rights and privileges as the church by law established would have met with approval by all orthodox Anglicans. It was a statement of the church's religious dominance. We have noted the petition presented to the House of Lords in 1839 against the practice of religious services being performed in unlicensed places of worship. Though widely ignored, the law then required that a penalty of £50 be imposed if the number of people meeting in a private house for the purpose of worship exceeded 20. The petitioners asked that this, and other related statutes, be enforced. In reporting this the *Nottingham and Newark Mercury* observed that the current legislation (or 'this arrange-ment') 'was one of the strong links by which the State Church is enabled to preserve and extend a dominant power over the people, although it is calculated to retard the progress of piety.'[2]

---

[1] Wilkins, *Letter to Earl Grey*, 4.

[2] *Nottingham and Newark Mercury*, 16 Aug. 1839.

Opposed to nonconformity (both papist and Protestant) and evangelical zeal as he was, George Wilkins would have agreed with the *Mercury*'s first sentiment but would strongly reject the second. For him the Church of England's 'dominant power' in the political, social, spiritual and moral life of the nation alone promoted piety and must be preserved and protected.

It must also be protected because, for Wilkins and the majority of his contemporaries, the established church was the epitome of reasonable Christianity, that is of orthodoxy untainted by enthusiasm. In his *The Village Pastor*, published in 1825 when he was vicar of Nottingham St Mary, Wilkins argued that 'Christianity is a religion not of feeling but of principle. The doctrines it enforces are addressed to the understanding; the duties it enjoins are submitted to reason. Whilst it aims at the salvation of the soul it does not reject either the wants or the co-operation of the body.' Thus, he rejected enthusiastic Christianity as 'that overheated furnace which mistaken zeal, like the officers of Nebuchadnezzar, lights for its own destruction.'[1]

If for no other reason the Church of England must be protected against zealous reformers, either within or outside its ranks. Wilkins's *The Convert*, published in 1826, is, like virtually all his writing, a polemical work. Here he takes issue with, successively, sceptics, Unitarians, Calvinists, materialists, Baptists, 'Papists' and Quakers. He does this in the light of the 'prevailing disposition of the times to consider every thing which has been long established as not merely capable of amendment, but as absolutely requiring reform; and in that unlimited toleration which it is the boast of this country to extend to all religious opinions' and which regarded the Church of England 'as no longer entitled to the distinction of a *National Church*.[2]

Wilkins was particularly critical of those zealous 'reformers' within the Church of England, the evangelicals, or, as he designates them, 'Evangelists'. An early example is to be found in 'The Clerical Conference' in his *Body and Soul*.[3] This records an imaginary conversation between Dr Freeman, who is the incumbent of a heavily populated urban parish, his curate Mr Deacon, and an evangelical clergyman, Mr Wiseman who is supported by two members of the Church Missionary Society. Freeman is clearly a self-portrait of Wilkins, himself a DD and

---

[1] 'One of the authors of *Body and Soul*' [George Wilkins], *The Village Pastor* (1825), 90–1.

[2] 'The author of *The Two Rectors*' [George Wilkins], *The Convert* (1826), vi.

[3] *Body and Soul* (1824 edn).

vicar of St. Mary's, by far the largest of the three Nottingham parishes. Freeman confronts his opponents' definition of 'evangelism' and 'evangelicals'. For him 'evangelical' should mean 'the whole Christian world' but the word 'has been assumed by, not given to, a portion of the Clergy of the Established Church as a mark to designate them from their less serious, but, let us hope, not less pious brethren.' Freeman rejects this as 'a most invidious and untrue distinction'. His central theological objection to evangelicals 'of his own Church' was that they had 'wrested the articles of her faith from their legitimate interpretation, and added to the perversion of them a conduct of austerity as far removed from the genuine spirit of Christianity as it was from the constitution of human nature.'[1]

Wilkins rejected the doctrine of the 'total corruption of human nature' as contrary to scripture, and evangelical notions of 'justifying grace' as 'misunderstood.'[2] For Wilkins the doctrines and behaviour of Anglican evangelicals undermined the very establishment whose privileges they enjoyed. For him they effectively constituted a protestant sect which threatened to subvert the constitution and doctrines of the established church from within. Wilkins's criticisms were immediately rebutted. The rector of Cotgrave in Wilkins's archdeaconry was John Henry Browne (1779–1858), rector of Cotgrave (1811-58). He was also the archdeacon of Ely (1816–58) and an equally combative polemicist. Browne published rebuttals of *Body and Soul* in *Five Letters Addressed to Revd George Wilkins, Containing Strictures on Some Parts of a Publication Entitled 'Body and Soul'* (1823), and in *A Letter to Revd George Wilkins in Reply to a Chapter in the Second Volume of 'Body and Soul' Entitled 'Evangelism'* (1823). We will return to Wilkins's confrontation with the evangelicals and to their response.

Wilkins therefore refused to accept that the church could be reformed either by parliament from outside or evangelicals from within but only at the behest of the monarch as its temporal head by divine right. The monarch alone could reform the Church because the monarch alone was, under God, its defender and champion. Wilkins admitted that 'the King, as supreme, can exercise his power and prerogative only through his responsible officers of State', but the principal officer of state was the prime minister 'whose especial office it is to direct the prerogative of our supreme, temporal Head − the King'. For this reason reform of the church could never be sanctioned by parliament alone, least of all by the

---

[1] Ibid., i. 14.

[2] Ibid., ii. 191.

lower house which has 'among its members so many who were either indifferent or hostile to the Establishment, that its countenance and favour have been sparingly given to it.'[1]

So (to introduce here issues to which we will return later) Wilkins duly, and apparently willingly, completed the returns for his several benefices to the Ecclesiastical Duties and Revenues Commission in the early 1830s, evidently because it was a royal commission headed by the archbishops of Canterbury and York, which reported directly to William IV, but he dismissed the 1851 census of religious worship because it possessed neither episcopal nor, he claimed, legal authority, and was subject both to nonconformist bias and to civil service indifference.[2] The return for Southwell St Mary was completed in a very cursory fashion and signed not by George Wilkins as permanent residentiary canon or John Murray Wilkins as rector, but by Peter Coxon, the 29-year-old parish clerk and verger.

Similarly, in a letter to Lord Russell, George Wilkins strongly opposed all attempts to abolish church rates on the principal ground that abolition would dissolve the union of church and state and therefore threaten the monarchy.[3]

Wilkins's opposition to parliamentary reform of the Church of England included any direct interference in the payment of clergy. In his open letter to Earl Grey he argued that had they had access to 'the whole produce of the tithe of land', although their returns would not be 'fairly commuted', at least the average incumbent would not be poor. But for centuries 'so great a portion of the ancient revenues of the Church' had been alienated that, as Henry VIII had begun the process of alienation so only the king could make adequate compensation. Failing that, the prevailing system under which, in 'numberless instances', the 'largest portion of income is dedicated to the least quantum of duty' would continue, and villages 'which have grown into populous towns' and 'towns which have outgrown and outnumbered some of the largest cities' would not be provided with an adequate number of adequately remuner-

---

[1] Wilkins, *Letter to Earl Grey*, 4–5.

[2] *Charge*, 1854.

[3] George Wilkins, *A Letter to Lord John Russell on the Subject of Church Rates* (1832, 1854). The argument that to challenge the rights and privileges of the Church of England was to undermine the monarchy was frequently employed. In 1834 the duke of Gloucester, presenting a petition to parliament against the admission of dissenters to Cambridge university degrees, claimed that the removal of the religious test might 'make such an inroad' that 'Unitarians, Jews or Mohammedans' could become professors, and 'might ultimately affect the stability of the throne itself' (*Nottingham and Newark Mercury*, 26 April 1834).

ated clergy. Again, large dioceses should be reduced in size, the majority of bishops should be paid equally, and their number in the House of Lords be drastically reduced to enable bishops to spend much more time in their dioceses than they are currently allowed to spend owing to their parliamentary duties. Gone were the days when bishops should so 'consider their station designed as the reward of past services' that they 'pursued the aggrandizement of themselves and their families' by 'the traffic of exchanges, renewals and insurances' in a manner which 'forfeited their claim to any nice sense of Christian feeling.' For this same reason, Wilkins argued, the excesses of pluralism should be curbed and the residence and maintenance of the parochial clergy be addressed. But, and here the Church and King man spoke most emphatically, in every measure of reform there should be no interference 'with the *Spirituals* of the Church', nor 'any thing even remotely touching them be made the subject of Legislation, unless with the concurrence of the Hierarchy', the bishops in Convocation. Any notion that 'the validity of the assumption that Ecclesiastical property is under the controul of the State' must be vigorously opposed, but he added the caveat 'at least so long as the tenure, by which it is held, of efficiently and faithfully providing for the spiritual welfare of the Community, is fulfilled.'[1]

In his letter to Earl Grey in 1832 Wilkins bolstered these arguments with a detailed analysis of 'the condition and circumstances of the parochial Clergy' in his own archdeaconry. He did not pass up the opportunity to tell the prime minister how hard-pressed he was personally, and that his numerous ecclesiastical appointments did not, in total, produce an income that matched that of three benefices in his archdeaconry each with less than 400 in its population. He correctly noted that 'in populous parishes the income varies *inversely* as the quality of duty.'[2] The population of 20 of the most heavily populated parishes in the archdeaconry was 119,112, but the net income of these benefices totalled £3,149. This meant that the pastoral care of every 5,955 people had to be undertaken on an average benefice income of a mere £157. Wilkins contrasted this with another 20 parishes in the archdeaconry. The total population of these was 8,394 and the total gross benefice income (no curates were necessary) came to £14,380: 'which is a rate of £719 for every population of 419.' Wilkins chose these parishes for comparison to achieve the best case, but his general point was sound enough. Having criticised schemes for parliamentary reform currently

---

[1] *Letter to Earl Grey*, 7, 8–9, 10, 11, 13, 15.

[2] Ibid., 25.

being proposed Wilkins nevertheless maintained that something must be done to 'enable the Clergy to uphold their respectability, and to extend their usefulness, by giving them a competent maintenance.' There was but 'one thing needful'. It was that 'our gracious King, as our supreme temporal Head, guided by the Spirit of Him "by whom Kings reign and Princes decree justice" should be the 'happy means of effecting these reforms', 'through you, My Lord, his Minister.'[1]

As we have seen, for theological and therefore constitutional reasons Wilkins was highly critical of evangelicals within the Church of England, and resisted all compromise with nonconformists, Roman Catholic and Protestant, outside it. For example, in his 1851 charge he denounced as 'papal aggression' the creation of the Roman Catholic archdiocese of Westminster and its twelve suffragan sees. He had earlier bitterly opposed the building of two Roman Catholic churches in his parish of Nottingham St Mary, not only because of what he regarded as the 'superstitions' and 'corruptions' of Rome, but because of its attempt 'to enter upon the field of my ministration, in order to draw away the flock authoritatively consigned to my care.'[2] He had no time, on the one hand, for those Tractarian Anglicans whose beliefs and practices aped Rome, or, on the other, for evangelicals who, he believed, consorted with Protestant dissenters and undermined the doctrines of the established church.

Wilkins had continued his pursuit of evangelicals in his 1841 charge. He condemned what he described as the 'Calvinistic' evangelicals within the Church of England both for their doctrines and also for their support of societies formed on 'an irregular and dangerous principle' such as the British and Foreign Bible Society, the Church Missionary Society, and the Church Pastoral Aid Society.[3] The evangelicals were 'disciples of

---

[1]   Ibid., 25–7, 32.

[2]   George Wilkins, *An Address to the Parishioners of St Mary's, Nottingham, on the occasion of commencing the Building of a second edifice for Roman Catholic Worship in the parish* (London and Nottingham, 1842).

[3]   *Charge*, 1841. His bishop, John Kaye of Lincoln, a moderate high churchman who had no time for evangelicals, and refused to support the Bible Society because it welcomed dissenters, nevertheless strongly supported the Church Missionary Society. In the same year Kaye wrote to the Society congratulating it and asking to be recorded as a subscriber (*Newark and Mansfield Times*, 11 Aug. 1841). In May 1841 two evangelical clergymen, Robert Simpson of Newark and Charles Plumptre of Claypole were present at the first meeting of the Southwell auxiliary of the CMS. In its report of this meeting the *Newark and Mansfield Times* for 12 May said: 'We are surprised to observe that none of the Clergy of the Southwell Collegiate Establishment were present: we hope their absence was occasioned by unavoidable circumstances, and not because of their disapproval of the Society … '.

the new School' who insisted on 'the extreme doctrines of Calvinism' and maintained their doctrines with 'narrow and unchristian feelings'. They 'carry out the extreme doctrines of the Genevan School' and 'throw discredit upon the framers of our Ritual for having embraced opposite opinions, and for having given expression to them in our Liturgy.' The evangelicals, Wilkins continued, 'throw censure upon the pious Reformers of the Church' and undermine episcopal authority in favour of private judgment on religious matters.[1]

Wilkins's bitter attack would hardly have gone unnoticed by Edward Garrard Marsh, a leading member of the Church Missionary Society, who, as prebendary of Woodborough, had served with Wilkins on the chapter of the collegiate church for eighteen years. In 1848 Marsh delivered the Bampton lectures to the university of Oxford. In the second of these he outlined and supported the very doctrine of human corruption that Wilkins found so abhorrent:

> ... let us with all humility receive the truth, as we find it recorded in our ninth article, that original sin is the fault and corruption of the nature of every man, that naturally is engendered of the offspring of Adam, whereby man is very far gone from original righteousness, and is of his own nature inclined to evil, so, that the flesh lusteth always contrary to the spirit, and therefore in every person, born into this world, it deserveth God's wrath and damnation![2]

Wilkins's assault drew several responses in kind. The evangelical vicar of Clarborough, Charles Hodge, wrote to the bishop of Lincoln, John Kaye, describing Wilkins's charge as 'objectionable both for its sentiments and also (more particularly) for imputing wrong motives to a particular section of the Church.'[3] Robert Simpson,[4] another evangeli-

---

[1] *Charge*, 1841, 13–25.

[2] Edward Garrard Marsh, *The Christian Doctrine of Sanctification* (1848), 28. Edward Garrard Marsh (1783–1862), Wadham College, Oxford, BA 1804. Fellow Oriel College. 1804–14. MA 1807, curate of Nuneham. In 1820 he bought a proprietary chapel in Hampstead for £2,900. He was Bampton Lecturer in 1848, prebendary of Woodborough 1821, vicar of Sandon, Herts., 1828 and of Aylesford, Kent, 1841 until his death. An evangelical and an influential member of CMS, Marsh was formative in the life of his brother-in-law, Henry Williams (1792–1867), one of the first missionaries to travel to New Zealand (in 1823) (Robin Fisher, 'Williams, Henry', *Dictionary of New Zealand Biography* (2002) etc.).

[3] LAO, Cor.B.5/8A/6, Hodge to Kaye, 9 July 1841.

cal and perpetual curate of Newark Christ Church, also wrote to John
Kaye. He accused Wilkins of libel for 'gross falsehoods' which were 'not
only unchristian, but also illegal.'[1] He asked the bishop to restrain
Wilkins from publishing his charge, and threatened legal action against
the archdeacon. As neither the request nor the threat succeeded, Simpson
published his objections to Wilkins in *Observations on certain statements
contained in the Charge of Archdeacon Wilkins delivered at the
Visitation holden in Nottingham, Retford, and Newark, in May, 1841.*
Simpson, who was present when the charge was delivered, was shocked
by what he heard. The archdeacon had made charges of 'a very offensive
character ... without affording to the accused any opportunity of
answering for themselves; *and charges which have not the slightest
foundation in truth ...*'[2] Simpson then defended evangelicalism by
answering each of Wilkins's charges with a detailed line-by-line rebuttal,
citing Hooker's *Polity,* the *Book of Common Prayer,* the Articles of
Religion and the very nature of the Anglican establishment itself. He
accused Wilkins not only of an 'unfairness' which was as evident as the
'the spirit [of the charges] is unchristian' and the 'mode of making them
irregular' but also, and tellingly, because while Wilkins condemned the
evangelicals, in the same 1841 charge he had applauded the authors of
Tracts for the Times as 'men of deep piety and erudition' and 'character-
ized by the most perfect moderation and forbearance',[3] and this in the
year that the most controversial of the *Tracts, Tract XC,* was published.[4]

Quite unmoved by these bitter criticisms George Wilkins defended his
theological and political opinions, and continued to exercise his
responsibilities as archdeacon with similar outspokenness until his death
in 1865.[5]

---

[4] Not the Robert Simpson who wrote *The State of the Church in the County of
Nottingham,* who was now vicar of St Leodegarius, Basford.

[1] LAO, Cor.B. 5/8/2, Simpson to Kaye, 28 May 1841 and 1 June 1841.

[2] Simpson, *State of the Church,* 5.

[3] Wilkins, 1841 *Charge,* 12; Simpson, *State of the Church,* 25.

[4] Newman's *Tract XC* encouraged a catholic interpretation of the Thirty-Nine Articles
of Religion. It was condemned by bishops but defended by many high churchmen. Its
publication and the criticism it engendered brought the series of *Tracts for the Times* to an
end.

[5] On Wilkins's position on church reform, the evangelicals, and other controversies, see,
in addition, Job Bradshaw, *Church Rates and Church Rights. The true view of the Church
Rate Question* (1854); George Wilkins, *A Letter to Earl Grey on the Subject of Ecclesiastical Reform* (1832); Richard Alliott, *An Apology for Calvin and Calvinism, in two letters
addressed to the vicar of St Mary's, Nottingham* (1823); George Wilkins, *The Pastor's
Address to his Flock, warning them of the efforts of the Romanists to supplant the*

The slow death of the Southwell college of canons

Up to the reform of the Southwell college of canons the archdeaconry comprised the four rural deaneries of Nottingham, Bingham, Newark, and Retford within the archdeacon's jurisdiction. Outside his remit were the 28 parishes in the 'deanery and jurisdiction of Southwell'. The archdeaconry was transferred from the diocese of York to Lincoln in 1839, and in 1841, when the dissolution of the college of canons began and the peculiar abolished, the parishes in the peculiar came under the jurisdiction of the archdeacon and were transferred also. This major reform was undoubtedly undertaken because, as one nineteenth-century historian has described them, the Southwell canons were 'a useless waste of ecclesiastical revenues which could be put to much better use',[1] together with much 'useless waste' in every other ancient foundation. John Kaye, bishop of Lincoln, was a member of the commission which recommended the radical reform of cathedral and collegiate church foundations, defending the reforms in his *Letter to the Archbishop of Canterbury* in 1838. Lengthy objections were made by the chapters of cathedrals and collegiate churches to the commissioners' proposals to reduce the number of canons, the size of choral foundations and the endowments and rights of patronage that they enjoyed in order that poor livings could be augmented. Southwell was by no means alone, but its struggle to maintain its privileges was not fought as strenuously as other foundations fought for theirs.[2]

The order in council relating to Southwell, dated 14 October 1841, determined *inter alia* that

Protestant Catholic Church in England (London and Nottingham, 1842); George Wilkins, *An Address to the Parishioners of St Mary's, Nottingham on the building of a second edifice for Roman Catholic worship in the parish* (Nottingham 1842); William Howitt, *W.H.'s vindication of his 'History of Priestcraft' against the attack of Archdeacon Wilkins* (2nd edn, 1833). Wilkins attacked nonconformity in his 1834 and 1837 charges. For his high church orthodoxy see, in addition to his annual charges, his novels *Body and Soul* (1822), *The Two Rectors* (1824), *The Village Pastor* (1825), and *The Convert* (1826). For further comment on aspects of Wilkins's pastoral practice and archdeacon's duties, drawing on Wilkins's correspondence with John Kaye, see Francis Knight, *The Nineteenth-Century Church and English Society* (1998), 87–8 et passim.

[1]   W.E. Hodgson, 'Southwell', in *Memorials of Old Nottinghamshire* (1912), 266, quoting (and acknowledging the accuracy of) Arthur Dimock, *The Cathedral Church of Southwell* (1898), 124.

[2]   For the correspondence see *Parliamentary Papers*, 1837 (204) (327), *Church Commission. Copies of communications addressed to His Majesty's Church Commissioners with reference to ecclesiastical duties and revenues*, etc.

so soon as convenient may be, the vicarage of Southwell shall be endowed with such portion of the tithes, or with other provisions, as by the like authority may be determined on, and may be consituted a rectory with care of souls. By reason of the vacancy of certain canonries and prebends in the Collegiate Church, certain lands, tithes and other endowments and emoluments, have accrued to, and become vested in us, under the providence of the said act &c., we propose the vicarage shall be a rectory &c. The rector to employ a person, licensed by the Bishop of Lincoln, and not being a minor canon of the said church, to be his assistant curate. Such stipend to be assigned him, not exceeding the sum of a non-resident incumbent. And we further propose, out of the proceeds aforesaid, the sum of £300 shall be paid to the rector of Southwell, first payment made November next, 1841. Further, nothing herein contained shall prevent a further augmentation. When means are sufficent for the purpose at any future time, a gross sum of stock in government funds, shall be apportioned to the rectory, or the tithes, when they shall become vested in us, or any portion thereof, shall be conveyed to the rector, the said act to take effect after it has been published in the Gazette.[1]

The sixteen prebendaries, each keeping residence for three months on a four-year rotation, had drawn their income from the fees, farm rents, fines, dividends and interest on securities arising from their prebendal estates. These revenues varied considerably from prebend to prebend. For example, in the three years to 31 December 1831 the wealthiest prebend, Oxton I,[2] produced a gross income of £84 (£74 net) for its prebendary, James Jarvis Cleaver, whereas the prebendary of Eaton, William Barrow, received a mere £10 gross (£3 net) from his prebendal assets.[3] Each prebendary also received £85 towards the expense of keeping residence. In addition, the prebendaries divided the chapter's surplus net revenue equally among themselves. They did well for themselves. Even the hostile local shoemaker John Holmes came to regret the dissolution of

---

[1] *London Gazette*, 9 Nov. 1841.

[2] There were two Oxton prebends, Oxton the first part (or Oxton I) and Oxton the second part (Oxton II).

[3] Cleaver was also rector of Hawerby in Lincolnshire (in the gift of the Southwell chapter), of Holme Pierrepont in Nottinghamshire (in the gift of earl Manvers) and vicar of Appleton le Street in Yorkshire. His gross income from Holme Pierrepont alone was £747 a year. Barrow was also rector of the relatively wealthy chapter benefice of Beelsby in Lincolnshire.

the college, for, he said, each prebendary when in residence 'kept a great deal of company and spent a good sum of money in the town.'[1]

If for no other reason the chapter, as we will soon see, fought strongly to retain its privileges. It had some experience of doing so. For example the 1822 Marriage Act deprived all but the two archbishops and the diocesan bishops of the right to grant marriage licences. The Southwell chapter and its vicar-general, William Barrow, immediately petitioned parliament arguing for the restoration of this ancient right. The dean of Battle, and the dean and chapter of Lichfield, who also exercised peculiar jurisdiction, appealed as well. Within a few months the Act was amended and the clauses that removed the power to grant licences (and to collect the fees for doing so) were restored.[2] In his analysis of the 1835 Ecclesiastical Duties and Revenues commissioners' statistics for Nottinghamshire Robert Simpson noted that the average annual gross revenue for the three years to 31 December 1831 produced by the Southwell chapter's assets was £2,211 (£954 net). The average total gross income of the 16 prebends was £561 (£440 net). Taking together the chapter and prebendal revenues, the gross income of the collegiate church in Southwell was therefore £2,772 though this was exceptional.[3]

The suppression of the college in 1840–1 was strongly opposed by the young MP for Newark, William Ewart Gladstone. In Gladstone's view the college's assets should have been retained for the future needs of the Church in England in Nottinghamshire. And so it turned out. After its creation in 1884 the first bishop of the new diocese of Southwell, George Ridding, was to regret its barely adequate endowments.

As the prebendaries resigned or died so their canonries ceased to exist and their prebendal properties vested in the Ecclesiastical Commissioners. Thomas Henry Shepherd, rector of Clayworth and prebendary of Beckingham, was the last member of the ancient chapter. When he died on 12 February 1873 the old order came finally to an end.[4] Richard

[1]   'The Life of John Holmes written by Himself' (MS in private hands, 1880), 100.

[2]   R.B. Outhwaite, *Clandestine Marriage in England 1500–1850* (1995), 155.

[3]   Of the chapter revenues, Robert Simpson noted that 'the net yearly produce is considered higher than the average amount for the future, there having been a short time ago an extraordinary fine upon a lease which had been neglected to be renewed at the customary period. Looking at the average of the five preceding years, it may be presumed that the future dividends will be much less than heretofore.' A fine was money paid by an incoming tenant, or a tenant renewing a lease, in consideration of a small rent.

[4]   For a brief account of the dissolution of the Southwell chapter see M.R. Austin, 'The Many High Proude Ones: The Church of England and the People 1884–1927', in S. Chapman and D. Walker (eds), *Southwell, The Town and its People*, II (Southwell, 2006), 173–4.

Beaumont has suggested that the ancient chapter was 'gradually strangled to death' but the judgment of the bishop of Lincoln, Christopher Wordsworth, was that it died by its own hand. In 1873 he began his first triennial visitation of Lincoln cathedral in its chapter-house and completed it in the chapter-house of Southwell. In Southwell, having noted that its capitular foundation, now at an end, had a longer history than the monarchy, Wordsworth observed 'that no institution was ever destroyed except by itself [by] showing how Southwell had been ruined by non-residence, pluralities, want of definite work, and consequent secularity.'[1]

This present study demonstrates the truth of that judgment.

The Southwell chapter: policies and personalities

In the late 1830s the future of the centuries-old college of canons and the threat to its authority created a major fault-line in the chapter. The chapter's minute and account book has, remarkably, no record of these discussions, but the division of opinion is evident from three 'memorials' (statements of fact as basis for a petition) submitted to the Ecclesiastical Duties and Revenues commissioners in May and June 1836.[2]

The commissioners' proposal was initially to reduce the size and expense of cathedral and collegiate church establishments in order to augment poor benefices and to endow new parishes in heavily populated areas. In the event the Southwell revenues augmented the endowment of the new sees of Manchester and Ripon, though it was argued that Lancashire and Yorkshire could well provide sufficient endowment income for their two new bishops.

In their second report the commissioners proposed that the parish of Southwell, hitherto served by a vicar choral, should become a rectory, with the archdeacon of Nottingham as 'Head of the Church, and Rector of the Parish' with one assistant minister; that two vicars choral should maintain the choral services in place of the current six; 'and that the separate Estates [of the prebendaries] should be dealt with, as in the Case

---

[1]   J.H. Overton and Elizabeth Wordsworth, *Christopher Wordsworth, Bishop of Lincoln, 1807–1885* (1888), 277–8.

[2]   Parliamentary Papers, 1837 (204) (327) *Church Commission. Copies of communications* etc., 61–2 (HC 204 [1837], xli, 37).

of the Cathedrals of the Old Foundation'[1] that is, that they should be transferred to the commissioners. At its meeting on 19 May 1836 the chapter instructed George Hodgkinson Barrow, its registrar, to write to the Commission. He did this the following day. He noted that Southwell collegiate church had existed as a choral establishment 'for above twelve hundred years'; that, apart from a grant from the Queen Anne's Bounty commissioners for £400 to found a divinity lectureship, the college was self-supporting; that a choral establishment 'so reduced' could not be maintained other than 'under a body of residentiaries'; and, as a decisive argument, that 'the funds of the Chapter are adequate to the maintenance of such an establishment … still leaving a surplus available to the purpose of the augmentation of small benefices, as your memorialists are prepared to prove, if required.' This last point, at least, was disingenuous, as for very many years the chapter had failed to augment the very poor benefices in its own gift. In brief, the chapter, under John Thomas Becher's leadership as vicar-general, argued that the Southwell establishment should remain virtually as it had always been.

On 21 May George Wilkins, writing from Nottingham, sent his own memorial to the Ecclesiastical Duties and Revenues commissioners. He rejected the chapter's position. It was, he wrote, 'not for the advantage of the public that the chapter establishment of Southwell should be maintained in greater efficiency, but … if preserved at all it should be reduced.' Wilkins noted that the town had a population of 3,384. The collegiate church was the parish church and was capable of holding one third of the population. However, he pointed out that

> [the] greater portion of the inhabitants are averse from the *choral* services, in consequence of which the building and maintenance of a church wholly parochial has long [been] deemed a *desideratum*; that with respect to the daily services, it has been correctly stated that the number of persons attending them, even in the summer months, does not average *one per diem*; that it is the belief of your memorialist, that were there … a parochial chapel, the collegiate church would be forsaken on the Sabbath by all but a few, and that few would remain from attachment to the venerable pile, and from their delight in sacred music.

---

[1] Parliamentary Papers, 1836 (86) *From His Majesty's commissioners appointed to consider the state of the Established Church with reference to ecclesiastical duties and revenues* etc., 12 (HC 86 [1836], xxxvi, 1).

Wilkins proposed that daily morning prayer should be said, evening prayer 'chaunted', and 'that on Sundays and great fasts and festivals ... the morning service be wholly *parochial* and the evening choral, with the lecture or sermon.' The establishment could therefore be reduced to beneficial effect.

A few weeks later Edward Garrard Marsh, prebendary of Wood-borough, wrote from his home in Hampstead to the archbishop of York who was one of the commissioners, with a compromise proposal. He wrote on his own behalf, but he clearly reflected the opinion of several of the chapter. Marsh indicated the chapter's dissent from George Wilkins's 'counter memorial'. He claimed that the chapter was not in disagreement with the commissioners' proposals *per se* but differed from them only on details. While the chapter did not disagree with the appointment of the archdeacon of Nottingham (George Wilkins) as rector of Southwell, it believed that the commissioners' proposal of 'a scheme for an inefficient choral establishment' would involve abolition of the paid choir.[1] Marsh suggested that an efficient choral establishment could be maintained if the three wealthiest benefices in the chapter's gift (Barnborough at £650 a year), Beelsby (£450) and Waltham (£300) were annexed to the chapter so that their revenues could be used to augment the payment of four residentiary canons including the rector, an assistant minister, and two vicars choral.

The details of Marsh's scheme, and of an alternative that he proposed, are of little direct relevance here, but the correspondence indicates the depth of disagreement between those, undoubtedly led by the vicar-general John Thomas Becher, who opposed any interference whatever with the traditional forms of governance and of worship of the collegiate church, and George Wilkins, archdeacon and prebendary, who, as vicar of a very populous parish in Nottingham, recognised that the religious needs of the people in Southwell were not being met by a choral establishment enjoyed by a few. But there was more than disagreement between Becher and Wilkins. There was also a degree both of rivalry and of personal animosity.

---

[1]   In 1818 there were five 'singing men' or lay vicars, each paid £10 a year. There was provision for six in the constitution but the number had been reduced to five 'a few years since ... to augment the salaries of the remainder.' The organist, who also served as the rector chori and auditor, was paid a total of £25 'and several other perquisites, all of which have been considerably advanced' (Richard P. Shilton, *History of Southwell* (Newark, 1818), 111).

John Thomas Becher:
vicar-general, magistrate, and poor law reformer

The college reached its widest influence in the years before it was dissolved – a dominance epitomised by the hugely energetic, able, autocrat John Thomas Becher (1770–1848), pluralist, magistrate, and ostensible social reformer, appointed prebendary of South Muskham in 1818 and the chapter's vicar-general in 1830.[1] Becher's powerful influence, and the institutions that he created, long outlasted his life. His determination to reduce poor relief and therefore the level of rates that supported it, his promotion of self-help through his proposals to regulate friendly societies, and the regimes he imposed in the Southwell workhouse and the house of correction (both of which he rebuilt or extended and superintended as visiting magistrate) are well known. Although he made a distinction between the 'legitimate Poor' and the 'abandoned Class' marked by 'wilful Pauperism', he was in practice resolutely intransigent to those he defined as the 'lower orders', the 'inferior classes' and 'mechanics'. Having initially been sympathetic to the distress of poor framework knitters he was to say of them that 'the lower orders were almost universally corrupted by profusion and depravity, scarcely to be credited by those who are strangers to our district … '[2]

---

[1] Strictly, a vicar-general was appointed by a bishop or archbishop to represent him in the exercise of his jurisdiction – in this case in the archbishop of York's peculiar jurisdiction of Southwell. Thus, the vicar-general conducted an annual visitation of the 28 parishes in the peculiar, calling their clergy and churchwardens before him in the chapter house for the same purposes as the archdeacon of Nottingham held a visitation in four centres in his jurisdiction. However, at least by the early nineteenth century the vicar-general of Southwell was elected by the chapter from among its number. He acted for the archbishop of York in the exercise of his episcopal functions (other than ordination and confirmation) and in his legal and administrative responsibilities, and also on behalf the chapter other than in those duties which devolved to the prebendary (that is the canon) in residence. Before the reform of the chapter and the dissolution of Southwell's peculiar jurisdiction the canon in residence (for three months on a four-year rota) was, as Richard Shilton noted, 'the director concerning all matters of internal government' in the collegiate church, 'and in some degree answers to the Dean of other ecclesiastical bodies of this description'. Every member of the chapter was required by the Southwell statutes to pay 'complete obedience' to him (Shilton, *History of Southwell*, 80–1). The canon in residence presided over meetings of the chapter and managed its revenues. After Becher's death George Wilkins styled himself permanent residentiary canon.

[2] Cited in Chapman and Walker (eds), *Southwell*, II, 20. The framework knitters in Nottinghamshire and Derbyshire (over 16,000 in 1844) suffered very badly in the repeated slumps in the hosiery industry. In 1844 the *Report to the Commission to Enquire into the Condition of the Framework Knitters* reported that the general state of the framework knitters in the two counties was 'very deplorable' (quoted in Christopher Weir, *As Poor as Stockingers* (Nottingham, 1998), 24).

In 1812, at a time of Luddite machine-breaking in a deep depression in the hosiery trades in Nottingham and its satellite industrial villages, Becher, as one of the county justices, published *Observations on the Punishment of Offenders and the Preservation of the Peace, occasioned by Trespasses, Riots and Felonies, now prevalent in the County of Nottingham*. This was a 56-page booklet in which he summarised the law relating to conspiracy, common assault, battery, assault with intent to murder, affray, larceny, robbery, the illegal levying of contributions (from 'the terrified inhabitants of country villages' by 'delegates from the Societies at Arnold, Bulwell and other places'), burglary, sending threatening letters, malicious mischief, cutting down and destroying trees, being accessories before and after the fact – and much else, including rewards that could be paid to informers, the remuneration of special constables, and the use of the militia. Becher concluded that it was not the responsibility of the magistracy to seek 'the adjustment of differences between workmen and their employers' but neither did he suggest where, or how, such an 'adjustment' should be sought. He was not unaware of the impact of irregular and low wages. Later, in evidence to a committee of the House of Lords, he argued that were farmers able and willing to increase average wages for their labourers from eight to twelve shillings a week this would reduce the rates and depauperize the poor. In 1828 he acknowledged that the weekly wage of stockingers in Nottinghamshire was on average 'only about Ten Shillings clear of the regular deductions' and that they earned less than 'the Common Labourer.'[1] But as a magistrate he was solely concerned with the maintenance of law and order and with ensuring that his fellow magistrates were fully aware of criminal charges that could be brought and penalties that could be imposed.

Similarly, Becher's reform of the operation of the poor law in the parishes within his jurisdiction, most significantly his support of the abolition of out-door relief, was designed primarily to reduce the burden of the poor rate levied on his own class. The reform served the interests of the 'Relievers' before that of the 'Relieved'. Although Becher appreciated that modifying the system of relief should not be undertaken solely to lessen 'the pecuniary expenditure on account of the Poor' and that 'religious impulse' and 'moral influence' and the inculcation of

---

[1]   J.T. Becher, *The Antipauper System, exemplifying the Positive and Practical Good realized by the Relievers and the Relieved under the Frugal, Beneficent and Lawful Administration of the Poor Law prevailing at Southwell and the neighbouring district* (1828, 1834), xxii–xxiii.

'virtuous habits' among the working class should play their part,[1] the fact that his reforms led to a drastic and lasting reduction in the poor rate was a matter of pride for Becher. He reduced expenditure in the parish of Southwell from £2,006 in 1821 to £517 in 1824 and to £606 in 1833 – a reduction of between 70 and 75 per cent maintained over 13 years.[2] This saving was also made in Bingham by Becher's cousin and friend, Robert Lowe, the rector, whose regime, once Becher's reforms had been introduced, reduced the cost of maintaining the poor in his parish from £1,231 in 1816–17 to £449 in 1831–2, a reduction of 64 per cent.[3] However, research has shown conclusively that expenditure on poor relief throughout this period generally rose and fell with the price of wheat, from a high in 1816–17 to a low in 1832–3. As magistrates were responsible for setting bread prices Becher would have been well aware of these changes. It is arguable that the burden on local ratepayers would have decreased dramatically without Becher's reforms.[4]

Becher took pride in his achievement and was a resolute defender of his reputation. This is clear from a pamphlet that he published in 1828 on his anti-pauper system. In this he argued, against rival claimants, that he had been the first to initiate poor law reform. He wrote: 'If the Antipauper system had been transferred from any other place to Southwell, sincerity and self-respect would have prompted me to render the full measure of acknowledgement to its original author.' He claims never to have discussed poor law administration with Robert Lowe, who had imposed a harsh regime in his own parish in 1815, but it is hardly believable that Becher and Lowe never discussed a matter of such importance. Becher reveals the true motive for his reforms a few sentences later. Having noted that that one reason that he never conferred with Lowe was that he was conscious that 'on many important points, our opinions differ essentially', he then says, 'in fact neither the Overseers of the Poor at Southwell, nor myself, had heard of any reduction in the Rates at Bingham, until our Antipauper System was in full operation.' The test of the success of the system was whether or not the poor rate was consistently and drastically reduced – as it was in Southwell and its neighbouring villages, and eventually in Bingham.

Inevitably those who J.T. Becher sought to regulate had a low opinion

---

[1]   Ibid. xxii, xxxi.

[2]   Ibid., 2.

[3]   *Nottingham and Newark Mercury*, 20 April 1833.

[4]   J.D. Marshall, 'The Nottinghamshire Reformers and their contribution to the New Poor Law', *Economic History Review*, 2nd ser, xiii (1961), 382–96; see also P. Mandler, 'The making of the New Poor Law *Redivivus*', *Past and Present*, 117 (1987), 131–57.

of him. In May 1814 the First Peace of Paris seemed to signal the end of the Napoleonic wars. It was reported that Southwell's 'loyal trades-men, elated by so cheering an event, thought proper to appoint a day to celebrate'. A letter from a Southwell inhabitant to the *Nottingham Review* tells us what happened next. Though the correspondent does not name John Thomas Becher it is clear that the clergyman 'who plumes himself as being the despot of the town' could have been no one else. He summoned the town's tradesmen to appear before him and told them that if they persevered in 'meeting and eating their dinners together' he would flood the town with rival tradesmen and destroy their living, reminding them of the evils of insubordination and telling them that 'the Clergy are the only legitimate heads of the town, and every tradesman, let his property, his influence, or his character stand as they will with his fellow citizens, is bound to acknowledge and obey them as his superiors.'[1]

In 1834 one of Becher's contemporaries, a man who knew him well, Williamson Etches, who had been keeper of Nottinghamshire house of correction in Southwell (until he resigned claiming that his duties did not suit him)[2] publicly accused Becher of enjoying 'love of office and of its sweets', of exercising 'his own authority and dictatorial power', and of deliberately altering a report by Etches in order to support his, Becher's, case against Etches's proposals to change the disciplinary regime in the house of correction.[3] However, a rule that 'silence shall be strictly observed and enforced in every part of the Prison' was imposed.[4]

In the same year, Matthew Mole, Etches' spredecessor as governor, who had been dismissed by Becher for alleged financial impropriety,

---

[1]   Letter from 'A Briton', *Nottingham Review*, 9 Sept. 1814.

[2]   NAO, C/QAG/5/137: Etches' letter of resignation dated 22 Oct. 1834; C/QA/G5/138: report of visiting magistrates, dated 23 Oct. 1834, recommending acceptance of Etches' resignation because he was incapable of carrying out his duties relating to records and accounts.

[3]   *Nottingham and Newark Mercury*, 27 Dec. 1834. The context was Etches's recommen-dation that silence be imposed in the house of correction in Southwell. Becher, as visiting magistrate, maintained that to follow Etches's advice would require, at considerable additional expense to ratepayers, structural alterations to the building and the employment of additional turnkeys. Etches denied this. Becher's motives were clearly financial and not humanitarian. Further to this see the report of a meeting of the justices of the peace in Dec. 1834 to discuss *inter alia* the 'carrying into effect the system of silence' in Southwell house of correction (*Nottingham and Newark Mercury*, 13 Dec. 1834). Becher's rules for the workhouse show that he imposed a harsh disciplinary regime with regular whippings for disobedience. He also encouraged the establishment of a treadwheel in 1822 with the support of Bernard Hutchinson, surgeon of the house of correction, but against widespread evidence of its very harmful effects elsewhere.

[4]   *Rules for the Government of the Nottinghamshire House of Correction* (1834).

published a detailed defence, effectively claiming that he had been unfairly treated,[1] and John Cowell, assistant poor law commissioner, published a line-by-line rebuttal of 'certain charges and assertions' made about Cowell by Becher in his booklet on his anti-pauper system showing how Becher had consistently omitted or misapplied evidence in his (Becher's) favour.[2]

Several of Becher's social class were also highly critical of him. Under the Poor Law Amendment Act of 1834, local administration of the poor law was passed from local magistrates to the poor law commissioners, the former poor law unions reorganised, and a national system of workhouses on the Southwell model was established. Of the three national poor law commissioners, the leading figure was George Nicholls, who had served as overseer of the poor in Southwell from 1821 to 1826. To Becher's chagrin he later claimed to have initiated and developed the Southwell poor law reforms. It was reported to Nicholls in 1836 that the 'Thurgaton Incorporation[3] is defunct ... Mr Becher is *almost raving*. Sir Robt Heron is here – and the two Barts [the other was Sir Robert Bromley] congratulate very much on Becher's downfall – if he gets well they will not *allow* him to have anything to do with the *New Union*.'[4]

Leaving aside these personal animosities and rivalries, a Nottingham Baptist and former hosier, Absalom Barnett, writing in 1833 of Becher's local administration of the poor law before the 1834 Act, attacked 'the calculating, systematic and unyielding regularity of a Becher'. Barnett accused Becher of ignoring one section of the moderately reforming Act of 1782 and of violating another, and creating a workhouse regime 'especially intended to act *in terrorem* upon [the] able-bodied and

---

[1] Matthew Mole, *A Narrative of Eleven Years Governorship of Southwell House of Correction* (Nottingham, 1834). In the opinion of the Benjamin Hutchinson, Mole was 'a man of indefatigable vigilance and acknowledged humanity' (*Observations on Prison Discipline, exemplified by the Tread-Mill and Dietary adopted in the Nottinghamshire House of Correction at Southwell* (Newark, 1823), 48.

[2] John W. Cowell, *A Letter to the Rev. John T. Becher of Southwell, in reply to certain charges and assertions made in the introduction to a second edition of his Anti-Pauper System, recently published* (1834).

[3] The previous poor law union of 49 parishes.

[4] The National Archives, MH 32/28: letter from Edward Gulson, an assistant poor law commissioner, to George Nicholls, one of the three poor law commissioners, 1 March 1836 (I am indebted to Stanley Chapman for this reference). Bromley was later to regret the harshness of the regime imposed in the new Southwell poor law union.

improvident poor.'[1]

Becher was aware of the need to protect 'the rights of the poor' and sought, he said, to 'distinguish carefully' between 'Impotent' and 'Improvident' paupers. As an ancillary element of his anti-pauper system Becher established a Friendly Society for the 'laborious Classes' and promoted a number of other 'protective Institutions', but these supplemented 'coercion', for he readily acknowledged 'the impossibility of enforcing the Anti-Pauper System without the aid of a Workhouse.'

What has not been recorded is the reactionary position Becher adopted as vicar-general, not least after the reform of the college and the abolition of its peculiar jurisdiction in 1841. Change did not bring about transformation. For example, Becher and his predecessor, William Barrow, did little to maintain the fabric of the Minster. A lengthy programme of essential restoration of the neglected building was not begun until after Becher's death in 1848.[2] Least of all was Becher inclined to effect the transition from the Minster's position of regional dominance to that of one parish church among others. As the chapter continued to exist until its last prebendary died in 1873, those of its residual responsibilities not passed to the Ecclesiastical Commissioners such as patronage of its benefices,[3] conveyances of land, and the granting of leases were still exercised by the remaining prebendaries under the leadership of John Thomas Becher.

The relationship between Becher and George Wilkins, each in his own sphere a powerful, influential autocrat, seems always to have been fraught. It became more so as the years passed. An example of this increased tension concerned the granting of leases by the chapter. After

[1]   Absalom Barnett, *The poor laws, and their administration: being an enquiry into the causes of English pauperism, and the failure of measures intended for its relief: also, practical suggestions to reduce the amount of parochial assessments, and improve the condition of the poor* (1833), 2, 36. Gilbert's Act of 1782 confirmed the principle of outdoor relief. Further to Becher's motivation in promoting his reforms and his attitude towards the poor, see M.R. Austin, 'John Thomas Becher 1770–1848: reactionary reformer?', in Stanley Chapman and Derek Walker (eds), *Minster People* (Southwell, 2009), 61–75.

[2]   For the restoration begun by George Wilkins, see Harold Brooke, *Closed for Business: Ewan Christian's Restoration of Southwell Minster 1848–1888* (Southwell, 1997).

[3]   When John Murray Wilkins carried out the visitation of his rural deanery in 1855 nine benefices (Bleasby, Edingley, Farnsfield, Halam, Kirklington, Morton, Rolleston, Upton and Woodborough) remained in the chapter's patronage, the rectory of Southwell remained in the gift of the prebendary of Normanton, and Oxton, Blidworth and Calverton in that of the prebendary of Oxton. By this date patronage of the former prebendal benefices of Caunton, Halloughton, North and South Muskham and Norwell had passed to the bishops of Manchester and Ripon alternately. The former prebendal estates which provided income for these bishops carried with them rights of presentation.

the reform of the chapter in 1841 George Wilkins argued that its remaining common assets be placed with the Ecclesiastical Commissioners (to whom the prebendal estates passed as each prebendary resigned or died) and, as leases on properties expired, not to renew them. Becher was opposed to this. The chapter seal was required on all leases. At a meeting of the chapter on 21 October 1847 it was noted that

> the Common seal of the Chapter having been abstracted and removed from the Fire Proof Box in the Record Room previous to the last Chapter held on the twenty-second of July last, and not being available for Chapter purposes, Decreed that a new Common Seal be adopted by the Chapter ...

The chapter ordered that the old seal 'be destroyed in the presence of the Chapter as soon as the same shall come into their custody or possession.' The previous meeting of the chapter, held on 22 July and chaired by Becher, had been almost exclusively devoted to the granting of new leases. Wilkins was present at that meeting but, alone among the prebendaries attending, had refused to agree to new leases being made and remaining leases being renewed. He had evidently previously appealed to the bishop of Lincoln to restrain Becher and the chapter in its policy. At this same meeting, the chapter had ordered its clerk, Richard Bridgman Barrow, to seek legal opinion on the question of the chapter's right to manage its own assets. At its meeting on 2 November 1847, chaired by Wilkins as canon residentiary, it was ordered that 'the late Common Seal of the Chapter now delivered up by the Canon of Normanton be destroyed and defaced.' The canon of Normanton was George Wilkins. He had 'abstracted and removed' the old seal in an attempt to prevent Becher granting leases, only to be outmanoeuvred by him. This incident must have marked the low point in the relationship between the two men. In his many letters to the bishop of Lincoln, Wilkins occasionally dropped the courtesy title 'Mr' when referring to J.T. Becher, notably when, in April 1847, he reported to Bishop Kaye that although 'our chapter day passed over without bloodshed ... Becher is resolved that every impediment should be placed in the way of doing any business, save and except the renewal of leases.'[1]

Wilkins's exasperation with Becher was expressed later that year when, in reporting Becher's illness (and remarking on his calm state of mind), he told Kaye that 'I have been expecting every day lately to

---

[1]   LAO, Cor. B.5/8/8/1, letter from Wilkins to Kaye, 23 April 1847.

announce the death of Mr Becher; but he is yet alive – and that is all.'[1]

There is no doubt that Becher resisted change. For him the old order must continue and the statutes of the collegiate church be upheld. For example, he insisted that the prebendal cycle of residence must be continued after the reform of the chapter even though as predendaries died or resigned they were not replaced. In 1845 George Wilkins, writing from Southwell, asked the bishop of Lincoln whether any arrangements had been made

> for the appointment of a substitute for each of the turns of residence connected with the vacant Canonries here. The Rota, or new Cycle of Sixteen turns commenced on 1st February, and the first turn is for a vacant stall. Mr Becher has done no act in the Church beyond reading the Communion Service some six or seven times – and in his absence when unable to attend the same, it has devolved on *me*, for I think 4 or 5 turns.[2]

Similarly, Becher insisted that the pattern of services in the Minster must be continued even though there were no longer six vicars choral to conduct them, and after their successors, the minor canons, had been reduced to two. He was intent on treating the parish vicar and, after 1841, the rector (George Wilkins's son) almost as curates under his direct supervision. In January 1839 Becher reported to the chapter that the parish vicar, Morgan Watkins, had, at a wedding that he had conducted on New Year's day, acted in an objectionable (but unspecified) way. The chapter, presided over by Becher, instructed its clerk, Richard Bridgman Barrow, to seek legal opinion 'as to what proceedings may be thought advisable for an exemplary prosecution' of Watkins. This instruction was noted in the chapter minute book. Wilkins had not attended that meeting but subsequently wrote against this minute: 'NB The spiritual duties are the duties of the parish vicar *only*, but may be discharged on particular occasions by a Clergyman obtaining his permission — Mr Becher denied such permission being necessary and persisted and resisted — And was in the wrong.' At the following chapter meeting, this time attended by Wilkins, Morgan Watkins, having admitted the 'error you acknowledge to have committed on new year's day at the Altar of the Church', was formally admonished. The chapter had been prepared to impose a more severe penalty but, the minute

---

[1]   LAO, Cor.B.5/8/8/4, Wilkins to Kaye, 14 Dec. 1847.

[2]   LAO, Cor. B./5/8/20/1, letter from Wilkins to Kaye, 3 Jan. 1845.

records, had been 'induced to adopt this mild form of proceeding' on the recommendation of the vicar-general, J. T. Becher – though Watkins must not again 'manifest any disrespect towards the person of the Vicar General.'[1]

George Wilkins may well have seen the rebuking of Morgan Watkins as a criticism of himself, for he had appointed Watkins as parish vicar and had been related to him by marriage. In 1842 Wilkins reported another example of Becher's assertion of authority. He complained to the bishop of Lincoln that Becher had insisted that a sermon be preached at 'the third service' on Sundays, evidently against the wishes of the newly appointed rector of Southwell, John Murray Wilkins, George's son. Becher had placed an injunction on 'Mr Turton', a minor canon, to do so, even though the statutes of the collegiate church did not require it.[2]

But these personal rivalries and policy differences were internal to the chapter. The members of the college had little personal contact with the ordinary people in the town, unless, as justices of the peace, they faced them from the bench of the magistrates' court. A local shoemaker, John Holmes who was born in the town in 1821, sums up the impression they gave when he described with bitterness the Minster's clergy as 'the many high proude ones' who were 'well knowen [for] ... grasping at all they can lay thir hands upon.'[3]

---

[1]   NAO, SC/01/16, Chapter minute book, 24 Jan. 1839, 18 April 1839.

[2]   LAO, Cor. B./5/8/36/15, letter from Wilkins to Kaye, 7 June 1842. 'Mr Turton' was William Parsons Turton (1819–96).

[3]   'Life of John Holmes', 75 (his spelling).

3

'A most deplorable spirit': church, politics, and class

In a letter to the *Nottingham and Newark Mercury* in 1827, George Wilkins wrote:

> ... I maintain my position, that of the two classes of the people, not of Nottingham alone, but throughout the whole Kingdom, viz. the Dissenters from the Church [of England] on the one hand, and the disaffected to the Government on the other — that both these are disposed to receive with avidity, any report that makes against the character or the conduct of the Clergy of the Establishment.[1]

Wilkins recognised that hostility to the Church of England, of which the clergy were the identifiable symbol, was driven by political, social and theological motives, yet each was bound up with, and expressed through the others. In urban parishes this opposition was most publicly and regularly (though by no means exclusively) expressed when church rates were levied by clergy and churchwardens at annual vestry meetings, while the social privileges that were its root cause were given visible identity in the arrangement, quality and possession of seats in parish churches, both urban and rural. The annual vestry meeting was the public focus of this opposition, particularly in towns.

The vestry: the clergy and civil administration

The Church of England made personal contact with the majority of the people on those few occasions in their lives when its clergy officiated at their weddings, baptised their children and buried their dead. Certainly in the early years covered by this study, the population of much of central Nottinghamshire would have lacked routine pastoral care because

---

[1] 10 March 1827.

many parishes lacked parsonage houses and resident clergymen. In these parishes the clergy touched the day-to-day lives of the majority indirectly through their role in local government and the administration of the poor law, and in the administration of justice. Until well into the second half of the nineteenth century there was a firm clerical hand on the instruments of social control in this part of the county. The parish vestry (so named because in the early middle ages these annual meetings were held in the parish church or its vestry)[1] was the only form of local government at this time, certainly in rural parishes. There were some 9,000 vestries nationwide, each under the chairmanship of the incumbent of the parish, but the system was by no means uniform. Where landowners had substantial estates, the vestry electorate might comprise less than a dozen. Over 700 localities lacked vestries altogether. In other places an oligarchical select vestry that had developed over time, or had been established by a local Acts of Parliament, usurped the functions of an open vestry. In some towns a chartered corporation carried out some of the functions of the vestry.

Originally the annual vestry meeting, presided over by the incumbent, appointed the churchwardens. They were responsible for the maintenance of the nave of the parish church[2] and churchyard and for financial provision for the church's services. Following the Poor Law Statute of 1600 the vestry also appointed the overseers of the poor and raised a rate for the maintenance of the poor through the provision of both indoor and outdoor relief, and for highways and sometimes other parish facilities such as the stocks and cattle pounds.[3] For example, in Farnsfield in the 1830s the annual vestry received the appointment of a churchwarden by the vicar and elected a parish warden, but also appointed a pinder, a 'Buyer of Sparrows',[4] a mole-catcher, and overseers of the poor and a surveyor of highways. The Farnsfield vestry was also responsible for

---

[1] In the nineteenth century the annual vestry could be held in a local public house. For example, on 27 March 1860 the Southwell St Mary vestry was held in the Crown hotel (*Nottingham Review*, 30 March 1860).

[2] The maintenance of the chancel was generally the responsibility of the rector of the parish, that is, actually or notionally, the person who received the 'great' tithes, be he (or she) a clergyman or a lay person.

[3] The Poor Law Amendment Act of 1834 transferred many of the powers of parish overseers to the new Poor Law Unions.

[4] The pinder was responsible for containing unattended and trespassing livestock in the parish pinfold (see, e.g., Farnsfield overseers' minutes for 22 April 1842). Sparrows were sold to the parish constable or, by the 1850s, to the parish Buyer of Sparrows, for 6d. per dozen for old birds, 3d. per dozen for young birds, and 2d. per dozen for sparrows' eggs (Farnsfield overseers' minutes, 6 May 1836).

letting the verges of the lanes in the parish for grazing to the highest bidders. Calverton's vestry appointed an assessor of taxes in addition to the other officers. In Southwell, as well as four churchwardens,[1] overseers of the poor and surveyors of highways, the St Mary's parish vestry nominated five constables. On 1 April 1857 the Southwell vestry meeting, with the Revd John Drake Becher in the chair, discussed, amongst other matters, 'the bad state of the sewerage in the town' and levied an additional rate to defray the expense of 'a certain portion being completed this year.'[2]

Critically, vestries were responsible for maintaining the parish church and churchyard through levying a separate church rate. Payment was compulsory until 1868, but caused great resentment in many parishes for many years before then. As churchwardens raised revenue their election was frequently contentious, particularly in urban parishes. Elections could be highly party political. The public poll might last two or more days on the model of a general or by-election with hustings, a high turn-out of qualified electors, and suspicions (often well-founded) of bribery. For example, in Newark in 1834, the year of the passing of the infamous Poor Law Amendment Act by Melbourne's Whig administration, in a hotly contested election five candidates fought for the three posts of churchwarden for Newark St Mary Magdalene. The *Nottingham and Newark Mercury* described the second day of the election:

> Last week we gave the state of the poll up to Friday afternoon at two o'clock. At seven o'clock the numbers were — Massey, 792; Crampern, 783; Clark, 1,016; Fillingham, 695; Bishop, 774. The poll commenced the next morning at nine, but went on very slowly till about eleven, when Bishop headed Crampern by one — and here commenced a beautiful race, they being neck-and-neck seven times before seven o'clock; at that time the Blues got the lead and kept it to the end, although the Red candidates polled for each other. About eight o'clock one of the candidates stated they had no more votes to bring up, and requested the poll might be closed, which was done accordingly, and after the numbers were pro-claimed by the poll-clerk, the vicar declared Mr Clark, Mr Massey, and Mr Crampern, duly elected as churchwardens for the ensuing year. A vote of thanks was given to the vicar and Mr Caparn, the

---

[1]   In addition two churchwardens represented 'the Trinity Church district', although Holy Trinity had become a separate parish in 1846.

[2]   *Nottinghamshire and Lincolnshire Advertiser*, 4 April 1857.

poll-clerk, and the meeting broke up. The Reds are very sore at their defeat, and say they will have a scrutiny, but that is impossible: the election was made in Easter week according to law. If they were permitted to scrutinize, they perhaps would be in a much worse condition, as both parties were not very nice who polled. The numbers at the final close were — Massey, 859; Crampern, 842; Clark, 1,042; Fillingham, 730; Bishop, 837.[1]

The work of vestries was overseen (more or less, according to their vigilance and independence) by the magistrates in Quarter Sessions. By the 1850s, in some parishes, powers had become separated between the vestry and the annual parish meeting, with the meetings held on different days. So, for example, by 1859 the Farnsfield annual parish meeting met early in April and appointed the overseers of the poor (in that year, John Wood, a carrier and farmer, and Thomas Hudson, a saddler); assistant overseer and surveyor of highways (Thomas Tongue, a cornwainer), the buyer of sparrows (also Thomas Tongue), the pinder (Thomas Pettener, cornwainer), and the mole catcher (W. Moody).[2] The annual vestry met a month later and appointed the churchwardens: William Todd was appointed by the vicar, and Richard Truswell was again elected by the parish. This separation of function anticipated local government reforms at the end of the century.

Only ratepayers (and then only male until 1831 when some female ratepayers were enfranchised) could vote or stand for office. Although the majority of the population could not vote, those appointed could be of modest social position.[3] There was no nationally uniform constitution determining the duties and powers of the vestry, and local custom and law resulted in very wide variation. The existence in many places of select vestries led to abuses of power, while the lack of efficient and

[1] *Nottingham and Newark Mercury*, 12 April 1834. The 'Red' candidates were Tories, and the 'Blue' candidates represented the Whig interest. At a parliamentary by-election in Newark in 1829 ratepayers were bribed or intimidated by the agents of the duke of Newcastle, the principal landowner, to vote for the Tory candidate. This led to a petition to parliament in 1830 and to a lengthy debate in the House of Commons. No action was taken as the duke's leases were due for renewal in 1836. The reference here to both parties being 'not very nice' may well allude to bribery.and intimidation. The existence of considerable, and long disputed, ecclesiastical charities in Newark would have been a further factor exciting interest in the election of its churchwardens.

[2] *Nottingham Review*, 8 April 1859.

[3] In 1854, for example, the annual vestry of Southwell collegiate church appointed a banker's clerk, two grocers and a builder as churchwardens, and a plumber, a glazier, two butchers and a cottager as constables (*Nottingham Review*, 12 May 1854). The two 'Trinity district' wardens were a painter and a 'gentleman'.

independent auditing resulted in widespread corruption. Even so, the annual parish vestry meeting was the first point at which local government met the ordinary people, the vast majority of whom were unenfranchised. In 1815 the parish vestries in England were responsible for levying and spending some £10 million in rates. The 1834 Poor Law Amendment Act and the 1835 Municipal Corporations Act brought some reform to the local government of towns by diffusing power, but apart from the major changes to the administration of the poor law, these reforms had little impact on the local government of rural parishes. It was not until the Local Government Act of 1894 that the parish vestries lost their powers except those relating directly to the maintenance and administration of the church and of ecclesiastical charities.

In any case, what the reforms of the 1830s did not do, at least initially, was to disturb the old authority structures based on class and money. But by the 1850s the middle classes were tasting power through a degree of ratepayer democracy, and the mass of the urban working class had long recognised that it had no political power at all. So it was that, as Richard Price puts it, 'mid-Victorian urban politics were dominated by contests around obscure offices like the highway surveyors or churchwardens as old and new, Anglican and dissenting, Liberal and Tory, and middle- and working-class groups jostled for leverage in the new system.'[1]

The deeply rural agricultural parishes were not usually the scene of these often bitterly fought contests between newly enfranchised voters and vested interests, nor did they hear the complaints of the ordinary people against both, but the industrial villages certainly were, and here church rates were fiercely debated at annual vestry meetings.

The church rate question

Church rates were paid by all ratepayers, whether Anglican or not, for the maintenance of parish churches to provide services to which all parishioners had access, not least for marriages. Under Hardwicke's Marriage Act of 1753, and until civil marriages were allowed in 1837, all marriages in England (except those of Jews and Quakers) had to be solemnised by the Church of England. The argument in favour of the imposition of a church rate was that as all used their parish church so all

---

[1] Richard Price, *British Society 1680–1880: Dynamism, Containment and Change* (Cambridge, 1999), 181.

must pay for its maintenance. In 1813 church rates were made recoverable before justices of the peace where the amount did not exceed £10 and the validity of the rate was not in dispute. Quakers had been compelled to pay church rates under legislation passed in 1696. Dissenters saw the imposition of the rate as a denial of their religious freedom. On the political front, Chartists saw church rates as a battle ground in their pursuit of at least three of the six points of their Charter – universal manhood suffrage, vote by secret ballot and abolition of property qualifications for electors.

Thus the compulsory church rate was a cause of bitter contention in many urban and industrial parishes, and, as time passed, in some rural parishes also. So it was that the Anti-Church Rate Liberation Society (known also by a title with a much wider remit, the Society for the Liberation of Religion from State Control) held meetings in nonconformist chapels in Nottingham throughout these years and attracted large and vociferous crowds. In April 1850 a contentious meeting in the Exchange Room passed the resolution 'that the union of Church and State is injurious to religion, destructive of the independence of the Church and incompatible with the existence of religious equality among the people.' An Anglican clergyman, William Clementson,[1] had attempted to put the case that the Church of England by law established (and therefore supported by church rates) was a national blessing but had met with 'loud groans and hissings.' Before the resolution was put, so the *Nottingham Mercury* reported, 'a working man addressed a few words to the meeting, recommending his fellow workmen to have no part or lot in the matter for that it was evident that both parties [the Church of England and nonconformity] were rogues and cheaters of the poor man.'[2] The *Mercury* did not name him, but he was no ordinary working man. He was George Woodward, born in Bulwell but then living in the parish of Nottingham St Mary. This 41-year-old framework knitter was one of the earliest Chartist leaders in Nottingham with, among a few others, George Harrison, a preacher from Calverton.[3] The issue of church rates was an issue for nonconformists and Chartists alike. For nonconformists it was a question of religious freedom, for Chartists it was a question of electoral reform. George Woodward could see the

---

[1]   Dublin AB 1844, AM 1847, Oxford MA 1847, d. 1844, p. 1845; 1852 Superintendent of the Special Mission to Roman Catholics in Great Britain (Protestant Truth Society); vicar of Womenswold (Kent) 1877–80.

[2]   *Nottingham Mercury*, 12 April 1850.

[3]   *Nottingham Journal*, 12 April 1850; 1851 census; Roy A. Church, *Economic and Social Change in a Midland Town: Nottingham, 1815–1900* (1966), 128.

difference. For him, as the *Nottingham Journal*, naming him, reported, the churches, nonconformity and the Church of England alike, were no more than 'thieves falling out.' Woodward recognised that working men must achieve the franchise before they would have any chance of 'getting their rights', and recommended that they should not side with any church.[1]

A very considerable number of the people whose lives were affected by the decisions of the vestries and their officers were not Anglicans. By the 1840s it was not unusual for the incumbent as chairman of the annual vestry to be confronted by a hostile crowd, especially in towns and industrial villages. Inevitably there was a sharp political edge to this hostility. In many places nonconformist rate-payers had for years used the annual vestry meeting to object to paying the compulsory church rate. To oppose the rate, together with the payment of tithes and the appointment of clergymen magistrates, was one of the few ways in which nonconformists (and then only rate-paying nonconformists) could register their opposition to political privilege represented by the Church of England. At least one nonconformist, John Thorogood, a Chelmsford cobbler, was imprisoned for non-payment in July 1839. It required an Act of Parliament to release him.

The Nottingham press was sharply divided on the great issue of the relationship of the state to the Church of England, of which the question of church rates was a focus. Inevitably the Tory press favoured the maintenance of these payments, and the radical press was against them. In the 1830s there was little balanced marshalling of evidence for and against. Twenty years later, in 1855, in his *Stevenson's Penny Times* the Nottingham newspaper proprietor Thomas Stevenson produced what he believed was a convincing argument for abolition. He cited the cost of public worship in Boston in the USA. The value of church estates in the city was, he noted, about four million dollars, and the expenses of the 20 different churches varied from 1,500 to 5,500 dollars a year, so 'the cost of public worship in the churches occupied by the wealthier portion of the citizens will average about 100 dollars a Sunday.' The clergy were well paid and churches were very well attended, leading Stevenson to observe that 'the above facts show that it is safe to divorce the Church from the State, and allow the most perfect religious freedom to prevail … The figures given above will allow that no compulsion is needed to

[1]   Ibid.

insure a liberal support for public worship in the community.'[1] By 1855 this argument was beginning to be heard but, with no state church in the USA, it had little relevance to the argument about church rates or the wider question of the relationship of church and state.

Church rate disputes could be fierce and even violent. For years the refusal of the annual vestry at Nottingham St Mary, of which George Wilkins was the incumbent, to pass a church rate[2] had meant that the maintenance of St Mary's had been neglected, and in 1842 the church was declared structurally unsafe with £4,600 needed for repairs. A churchwarden, George Eddowes, had refused to ask the parish to set a church rate for many years and said that he did not care whether one was passed or not.[3] The church was closed for worship from 1843 to 1848. Wilkins placed the blame on 'the Dissenters' who, he claimed, in 1834 'came to a determination that they would no longer suffer the Law to take effect in regard to the making of a Church-Rate' and

> upon every occasion of an attempt to make a Rate, such scenes of turbulence were enacted – such acrimony and bitterness vented against the Church, as for some time deterred its members from entering into further conflict. Indeed, no language can describe the methods used to intimidate and overawe: – no pen can paint the appearance or character of those swarms of wretches, whom, on these occasions, the ringing of the Crier's bell summoned from the beer-shops, and who, headed by Leaders, assembled in mock vestry to throw their venom upon everything sacred – creatures scarcely human, and so besotted as to be ignorant of every thing, save to raise the shout of clamour at the pre-concerted signal for expressing their disapprobation.[4]

Wilkins needed to make a case, hence his over-blown language, but his

---

[1] *Stevenson's Penny Times, Weekly Newspaper and Model Epitomist*, 29 Sept. 1855. The newspaper was published from premises in Wheeler Gate in Nottingham.

[2] During George Wilkins's incumbency of Nottingham St Mary, the church rate was regularly refused. See M.W. Bowen, 'The Anglican Church in the Industrialised Town: St Mary's Parish, Nottingham, 1770–1884' (Uunpublished M.Phil. thesis, University of Nottingham, 1997). See also a letter from a correspondent resisting the payment of church rates in Lenton in the *Nottingham Review*, 10 April 1846.

[3] *Nottingham Review*, 13 Jan. 1843. Lengthy correspondence in the Nottingham newspapers before and after this date record in great detail the story of the St Mary's church rate disputes, and the condition of the parish church.

[4] George Wilkins, *A Letter addressed to Lord John Russell in 1837 on the subject of the Church Rates* (2nd edn, 1854), 14.

account does not exaggerate these incidents: on one occasion Wilkins was saved from personal violence only by the intervention of 'a body of police'.[1]

Less violent but equally bitter campaigns were waged against the payment of church rates (and indeed any rates) in the industrial villages of Lenton, Basford, Arnold, Radford and Calverton, and in larger villages like Blyth. In Radford, the Nottingham press reported annual vestry battles. On 16 May 1850 the democratic *Nottingham Review* noted a dispute at the 'rather ungovernable' adjourned meeting of the church vestry called to rescind the operation in the parish of the Small Tenements Rating Act passed in the same year. The *Review* observed that at the first meeting of the vestry it had been evident that 'a petty spirit was at work'. What was at issue was less the operation of the Act than that many small ratepayers believed that they had been disenfranchised by trickery. Those paying less than £6 a year 'had been struck off the book and therefore denied a vote'.[2] For some the vestry allowed them to object to those with money determining a raft of local questions. One man claimed that he would not have attended the meeting had it not been 'that many of the wealthy were going to be present, who were opposed to the establishment of a free library.' Those paying less than £6, he asserted, were being classed as paupers.

Eight years later a special meeting of the Radford vestry was convened under the chairmanship of the 'senior churchwarden', a Mr Bostock. This was called to consider 'what means should be adopted in reference to the highway accounts recently disallowed by the magistrates.' The meeting was adjourned from the vestry itself to 'the entrance end of the church' to accommodate the 50–60 people who had attended, 'by far the greater proportion being working men'. The vicar, Samuel Creswell,[3] asked that the vestry be conducted in an orderly manner and in 'a spirit of forbearance.' It was not to be, and a highly contentious

---

[1]   Opposition to the payment of church rates was a feature of the annual vestries in the other Nottingham parishes: see, e.g., *Nottingham Journal*, 9 May 1845 for the dispute at St Peter's, where a churchwarden, Henry (?) Shipley, said that he 'did not care a straw whether the rate was carried or not'. On this occasion a rate was being raised merely to replace the church clock.

[2]   Under the Small Tenements Rating Act (13 and 14 Vict. c. 99) a landlord could be rated rather than a tenant where the rateable value of the premises did not exceed £6. This disenfranchised tenants who paid rates on these properties.

[3]   Born in Nottinghamshire in 1806, St John's College, Cambridge, BA 1827, MA 1830, d. 1828, p. 1829 (archbishop of York). He was married in Radford St Peter in 1832 to Mary Louisa Kreisa, and became vicar of the parish in 1840. He succeeded his father Edward who had been vicar both of Radford St Peter and of Lenton Holy Trinity since 1803.

meeting again passed the accounts that the magistrates had rejected. The *Review* observed that 'it will be seen that the meeting "passed" accounts that were not before it, and which have been disallowed by the magistrates. Comment is needless'.[1]

When Samuel Creswell became vicar of Radford eighteen years earlier the church rate had been passed without dissent. He was a well-liked incumbent, and had, within months of his appointment, established an allotments scheme in Spring Field in the parish which allowed poor labourers to rent land for cultivation at below the market rate.[2] But within a few years he had become well used to acrimonious vestry meetings in his parish. Here is another example of many of the vestry being the focus of opposition to the payment of rates in Radford. The Tory *Nottingham Journal* for 21 February 1845 reported the determination of the church rate at the annual vestry meeting. A proposal was made that the rate be set at one and a half pence in the pound. But

A Mr Milward, after much vituperative language, proposed an amendment, to the effect that the meeting do adjourn for twelve months, which was seconded by Mr Morrison, in a speech of some length, teeming with audacious falsehoods, and equally great absurdities. Amongst the rest, he attempted to give a statistical account of the wealth of the bishops – the riches of our National Church, which he stated was richer than all others put together – the number of livings in the hands of the aristocracy &. He also said that the union of Church with the State tended to demoralise the people and lower them in the scale of civilized society! This speech was continually interrupted with hisses, groans, and cries of 'Question' 'Chair' 'Order' &c., but Mr Morrison declaring that he was determined not to be put down until he was done, and that no motion should be put until he had been heard, he was permitted to proceed. At this stage several gentlemen left the church, disgusted with the speaker and with the disgraceful conduct of many of his friends. A second amendment to the effect 'That the rate be abandoned and a voluntary subscription immediately commenced' was proposed by a Mr Wilson, a gentleman who styled himself a churchman, but who said he was conscientiously

---

[1] *Nottingham Review*, 3 Sept. 1858.

[2] This provoked opposition from another landlord who leased land 'at a most grinding rent' to the poor. He attempted to vilify Creswell, but five 'Protestant Dissenters' defended Creswell to the bishop of Lincoln (correspondence cited in Frances Knight, *The Nineteenth-Century Church and English Society* (Cambridge, 1998), 74).

opposed to church-rates. This amendment was also seconded. In the midst of a scene of uproar and confusion which defies description the chairman [the vicar, Samuel Creswell], who had refused to put any amendments, put the original motion. On a show of hands being taken more than fifty were held up in its favour, and but one against it; the chairman therefore declared the rate carried. The opportunists, however, immediately proceeded to elect another chairman, when the reverend gentleman, after some conversation with the leaders of the opposition, agreed to put the first amendment, which was carried by a large majority, so that the [church] rate was actually lost. The other amendment was likewise put and agreed to unanimously, after which the meeting broke up.

The campaign to abolish compulsory church rates was a plank in a wider radical platform. Their abolition was a focus of Chartist agitation in Radford. At the Radford annual vestry in 1850 John Bagley, a Chartist, was elected churchwarden 'in consequence of the "unwashed hands and unshorn chins." ' In reporting this the *Nottingham Journal* said that

> it is passing strange that men whose consciences are so tight as not to allow them to pay church-rates, should, without hesitation, send one of their friends before the dignitaries of the Church, to which they are so bitterly opposed, to declare in God's house, and before the congregation that he will truly and faithfully execute the office of churchwarden. We trust that Mr Bagley has more sense.[1]

The Nottingham parliamentary by-election in April 1841 indicated that church rates had been a target of the Chartists for many years. The two candidates were John Walter, a Tory and editor of *The Times*, and Sir George Gerard de Hochepied Larpent, who described himself as a Whig Liberal. Three days before the election the radical *Nottingham Review* tested their positions on four issues: fair trade and repeal of the Corn Laws, extension of the suffrage, secret ballots, and the abolition of church rates. The *Review* noted that Walter was silent on all four, but that Larpent was in favour of each. As to the last, he said, 'I do not approve of taxing, by means of church-rates, persons who not belong to the Church of England, and I shall therefore vote for abolition.'[2] Nevertheless Larpent lost that by-election, though only by a narrow

---

[1] *Nottingham Journal*, 5 April 1850.

[2] *Nottingham Review*, 23 April 1841.

margin: 1,745 to 1,913. He blamed this on 'the union of the Tory party with the Chartists'. No doubt this was true. His platform and that of the Chartists were practically identical but such was the opposition in Nottingham to the Poor Law Amendment Act, passed by a Whig administration in 1834, that Larpent, despite his willingness to support amendment of the Act 'in such parts of it as seem to press hardly upon the poor',[1] was tarnished by association.

The significance of this election is that it shows how high on the political agenda the question of church rates was. By the 1850s, in many urban parishes, hostility was such that imposition of a compulsory rate had become a dead letter. This was not the case in the industrial village of Calverton, a benefice in the gift of the prebendaries of Oxton, where the dispute had a national political reference. It was an emblematic *cause célèbre* for the Chartists. It is worth considering in some detail as a local case study of the complex social interactions of class, politics and religion given additional traction by a history of oppression.

Church, chapel and Chartism

John Murray Wilkins, as rural dean, visited Calverton parish church on 10 May 1855. He subsequently added a pencilled note to his return. Against the articles relating to churchwardens the note reads 'Difficulties anticipated from the parish ch[urch]warden not finding rate etc.' The last three words are indistinct but that this is the correct reading is suggested by the article recording the church rate which reads 'Till this year – not refused.'

In the 1850s, and as it had been for several generations, Calverton was a village of framework knitters. The Anglican clergyman, William Lee, who had invented the stocking-frame in 1589, had been born in the village. By the 1840s there were 'upwards of 400' of these 'complicated pieces of machinery' in the village.[2] Framework knitters sold their products to Nottingham merchant hosiers who managed the market and controlled prices.

In 1843 the annual vestry meeting for the parish was held on 20 April. At this meeting the incumbent, Samuel Oliver, reappointed a Mr

---

[1] Ibid.

[2] White's *Directory and Gazetteer of Nottinghamshire* (1844), 545. William Felkin, *History of the Machine-Wrought Hosiery and Lace Manufactures* (1867), 467 puts the figure at 409 in 1844.

Baines as his warden[1] but, so the *Nottingham Journal* reported, when a Mr Haworth was nominated as parish warden, 'being proposed by the church party for re-election'

> an opposition was unexpectedly raised by the Chartists, who proposed Joseph Roe, one of their body. At the commencement of the poll (which was appointed for the next morning), the church party mustered a great strength, and, after waiting half an hour, during which time not a single Chartist made his appearance, the election was declared to have fallen upon Mr Haworth by the unanimous voice of the meeting. Mr G. Harrison, the noted Chartist leader, had previously been proposed to fill the office, but not being able to procure any ratepayer as a seconder, his nomination was not recorded in the minutes of the meeting.[2]

George Harrison was born in Nottingham in 1798. Roy Church describes him as accredited nonconformist preacher. He was a leader of Chartism in Nottingham from the earliest days of the movement.[3] He described himself as a cottager in the 1841 census and was then living, with his wife Elizabeth and their four children, in Calverton. He is absent from the 1851 return but in 1861 he was still living in the village and was employed as a framework knitter. By that time he was a widower aged 63 lodging with Richard and Clara Lee in Foxwood Terrace. The Lees were framework knitters, as were all their neighbours. In 1842 Harrison was one of the two representatives of the Basford district Chartists at the second 'Sturge' conference in Birmingham[4] and was very active in Chartist agitation. Roy Church notes the link, perhaps only tenuous, between trade union working-class Chartism and nonconformist working-class evangelical Christianity in Nottingham in these early years of the

---

[1]   As the custom then was – the practice was to continue for at least a century and a half. 'Mr Baines' may have been William Bains, who in the 1841 census described himself as a wheelwright, aged about 40.

[2]   *Nottingham Journal*, 28 April 1843.

[3]   See Church, *Nottingham*, 128–61.

[4]   *Northern Star*, 14 Jan. 1843. Joseph Sturge (1793–1859), a Quaker, founder of the British and Foreign Anti-Slavery Society and a middle-class champion of universal suffrage and of working class rights. He was an early member of the Anti-Corn Law League. Sturge called a conference in Birmingham in 1842 in which he sought the cooperation of the Chartists and the League to fight under his leadership for 'complete suffrage'. Leaders of the League and influential Chartists opposed him and the proposal was rejected. He stood unsuccessfully for election to Parliament for Nottingham in 1842, for Birmingham in 1844 and for Leeds in 1847 on a complete suffrage platform.

Chartist movement. Harrison certainly made the link. He believed that in preaching against oppression and tyranny he was following in the footsteps of the Old Testament prophets, Joel and Nehemiah.[1] Joseph Roe, who, so the *Nottingham Journal* reported, replaced Harrison to contest Haworth's re-election as a churchwarden at the Calverton vestry in 1843, was a less significant – and perhaps much younger – figure, but his family name was iconic in Calverton. The only Joseph Roe who lived in Calverton in these years was a framework knitter, son of Samuel Roe, also a framework knitter. In 1851 he lived in Top Buildings in Calverton with his wife Ann and two lodgers. He was then 26, and therefore (if this is the same Joseph Roe) would have been only 18 when proposed for election at the Calverton vestry in 1843.

Nothing came of this particular challenge, but this local *cause célèbre* shows that working-class Chartists were more than ready to oppose privilege, particularly in districts where skilled labourers were numerous and, if not formally organised, were well led. George Harrison was one of many working-class leaders for whom radical religious nonconformity and a radical political agenda were inextricably linked, the one providing the motivation for the other.

This was an exciting period for politically aware labourers and a worrying time for the comfortable classes. Late in August 1843 the great Robert Owen delivered a series of lectures in Nottingham. He was denounced as a socialist by the Tory *Nottingham Journal* as 'the inventor of the "Social System" ... with all its disgusting immoralities ... [and] pernicious doctrines.'[2] The report in the *Journal* would not have gone unread by the increasingly uneasy well-to-do worshippers in the parish churches in the Southwell rural deanery.

The opposition of the nonconformist working class in Calverton to the Church of England continued for many years. The *Nottingham Journal* for 2 June 1854 reported at length the visitation charge which the archdeacon of Nottingham, George Wilkins, had recently delivered in Southwell. Having delivered his charge, Wilkins asked the churchwardens of Calverton to come forward, together with those they had defeated at the vestry election earlier in the year. Wilkins did this because, the *Journal* reported, one 'respectable gentleman' (evidently the churchwarden elected by the parish the previous year) had been 'turned out'. This, Wilkins said, was 'much to be regretted.' He put a series of questions to the newly elected warden, and, reported the *Journal*, he

[1]   *Nottingham Review*, 29 March 1839. See Church, *Nottingham*, 129.
[2]   *Nottingham Journal*, 1 Sept. 1843.

discovered that the opponents of the former warden

> had manifested 'a most deplorable spirit' and that Mr Ward, the
> newly elected churchwarden, was, in fact, a dissenter, he having
> only twice attended church within the last two or three years – one
> occasion being a funeral and the other the special service on the
> day of humiliation.[1] The majority, however, was composed of
> persons who had not paid their rates, and were not, therefore,
> legally qualified to vote. If these votes were struck off ... it would
> leave the majority of 100 to 9 in favour of the old churchwarden.

Therefore Wilkins was, he said, minded to refuse to allow Ward to make the appropriate declarations required before being sworn in as a churchwarden, but rather to 'receive the gentleman who, he believed, was legally elected.' Wilkins said that he had in his possession a paper 'thrust into the hands of various people' by canvassers for Mr Ward, and 'a more infamous one he had never seen put into print'. This pamphlet was entitled *Twenty Good Reasons Why I am not a Churchman*. It had been printed by a person named ('and truly he deserved it' said Wilkins) James Vice of Petergate, Nottingham. Wilkins told Ward that if he were to be admitted as a warden it would only be after legal process, and that those who distributed the anti-church pamphlet might be called before an ecclesiastical court. It appears that the threat (with the implication of considerable legal costs) had an effect. The former wardens were deemed to have been appointed and were admitted to office after taking the required oaths.

Who was the dissenting Mr Ward? He may have been either Robert Ward, who, according to the 1841 census, was a harness-maker aged 25, living in Town Street, Calverton, next door to Samuel and Ann Roe or Samuel Ward, then 72, the long-serving minister of the Particular Baptist church in Calverton. But it is much more likely that the dissenting Mr Ward was William Ward, 51, farming 100 acres and 'employing [a] labourer', and living in Main Street. It is probable that Robert Ward and William Ward were related to Samuel Ward, the Baptist minister. The report in the *Nottingham Journal* of the Calverton vestry meeting held on 27 March 1854 does not record the appointment or election of churchwardens, but it does note the election of William Ward and a Samuel Farley as overseers of the poor, John Wood as overseer of the

---

[1]   This was the Day of Fasting and Humiliation on 26 April 1854 called by Queen Victoria for prayer for the armed forces engaged in 'the just and necessary war in which we are engaged', i.e the Crimean War of 1854–6.

highways, and Richard Milne as assessor of taxes.[1]

That Robert Ward lived next to a framework knitter called Samuel Roe and that a Joseph Roe, a Chartist, was proposed to contest the parish churchwarden election in 1843 in place of George Harrison is significant. White's *Directory and Gazetteer of Nottinghamshire* for 1844 records the existence of

> a small meeting house of the followers of John Roe,[2] a dissenting preacher, who bid defiance to the discipline of the established church, respecting matrimony, and for some time persisted in marrying his flock 'in his own way', in opposition to the threats of the clergy and magistracy: the consequence was that two of his female followers suffered a long imprisonment in Nottingham gaol for refusing to swear [as] to the fathers of their children, and for declaring that they were as firmly united, in wedlock, as it was possible for the mother church to make them.

This brief note summarises an extraordinary story of working-class nonconformity and courageous resistance to oppressive authority. John Roe (1732-1823) was the first son of William Roe. The family lived at 21 Main Street in Calverton. By the mid eighteenth century Roe had established what he described as 'a society of Protestant dissenters' in his home village 'calling themselves Reformed Quakers.' This Calverton community was Quaker in theology but, having their own minister, did not share Quaker church order – so it was that John Roe's Quakers described themselves as 'Reformed.' It was a strictly regulated community. Young men and women were forbidden to choose their own marriage

---

[1]　The 1851 census records a William Ward, 51, living in Main Street with his seven children Ann (26), Helen (18), William (16), Mary (13), and Sarah (11), Joseph (9) and Hannah (6), with Richard Blackall, (17) a farm servant. It also records a Samuel Farley, a hosier aged 54 and born in Nottingham, living in Calverton with his wife Mary (54), and their children Samuel (20) a brazier, Elizabeth (22) a seamer, and George (18) a cordwainer. The occupations of the children suggest that Farley was not a hosier of substance. However, as he could be elected to office at the annual vestry he would have been a ratepayer. This suggests that he employed framework knitters. In the same census a John Wood, aged 32 and unmarried, was a farm bailiff living in Calverton with six farm servants, and a Richard Milne, unmarried, aged 56, farming 84 acres, lived in Main Street with one living-in servant and two farm servants. That William Ward and Richard Milne lived in Main Street with their labourers suggests that they were tenant farmers of land with no farm houses or labourers' cottages.

[2]　There is no record of the existence of this meeting house in the Calverton returns to the 1851 census of religious worship. Its nearest equivalent in theology and political orientation would have been the chapel of the Particular Baptists (erected in about 1820 by the 'New Methodists') and, in 1851, still with Samuel Ward, then 82, as its minister.

partners, and so courting was disallowed. A committee of twelve selected marriage partners for these reformed Quakers by lot so that 'the will of heaven' should be known. John Roe's own wife was selected for him in this way. She was Mabel Morris, sister of Elizabeth Morris who was married to Thomas Bush. As Quakers rejected the Church's sacramental disciplines, so they rejected Anglican marriage. In 1785 Mabel Roe and Elizabeth Bush were gaoled for flouting the marriage laws. The story of Elizabeth Bush was recorded in Throsby's edition of Thoroton's *Nottinghamshire*[1] and in more detail by the radical John Blackner in his *History of Nottingham* in 1815. Blackner records that Mrs Bush, on refusing to name the father of her child, 'was then driven knee-deep in snow to Southwell House of Correction, where, under the care of Keeper Adams, a man whose cruelty and avarice went hand in hand, she lay-in, in a room which had an unglazed window, and through which the snow blew in flakes upon her bed of straw.'[2] After the birth of her child, Elizabeth Bush was released but was cited to appear before what Blackner calls 'the Spiritual Court' by which he must mean the archdeacon's court. Elizabeth refused, as did Mabel Roe, and the two sisters were confined to Nottingham goal until they agreed to be married according to law. This they refused to do, and, notwithstanding appeals from John Roe and from William Roe to Lord George Gordon,[3] they remained in goal until 1798 when, it seems, they were allowed to escape having become an embarrassment to the civil and ecclesiastical authorities.[4]

[1]   Vol. III (1796), 43.

[2]   J. Blackner, *The History of Nottingham* (1815), 58. The poor condition of the Southwell House of Correction at this time had been recorded by John Howard following his visits in 1775, 1776 and 1779.

[3]   In June 1780 Lord George Gordon had led a peaceful procession to parliament to present a petition opposing concessions to Roman Catholics under Lord North's Relief Act. The demonstration got out of hand, and led to rioting and looting in London which lasted a week. Gordon was tried for treason, was acquitted and remained a focus for Protestant resistance.

[4]   On John Roe see *The experiences of John Roe, late minister of a society of Protestant Dissenters in Calverton, calling themselves Reformed Quakers. Written in the year 1759, for a play-fellow, a fellow-singer, and a fellow-sinner* (Sutton & Son, Nottingham, 1882). On the imprisonment of Mabel Roe and Elizabeth Bush see *A Letter from John Roe, Minister of the Protestant Dissenters at Calverton, near Nottingham. Concerning the imprisonment of their wives for life, for Nonconformity to the Church of England, by force of the writ Excommunicato Capiendo. Addressed to the Rt. Hon. Ld. George Gordon, President of the Protestant Association* (Nottingham, 1789); a letter from William Roe of Farnsfield to Lord George Gordon in the *Nottingham Journal*, 12 Feb. 1787 and Lord George Gordon's letter to the archbishop of York in the *Nottingham Journal*, 31 March 1787. See also John Roe, *The Case concerning the marriage of Mrs Roe and Mrs Bush, belonging to the congregation of John Roe … with John Roe's answer to a scandalous letter published against him, by J. Morley, to which is added An Appeal from Scotland, by*

These imprisonments show the passion with which John Roe and the Calverton Reformed Quakers refused to submit to ecclesiastical authority. Of immediate relevance to the 1854 disputed vestry election was Roe's refusal, almost 70 years earlier, to pay the church rate. The closely interrelated religious, political and social class differences between Roe's Quaker community and their detractors is illustrated in a lengthy and bitter *Answer to Roe's Letters* by J. Morley of Calverton published in March 1787. Morley condemned Roe for founding a 'pernicious faction' and for 'always being a very troublesome mischievous Person in our neighbourhood'. Roe and members of his society, Morley said, were

> so perfectly illiterate that neither John Roe nor any of his society is capable of reading a Chapter of the New Testament with any tolerable Degrees of Propriety; and they have no more Notions of Sense and Argument than one of the brute Animals – But that is not to be wondered at – Knowledge and Learning are Subjects of their constant Raillery and Contempt ... Their Religion is an Heap of inconsistencies promiscuously jumbled together, and their preaching an invariable Compound of Railing Absurdity, Billings-gate and Blackguardness.

Inevitably, John Roe had objected 'to the payment of his parish assessments, there being no less than five Levies against him, which he absolutely refuses to pay, tho' he is the only person in the Village who is rated under the Commissioners Valuation when our Commons were enclosed.'[1]

That, despite this invective, Morley could profess himself 'a Favourer of the Dissenters' and 'as tenacious' of their 'civil and religious Rights of Mankind as any Person whatever' shows the depth of opposition to radical religious and political dissent at that time, an opposition which was to come to a head a few years later against a background of fears of revolution. In 1854 the coincidence of the names Ward and Roe in the dispute in Calverton suggests not only a close dissenting and politically radical relationship between these families in opposition to a repressive authority, at once ecclesiastical and political, who governed without the democratic consent of the unfranchised majority, but also that this opposition had continued for very many years. That those they repre-

---

Calvinus Minor (Nottingham, 1787). An account of the Roeites is in A. Stapleton, 'The Roeites of Calverton' and 'Roeites and Wroeites' in *Nottinghamshire Occasional Papers* (reprinted from the *Mansfield and North Nottinghamshire Advertiser*, 1911), 37–52, 178–81.

[1] Commons enclosed in 1780.

sented had suffered imprisonment for their convictions two generations earlier gives reason for their fierce, uncompromising and long continued opposition to the 'clergy and magistracy'. These working-class men and women found in the principles of Chartism a focus not only for their democratic aspirations[1] but also for their opposition to low wages, high food prices and, above all, to the harsh provisions of the new Poor Law of 1834. It also gave political definition to their religious nonconformity.

Another of the Calverton Chartists was Bill Smith, a great admirer of the Chartist leader Fergus O'Connor. In about 1844, and evidently homeless, Smith moved his wife Kitty and their small child, with some furniture, into Calverton parish church. He refused to move out, and, on being told that the vicar would turn him out, declared that he could not as 'It's the poor man's church. It's my church as well as his.' He was eventually persuaded to leave 'for a guinea and a half.'[2]

The vicar of Calverton, Samuel Oliver, had been incumbent since 1826, the year he was ordained priest. He remained in the village until 1864. He was confronted by radical nonconformity for much of this period, and engaged with it as best he could. Evidently in reply to the 'infamous' pamphlet *Twenty Good Reasons Why I am not a Churchman* Oliver produced *Plain Questions for Dissenters* and *A Plain Argument for the Church*, both printed on a card and costing a penny for easy and inexpensive distribution to labourers.

'Not a matter of conscience, but of revolutionary passion'

It was comparatively rare for there to be a dispute over church rates in rural villages, but in November 1863 the very modest church rate of three farthings in the pound proposed by the churchwardens of what was described as the 'quiet village' of North Muskham in the rural deanery of Southwell was rejected by a show of hands at a vestry meeting. The proposers of the rate requested a poll of ratepayers. This was set for 26 November in the National schoolroom in the village. The *Newark Advertiser* subsequently reported that

It appears that great efforts were made by all parties from 3 in the

---

[1]   The six principles of a draft bill known as the Peoples' Charter were: universal male suffrage, no property qualifications for MPs, annual parliaments, equal electoral districts, voting by secret ballot, and payment of MPs.

[2]   'Calverton and the Chartists', *Nottingham Weekly Guardian*, 8 June 1901.

afternoon to bring up voters to the poll. Treating with ale and other disreputable proceedings were resorted to. After the close of the poll a rather angry altercation too place as to its legality, objections being made to the manner in which some of the votes had been obtained. As might be expected after such a contest there was much dissatisfaction with the result. It does not appear very clear why so much opposition should have been raised, as the rate was very small for the customary expenses of the church service … [1]

The clergy of the Nottinghamshire parishes looked to their archdeacon for support in this contentious matter. He did not disappoint them. In 1834 the Whigs had proposed the abolition of church rates and its replacement by a charge on the exchequer of £250,000. The bishops thought this too small, and nonconformists too large. In 1837 Thomas Spring-Rice, Chancellor of the Exchequer in Melbourne's second administration, suggested that if the property of the bishops were to be directly administered by commissioners there would be a saving of some £250,000 which, presumably, could be diverted to the parishes and enable compulsory church rates to be abolished. The bishops refused to agree, not least because this would have made them 'annuitants of the government'. In that year George Wilkins addressed his open letter to Lord John Russell on the 'Church Rate Question, then violently agitated'. He published a second revised and enlarged edition in 1854 when abolition was again on the political agenda with the immediate prospect that the issue was to be 'definitively determined'. For Wilkins the continuance of a compulsory church rate was as much a matter of constitutional and therefore theological principle as its abolition was a political issue for dissenters. The argument was again deployed that for the civil authority to tamper with the Church was to threaten the monarchy. Employing in combination the image of the indissolubility of the marriage bond and the threat of bloody revolution Wilkins maintained that to abolish a church rate levied on all ratepayers would call into question not merely the constitutional establishment of the Church of England, but the very constitution of the state itself. He argued that

> if the Government is to repeal the Law which for above one thousand years has been the unchallengeable law of the Country, by which the Nation at large is made to provide for the sustentat-

---

[1] *Newark Advertiser*, 2 Dec. 1863.

ion of the Churches *for the benefit of the whole community*; such
an act of repeal would at once dissolve the union of the Church
with the State — a tie fully as important to the one as to the other
— a tie which God Himself has joined together, and which man
at his peril here and hereafter will cut asunder ... Were this
obligation broken and dissolved, it is not difficult to divine how
much longer the Throne would continue. Such did come to pass
some 200 years ago, in the Great Rebellion.[1]

Wilkins dismissed both the objections of the dissenters and the proposals
to replace or modify church rates. Dissenters who pleaded 'tenderness of
conscience' in refusing to pay the rate were cowardly, Wilkins said,
lacking the courage openly to avow 'as others have manfully done, their
deadly hatred of the Church.' The true ground of opposition, quoting an
unnamed dissenter, was this: 'The Church-Rate gone, the Establishment
itself will be an easy prey.'[2] Wilkins believed that opposition to church
rates was 'not a matter of conscience but of revolutionary passion.'[3]
Quoting the somewhat disingenuous arguments advanced by Christopher
Wordsworth,[4] Wilkins maintained that dissenters ignored the benefits
that an established church, supported by rates, had brought to them: the
Bible in English, the English Reformation, the 'best English Comments'
on scripture, escape from 'the tyranny of Rome', 'the blessings of peace
and quietness', and the maintenance of 'a sense of true religion.'[5] Given
that the established church was the guarantor of 'the Religion of this
Land ... should not the Laws provide for the permanency of this
system?', Wilkins asked.[6] Therefore, paying rates to maintain the parish
church was as much a social obligation as paying rates to maintain law

[1]   George Wilkins, *A Letter addressed to the Right Honourable Lord John Russell, in
1837, on the subject of the Church Rates; second edition enlarged and adapted to the
present time: to which is appended a Scheme for making the law respecting them more
efficient* (J. Whittingham, Queen Street, Southwell, 1854), 3.

[2]   Ibid., 8, 9.

[3]   Ibid., 2.

[4]   1807–85, bishop of Lincoln 1869–85. Wilkins does not cite his source, but in 1859
Wordsworth defended church rates as 'a part of the royalty of Christ our Saviour, a part
of His royalties established for the propagation of His true doctrine, the maintenance of his
true religion, and the instruction of the poor.' He argued that the proper way to preserve
church rates was to provide more accommodation in churches for the poor (J.H. Overton
and Elizabeth Wordsworth, *Christopher Wordsworth, Bishop of Lincoln, 1807–1885* (1888),
170).

[5]   Wilkins, *Letter ... Lord John Russell*, 21.

[6]   Ibid., 11.

and order or to support the parish's poor. Indeed, a parish church rate is 'a charity, if not a due, of right, to the poor' to allow them to come to church and not to pay anything to do so.[1] Thus, 'it is becoming [of] the State, which requires the support and junction of the Church, to make some return for the acknowledged benefits of this union.'[2]

Several proposals had been advanced to replace or to modify church rates. The first, and at first sight the most persuasive, was to abolish them and to rely upon voluntary contributions. Wilkins would have none of this. The 'Voluntary System ... can never avail effectually, never can work well generally', not least because by no means all worshippers could afford to maintain their parish church. Citing his own parish of Nottingham St Mary Wilkins asked, 'in a congregation of 1500 persons what proportion of them could, even if they would, contribute more than an occasional donation towards the support of a Fabric requiring a constant and continual expenditure?'. The caveat 'even if they would' carried weight for Wilkins. Quoting Philip Dodderidge he noted that 'the general aversion of mankind from good is such, that if left to themselves, they would have no Religion at all.' Even if this was not the case, Wilkins argued, the voluntary system would make the clergy prey to the congregation, making their income very insecure and themselves liable to dismissal.[3]

Another proposal, made by Lord John Russell himself, was that only village churches should be supported by a compulsory church rate. It would be levied on land in cultivation, with town churches depending on what Wilkins called 'the precarious and inadequate sustentation of voluntary contributions.' Wilkins regarded this suggestion as both unworkable and essentially unjust. Hitherto all property, whether land or buildings, had been chargeable to the church rate. Were the proposal to be accepted town churches would be disadvantaged, and 'the Law, which is not just, would become partial.'[4] Wilkins dismissed every other proposal to replace or modify church rates. To replace them by an annual payment made to every parish from the Consolidated Fund would be very expensive to administer and would lead to 'endless disputes within and without the walls of Parliament'. To exonerate dissenters from church rates on their being registered before magistrates sitting in quarter sessions would both 'put a *bonus* on dissent' and lead to the doubling of

---

[1] Ibid., 19.

[2] Ibid., 25.

[3] Ibid., 16, 18, 19.

[4] Ibid., 28.

the assessment 'and placing it upon another, and thus tend to "unchurch"
both'. That all rateable property should be subject to one rate 'and then
subject to redemption either by a *fixed* annual payment, or by the option
of commutation', would be, Wilkins implied, extremely difficult to
arrange and to operate.[1]

Wilkins concluded his revised letter to Russell with detailed suggestions for the more efficient collection of church rates. He ended it 'on
behalf of the Nation at large now visited by the sore judgments of God
for national sins' by 'fervently' imploring that Russell might be made
'the instrument for securing to His Church its temporal rights, and of
furthering her spiritual efforts to turn away His wrathful indignation from
us' — the no doubt sincere theological warning with which he had begun
his letter.

But Wilkins was pushing at an open door. Lord John Russell was a
resolute defender of the principle of compulsory church rates for much
of his political career. He opposed the 'voluntary system' as this would
make the Church of England an exclusive, sectarian, church. In his view
compulsory church rates guaranteed the maintenance of the Church of
England as an inclusive broad church open and of service to all. Yet in
1859 he changed his mind, no doubt disappointed by the failure of all
attempts to compromise with abolitionists, and in face of evidence that,
in many places, voluntary contributions from parishioners raised more
income that compulsory church rates.[2]

Disputes over church rates, as a focus of the debate about the relation
of church and state, continued until 1868 when the levy ceased to be
compulsory. In his charge in 1856 George Wilkins criticised a church
rate abolition bill brought before Parliament 'by the party calling
themselves the Religious Liberty Parliamentary Committee.' In March
1859 the *Newark Advertiser* reported another Nottinghamshire dispute,
in this case not over the principle of the rate but about the unfairness of
its imposition. Bryan Clark, a farmer of 50 acres, aged 46, refused to pay
his church rate in Tuxford. He was charged before the Tuxford magistrates, on a summons by James Wood, a churchwarden, that he had
refused to pay his assessed rate of £1 7s. 10½d. Wood said that the rate,
for the enlargement of the churchyard, had been duly passed after a poll
lasting four hours. Clark objected, questioning the legality of the rate. He

---

[1]   Ibid., 26–8.

[2]   Further to this see J.P. Ellens, 'Lord John Russell and the Church Rate Conflict: the
struggle for a Broad Church', *Journal of British Studies*, 26 (1987), 232–57, and William
L. Sachs, *The Transformation of Anglicanism: from state church to global communion*
(Cambridge, 2003), ch. 3.

said that he did not object to paying a rate but he did object that not all the land and property in the parish had been rated. He further protested that the church was profiteering: 'the land will cost the parish £500 an acre, and the vicar and his churchwardens are to sell it out again at no less than £20,000 an acre', and also that 'the original fee for a tombstone [was] a guinea, but now they have raised it to ten for a tombstone of two yards. [The fee for a] common headstone had been raised from six shillings to a guinea ... ' The case against Clark was dismissed. A leader in the same edition of the *Advertiser* weighed in against the government's church rate commutation bill then before parliament:

> Anything more invidious or bungling we have rarely seen than the Church Rate Bill introduced a few evenings ago by the present Government ... first of all, it denationalises the Church of England, separating her by law into an exclusive sect. Well, let that be either a good or an evil, as you please to consider it. We simply note the fact. Her vestries are to be henceforth snug counting-houses of a corporation for 'taking and holding' money, but they are not in any sense to belong to the parish – all who have consciences that object to the employment of force in the kingdom of love being excluded. Secondly, the operation of the Bill when it becomes law, will be enormously to increase the number of Dissenters. Myriads of people, who never troubled themselves much about conscience before, will, when the warden comes to take their money, suddenly find themselves in possession of that article, and refuse to pay. JOHN SMITH, landlord of the 'Pig and Whistle', who was never inside a Dissenting chapel in his life, will most 'conscientiously object' to the demand of the 'corporation', and henceforth be a Nonconformist. How much better, nobler, wiser would it be for the honour of Churchmen, for the peace of the country, and for the credit of Christianity, to abolish Church-rates at once, and for ever, without condition and without equivalent. By the voluntary gifts of members of the Church of England, enough and more than enough, would be raised to meet all that it required.[1]

---

[1] *Newark Advertiser*, 9 March 1859; census returns, 1851 and 1861.

'Invidious human distinctions':
social class and seats in church

Not directly political, but much more socially divisive, was the other method by which clergy and churchwardens maintained their parish churches, and, in many cases secured the incomes of incumbents — the trafficking in seats in church. It was less stridently debated across the denominational divide because most churches and chapels, Anglican and dissenting alike, employed the practice.

The 1851 religious census returns asked for details of the numbers of free and appropriated seats. Of the churches and chapels in and around Southwell supplying figures for seating, on average 37 per cent of seats were free and 63 per cent were appropriated (rented or freehold). If the poor had wished to attend church very few of them could have done so. And even had they done they would usually have been seated on benches in parts of the church where, as in the theatre, those who paid to attend refused to sit. Where members of a congregation sat in church was a matter 'touching caste' as Henry Mozley, a churchwarden, observed during an acrimonious pew dispute in St Werburgh's church in Derby in 1830-31. Those of a 'low caste', that is 'lower middle people, small tradesmen and clerks' sat in the nave, while the well-do-do sat in their one hundred guinea pews in the galleries.[1] In other churches the wealthy sat in the nave, but the social and physical distance between their seats and those of their social inferiors remained the same. As one of many examples, in 1845 the *Nottingham Journal* carried an advertisement by a family wishing to buy or rent pews in the extra-parochial area of St James, Standard Hill, in the city: 'Wanted in this Church, from the 25 March, Two good-sized FAMILY PEWS, in the Middle Aisle, at some distance from the Gallery – Also Two Pews in the South Gallery. Apply by letter to Z, *Journal* office.' The pews in the south gallery were for the servants of the family in the middle aisle who wished to place themselves 'at some distance' from them. In the same edition of the *Journal* and in the same church: 'To be let and may be entered upon immediate-

---

[1]   T. Mozley, *Reminiscences of towns, villages and schools* (1885), II, 80. For an account of pew appropriation in Derby and Derbyshire at this time see M.R. Austin, 'The Church of England in the town of Derby and the adjoining townships of Litchurch and Little Chester 1824–1885' (unpublished MA thesis, University of Birmingham, 1966), 190–206, and M.R. Austin, *A Stage or Two beyond Christendom: A social history of the Church of England in Derbyshire* (Cromford, 2001), 145ff.

ly, PEW no. 48'.[1] In 1851 St James's had seats for 1,540, with 140 (less than 10 per cent) of them free. The income of the incumbent, Henry Bell, was £200 a year, entirely drawn from pew rents.

By 1855, although opposition to the practice of pew appropriation had been expressed for some years, it remained well entrenched. In that year in the rural deanery of Southwell the majority of the seats in every parish church were appropriated, either rented to families or allotted to houses in the parish.[2] Many had been erected by faculty. Such free seats as there were were placed either in front of the congregation (perhaps to remind the congregation of the dominical injunction that they would always have the poor with them) as at Carlton on Trent where 'about 60' seats for 'servants and children' were situated in the chancel, or behind the congregation as in Edingley where, of 119 seats, the four free seats were placed 'at the back of the Gallery'. In Farnsfield the 70 free seats were in the north gallery. At Hockerton, seven of the 81 seats were free, with 14 pews allotted to houses in the parish, and six reserved for 'domestics from any House.' In Norwell parish church there were no free seats, although 50 children could sit in the gallery, and 70 seats in pews were reserved for 'Farm Servants etc'. But Norwell was in 'a most wretched state' with a floor 'as if there had been an earthquake [and] old high square pews, large enough to hold 8 or 10 in each, average occupants 2 or 3'. It is doubtful whether farm servants would have attended willingly.

Dissenter ratepayers objected to paying church rates but the older nonconformist denominations had little objection (or, for some, little alternative) to renting pews in their chapels. In 1851 in the parish of Nottingham St Mary, where opposition to paying church rates had been particularly bitter, 42 per cent of the seats in 20 chapels were rented. Of the 610 seats in the influential High Pavement 'Presbyterian or Unitarian' chapel less than 10 per cent were free. In Wesley Chapel, built in 1839, only a third of the seats were free, though there was standing room for a further 900. Even the Primitive Methodist chapels rented out the majority of their seats. In contrast to older nonconformity the newer Protestant sects willingly embraced the 'voluntary system'. Of the

[1] *Nottingham Journal*, 7 Feb. 1845. As pews could be bought and sold so they could be bequeathed. When Archelaus Rhodes of Sutton-in-Ashfield made his will in 1804 he left 'to my daughter Mary half of my Pew or Seat in Sutton Church' with the other half going to his son Matthew (G.G. Bonser, *A History of Sutton-in-Ashfield* (1949), 26.

[2] In 1855 about a third of the accommodation in the rural deanery parishes was free (see chapter 9). By 1884 free accommodation in these parishes had increased to 88 per cent (*Southwell Diocesan Church Calendar* (1885).

'Desciples [sic] of Jesus Christ or Christians' meeting in Salem Chapel
in Barker Gate the pastor noted in his return to the 1851 census of
religious worship that 'all our seats are free, we have no contributions
but what are purely voluntary and presented on every first day of the
week when we meet for worship.' Whereas nonconformity saw pew
appropriation in the Church of England as socially divisive, it allowed
the practice in its own chapels because, there, to rent a pew there was
seen as a token of God's favour on the thrift of those who sat in it.[1]
There is no evidence that respectable nonconformity played any part in
fomenting the wild scenes that marked the St Mary's vestry meetings
that, year after year, rejected the setting of church rates in the parish, for
these were primarily politically and not theologically inspired. Nevertheless the poor had as little a chance of finding free seats in nonconformist
chapels as they did in the Church of England – and as little an inclination to sit in them.

But, at least by the late 1830s, opposition was growing to the
appropriation of pews in church by the well-to-do. Early in 1843 the
Nottingham Journal reprinted an article from *The Spectator* which set out
the argument for the abolition of pew appropriation. It is worth quoting
in full because, by reproducing it, Job Bradshaw,[2] the proprietor of the
principal conservative newspaper in Nottinghamshire, made a very
pertinent theological point and an equally significant political observation, both of which went contrary to the opinions of very many of his
subscribers.

> ABOLITION OF PEWS. A change has begun in the mechanical
> arrangement of our churches, which, if it is carried out, must
> materially alter the relation of the church to the people – it is the
> removal or throwing open of the pews. The proceeding is con-
> demned by Conservatives of form, on the ground that it removes
> an outward and visible sign of the distinction between the
> Protestant and Roman Catholic Churches, and because it is
> supposed to be a concession to Puseyism:[3] it is vindicated on the

---

[1]   Further to this see Austin, *A Stage or Two*, 145–6.

[2]   Job Bradshaw and John Hickin became joint proprietors of the *Nottingham Journal* in
1832. From being a moderately Tory newspaper, it became much more pronounced in its
view, Hicklin seeking to 'check the spread of … democratical and irreligious doctrines'
(cited in Church, *Nottingham*, 18). Bradshaw became sole proprietor in 1841.

[3]   Edward Bouverie Pusey (1800–82) was the principal champion of the Tractarian
movement in the Church of England after John Henry Newman's secession to Rome in
1845.

ground that it abolishes a very unsightly encumbrance in our church architecture, which forms no necessary adjunct of Protestantism, while it is opposed to the spirit of Christianity, marking out invidious human distinctions in the sacred edifice, and even excluding people from worship by wasting space. Whatever the opinions as to the expediency, there is not doubt that the measure would in some respects assimilate our churches to those of Southern Europe from which they are now distinguished by two among other usages. The churches of the Continent stand open always, as places of religious solace and quiet to the afflicted or the meditative; our churches are oftener shut than open, if we may believe certain correspondents of *The Times*, not the money-changers, but the worshippers are sometimes rather abruptly driven from the temple. Within the churches of the Continent the distinctions of class disappear, and, with certain exceptions of State occasions, you will see young and old, rich and poor, prince and beggar, kneeling together. All are equal in the sight of God, 'as the saying is' here; on the Continent it looks as if they really thought so. It is good for others to consider how far these wooden penfolds are essential to the discipline of the Reformed Church. The politician, regarding the Established Church a means of civilisation, cannot but perceive that the new movement has a tendency more than anything to popularise the institution, and so to diminish the distance between it and the people. In the same sense, it would also tend to remove one instance, and one which makes others, of that harsh social severance into classes, which is one of the most mischievous features of our political state.[1]

The article in *The Spectator* reflected the developing debate about the theological significance of seats in church. Box pews were defended by evangelicals as 'The Wooden Walls of England'. They were 'those sturdy, significant, outward and visible Protestant Bulwarks against this system of levelling all bodies that they may level all minds'.[2] The low church religious justification for social distinctions embodied in church seating is very clear. It was strongly opposed by the Oxford Tractarians on theological grounds and by the allied Cambridge Camden Society for

---

[1]   *Nottingham Journal*, 20 Jan. 1843.

[2]   William Goode, *The Wooden Walls of England in Danger: a Defence of Church Pews* (1844), 14. See also *Twenty-four Reasons for Getting Rid of Church Pews – or Pues* (The Ecclesiological Society (late Cambridge Camden Society), 1844), et al.

reasons ostensibly architectural but no less theological. Open pews were
regarded as Puseyite and dangerously inclusive by Protestant Anglicans,
and box pews as Protestant, socially exclusive and discriminatory by
Catholic Anglicans. Writing of the 1850s Samuel Reynolds Hole, then
vicar of Caunton and later dean of Rochester, recorded that

> In a certain Lincolnshire village there was a movement in favour
> of restoring and reseating the parish church, which so sorely
> exercised the mind of the principal farmer that he wrote to the
> Bishop of the Diocese, protesting about the socialistic character of
> the alterations, and concluding his letter thus: 'I know, my Lord,
> that in heaven we shall all be equal, but so long as I am upon
> earth I claim the privilege of keeping myself respectable.' [1]

Apocryphal or not the story shows that many strongly opposed the
'levelling of bodies' that would remove social distinctions in church.

Shortly after *The Spectator* published this article the bishop of
Norwich, Edward Stanley, wrote to the press about 'the injustice and evil
tendency of pews.' It was a theme which was picked up by the new
satirical magazine *Punch* (first published in 1841) and reported in the
Nottingham Journal on 10 February 1843. However, pew-renting and the
buying and selling of pews continued to be socially divisive and
economically important for many years to come. Originally intended to
raise income to maintain church fabric, by the 1850s rental income was
being devoted to other needs. In May 1854 the bishop of London's bill
to allow pew rents to be used to augment benefice incomes passed its
third reading in the House of Lords.

The 'injustice and evil tendency of pews' locally was no better
illustrated than at Newark St Mary Magdalene. When the 1851 census
was taken, the incumbent, John Garrett Bussell, did not return a figure
for accommodation in his church either in total or in the number of the
appropriated and free pews. In fact he could not tell how many attended
his church on 30 March 1851 — the number in the general (or adult)
congregation, he noted, could 'not [be] accurately ascertained.' All he
could do was to produce a 'calculation' of the average number attending

---

[1] Samuel Reynolds Hole, *More Memories; being thoughts about England spoken in
America* (1894), 22–3.

all three Sunday services each week during the previous twelve months.[1]

The reason that Bussell could not produce these figures is that both the arrangement and mis-use of the seating in St Mary Magdalene's was chaotic. In March 1850 a correspondent to the *Nottingham Journal* wrote of

> the unmitigated ugliness of the pens on the ground floor, on surveying which from any of ... the galleries on the week-day one is involuntarily reminded of Smithfield Market when empty ... That this motley assemblage of deal boxes is allowed to exist in all its hideous variety and deformity [reflects] great discredit on the town ...

As disordered as the pews was their use:

> Many of the pews are in the hands of Dissenters (who refuse to give them up) and are never used; whilst, on the other hand, several belonging to members of the congregation of Christ Church[2] are in possession of others which, with true dog in the manger spirit, they neither make use of themselves, or allow other parties to do so; and again, even amongst attendants of the Church there are individuals laying claim to several pews each, which they never, or but very seldom, occupy, and have not the slightest occasion for, to the exclusion of those who would only be too happy to do so; indeed, the anomaly exists, that whilst numbers of pews stand empty Sunday after Sunday, many people are unable to procure seats, and in consequence leave the Church; whilst the poor are almost entirely deprived of their rights for, with the exception of some miserable little accommodation provided for them in the nave and aisles, they have not where to sit. I may add that it is but justice to the Vicar to state that he has done all in his power to remove the foregoing evils.

In a postscript this correspondent added that he was very much in doubt

---

[1]   This was 1,006, but as the number of Sunday scholars attending on 30 March (150 boys and 95 girls) was also the average attendance for the entire year, we can have little confidence in Bussell's calculations. John Welby, the registrar of births, marriages and deaths, attempted a more accurate return. He estimated the usual total number of attendants at all three Sunday services as 1,150 seated in 400 free seats and 213 appropriated seats – a total of 613. In the light of the following correspondence in the *Nottingham Journal* these figures are also suspect.

[2]   Built in 1837.

whether two thirds of the pew-holders had any legal title to their '*boxes*'. Nevertheless 'the practice of buying and selling seats, making merchandise of the House of God, is carried on, I fear, pretty extensively.' The proprietor of the *Journal* added that he too was 'grieved and pained to witness the deformities which ignorance, pride and self-righteousness had produced' in St Mary Magdalene's.[1]

The *Nottingham Journal* reprinted *The Spectator*'s attack on pew appropriation in 1843. Three years later it launched its own assault on what it rightly described as the 'vicious and unChristian' practice not merely of pew appropriation but also of patronage by trustees with which it was often closely associated. Where patronage trustees refused, or were unable, to raise sufficient endowment to provide a reasonable income for an incumbent he might be compelled to raise his income by leasing pews in his church. An example was the new parish of Holy Trinity in Southwell. As we have noted, in 1836 George Wilkins had suggested that a 'parochial chapel' be built in Southwell. He and others[2] recognised that the Church of England needed to offer, as it was put at the time, 'a simple form of congregational service in which all might be able to join, and which all would appreciate and understand', the choral worship in the collegiate church not being 'suited to the taste, nor to the understanding of the majority of the people, who are not qualified to appreciate its merits.'[3] Evidently, 'the majority of the people' were the poor who lived at a distance from the Minster – or at least so it was assumed by the Nottinghamshire press. It was a worthy object. The new parish (for such it was to be) was to have no formal connection with the Minster.

The newly built Southwell Holy Trinity, in Westhorpe, was consecrated on 31 March 1846. It was designed by Sheffield architects Weightman and Hadfield, and built by Nathaniel Parkin, a Southwell stonemason. The cost of the land and the building had been raised by public subscription (principally from two substantial contributions) and a grant from the Nottingham Church Building Society. The patronage of the new benefice was placed in the hands of five evangelical trustees. Although the church could accommodate 600 worshippers, the poor, for

---

[1] 'A Layman', *Nottingham Journal*, 22 March 1850. The letter provoked further correspondence. See letters in editions for 12 April 1850 from 'A Calm Observer' and 19 April 1850 from 'Parcus Deorum Cultor'.

[2] The *Nottingham Mercury* noted that Edward Heathcote was 'particularly deserving of honourable mention' in promoting the building of the new church.

[3] Quoted in Margaret Huthwayte and Penny Young, *Holy Trinity Southwell 1846–1996* (Southwell, 1996), 7.

whom it was notionally built, were, if not largely excluded, then certainly disadvantaged. In recording the consecration of the church the *Nottingham Journal* noted that

> in consequence of the very inadequate stipend provided for the clergyman, the best seats in the church, and the principal part of them too (probably about three-fourths of the whole) are numbered and are to be made [a] matter of merchandise to the rich, so that the poor will not profit by this addition to the church accommodation of Southwell, further than to sit at the rich man's footstool or partake of the crumbs which fall from his table. The patronage is invested in trustees, and, therefore, the permanent endowment is not likely to receive such an increase as to enable them to abolish the highly objectionable system of pew rents. For who can tell into what kind of hands trustee-churches may ultimately fall. The present patrons may be, as individuals, unobjectionable enough, but no security can be given that their successors will be equally eligible. Besides, third persons will not readily place their money at the disposal of private persons as they will in the hands of a high public functionary in the church, such as, for instance, the bishop of the diocese. While, therefore, the patronage remains in private hands the endowment is likely to continue small, and the chance of this really beautiful church being ever blessed with the title of 'the poor man's church' very remote indeed.

The following week the proprietor of the *Journal*, Job Bradshaw, had to publish a retraction – which he immediately retracted! He wrote:

> We were led into an error last week, when we state that no accommodation was made for the poorer classes by providing them with sittings in this church Our correspondent at Southwell has since been over the church with one of the Committee, and he finds [that] more than one-third are allotted as free sittings for the poor; and they are in the best situation in the church, and equally as good as any other pews – no distinction whatever being made between those for the rich and those for the poor. We deem it right to state this, as the Committee has taken special care to provide these free sittings: they are to number more than allowed by law – We have inserted the above from a correspondent at Southwell, but are by no means inclined to withdraw the statement we made last week from our own observation. The facts of the case are a complete refutation of our correspondent's assertion that the seats

for the poor are as good in their situation as those for the rich. The church accommodates 600 or which 400 are to be let, and 200, according to the above account, are to be what is called 'free'. Now we would ask, do not those seats which are to be reserved to be let occupy the whole of the nave from the chancel arch to the cross aisle at the font?, and is not the principal part of the free seats next to the walls on the south and north sides and at the extreme west end? We are not surprised that such should be the case, for it is not likely that those who buy admission into a place of worship will submit to be put into dusty corners and behind pillars; they pay for the best seats, and they ought to have their goods for their money. Besides, are the proportions of rich and poor reversed in Southwell? – are there only 200 poor persons requiring [free] accommodation and 400 who can pay? The system of pre-rents is vicious and unchristian altogether. Unfortunately it seems to be growing. We hope to see it abolished; and shall take an early opportunity to state some of the reasons which, in our mind, make such 'a consummation so devoutly to be wished.' Ed. *NJ*.

The *Nottingham Mercury* also reported the consecration of Southwell Holy Trinity. It noted that the population of the town in 1841 had been 3,481 comprising some 700 households 'of which number not 120 had sittings or pews; thus not less than 580 families were left without the means of attending divine worship' in the established church in Southwell. The collegiate church (or 'the cathedral' as the *Mercury* described it) held only 800. The *Mercury* noted that one-third of the sittings in the new church were to be free and unappropriated 'or, instead thereof, let at such low rates as the Bishop of the Diocese should from time to time direct'. The caveat 'instead thereof' is significant. Southwell Holy Trinity was built not for the poor but primarily for those Anglicans who did not care for the choral worship offered by the collegiate church. In both churches the poor were seated as befitted their station.

In a few parishes elsewhere incumbents ensured that the poor could sit where they pleased. On Sunday 17 August 1856, in the poorest part of Derby, the preacher and congregation in the small medieval parish church of St Michael's 'were startled by a strange rumbling sound' as their church began to collapse. 'Mothers ran eagerly to the gallery fearful for their children, forgetful of themselves. But, by God's mercy, no one was hurt.' The incumbent, John Erskine Clarke, replaced his church with a new building that contained 430 seats. He insisted that all these seats should be 'free and unappropriated' and distributed a handbill among 'the poorer parishioners and others whom it may concern' urging them 'to come in such clothes as you have, however poor they may be; make them as clean as you can and come' for 'the Church is not for showing off people's fine clothes, but for praying to God, for praising Him, and for learning something of that world where there is no more sin nor trouble (because there is no sin) and where poverty never pinches, and labour never wearies.' Another handbill announced that 'Handicraftsmen and labourers will be as welcome in fustian as if they were in broadcloth, and their wives as welcome in cotton gowns as if they were in silk ones.' Clarke was wealthy, the son of an official of the East India Company, and paid for the building of the new St Michael's.

There is no evidence that the clergy in and around Southwell would have adopted this radically Christian socialist approach in comparable circumstances, though, as we will see, Frederick William Naylor, vicar of Upton, came close to it. Although Naylor and Clarke shared a similar family background the social context of Naylor's parish was so different. Derby was a rapidly growing railway town, with (as in St Michael's parish) slum dwellings surrounding open cesspits within a stone's throw of the houses and businesses of the well-to-do. While some of the clergy in Derby were sympathetic to Clarke by no means all were. When Clarke chaired a meeting of striking ribbon weavers in the town in 1860 there is no evidence that any other clergy shared the platform with him, though, in the following year, nine Derby incumbents and six nonconformist ministers urged the establishment of a conciliation and arbitration board in the town. In Southwell, less than 25 miles away, the attitude of the clergy to the poor owed much to the influence of John Thomas Becher, who would have had no time for his younger contemporary John Erskine Clarke. In rural Nottinghamshire, as elsewhere, the clergy would have expected Anglican ratepayers willingly to have paid their church rate as they paid their poor rate and owned or rented their pews. They would have viewed 'Dissenters' with suspicion and 'Romanists' with fear. They would have felt ill-at-ease with labourers, and, while treating them as kindly as the law required and social ordering allowed, would have been untroubled by their relegation to the free seats in their churches, or even by their absence from worship altogether. The clergy, with few exceptions, shared the social and political perspectives of the class from which they had been drawn. But how many people attended church, irrespective of where they sat?

4

'These questions ought never to have been asked': counting the people

Much has been written about the first, and so far last, attempt to record the commitment of the English to religion measured by actual attendance at places of worship. This census, taken as part of the decennial census of 1851 was held on on Sunday 30 March 1851. The results were published in 1854. The Nottinghamshire material was analysed and published by Michael Watts in his *Religion in Victorian Nottinghamshire* in 1988.[1] It may not be entirely coincidental that the census took place at the height of Chartist agitation, the first sustained relatively peaceful attempt nationally to bring about democratic governance in this country.

Horace Mann, a barrister and a senior civil servant in the census office, was given the task of managing and interpreting the census. In his report he drew some arresting conclusions: as a percentage of population, more people attended places of worship in the country than in the towns, in the towns a higher percentage attended in non-industrial towns than in industrial towns, and in all towns, as a percentage of population, progressively fewer people attended the further down the socio-economic scale one went. Mann gave perceptive reasons for the failure of the working classes to attend church. These had to do principally with the lack of leisure and quiet withdrawal on which the development of the spiritual life depended, and, no less importantly, the lack of example provided by industrial employers compared to employers in rural communities.

Although the statistical methods Mann employed to interpret the raw data have been much criticised (he himself recognised their short-comings) there is no doubt that the evidence showed not merely that England was not as church-going as middle-class opinion had assumed, but, among those who did attend a place of worship on that day, not as

---

[1] Published by the then University of Nottingham Department of Adult Education.

Anglican. Not only did the raw data show how strong was the nonconformist challenge (in Nottinghamshire and Derbyshire, for example, there were more nonconformist than Anglican attendances on 30 March 1851) but also how relatively 'godless' the nation was. If, thoughtful Anglicans asked themselves, only some 40 per cent of the nation attended church that day, as Mann's raw data indicated, and that many of those who did attend were nonconformists, what did this say about the effectiveness of the Church of England as the church established by law to sustain the religious life of the nation?

There was widespread discontent among Anglican clergy about the propriety, and even the legality, of conducting this census. Many dismissed the findings – the bishop of Oxford, Samuel Wilberforce, claiming that 'ignorant Dissenting Ministers' could not be trusted to be as accurate or as truthful as Anglican clergy in compiling the returns! In Nottinghamshire several incumbents expressed their misgivings. George Wilkins's successor as vicar of St Mary's, Nottingham, J.W. Brooks, sent his return direct to the census office because, he said, he wanted to prevent 'any improper use being made of them by the officers appointed to receive them, the majority of whom in Nottingham are dissenters.'[1] The return for Southwell collegiate church was at best superficial and was signed off by Peter Coxon, the parish clerk. Returns for other parishes were so cursorily completed as to render them virtually valueless. Some clergy simply returned the forms uncompleted. Others selected the questions they would answer and refused to answer others. For example, Charles John Myers, vicar of Flintham, declined to answer questions about his benefice endowment and the attendance at the parish church because 'I consider them impertinent, in the original sense of the word; and because I know not to what use the required information might be put by an unscrupulous Ministry.' William Henry Walker, rector of Hickling, completed his return under protest, for 'these questions ought never to have been asked by her Majesty's Ministers, since they exclusively appertain to her Majesty's Bishops'. The return for Cotgrave All Saints was completed by a census official who noted that 'the above is the best information which I can obtain – the Rector and Sexton having positively refused giving any information whatever.' The rector since 1811 had been John Henry Browne, the archdeacon of Ely.

Perhaps following the collegiate church's lead the returns for a number of the parishes in the chapter's gift, or that of the bishops of Ripon or of Manchester (and formerly in the gift of individual prebends),

[1] Cited in Watts, *Religion*, ix.

were perfunctory and not completed by incumbents or curates – a higher proportion than elsewhere in the county. The return for Caunton parish church was completed by George Elvidge, the parish clerk and school-master, aged 20 years.[1] Both Joseph Leeson who completed the return for Halam and Richard Truswell, for Farnsfield, were so poorly informed that they wrote 'Name Unknown' against the dedication of the church whose returns they signed, though both were local farmers who had been born in their parishes. Truswell was currently both a churchwarden and the poor law guardian for Farnsfield.[2] The return for Edingley was signed by William Alvey, the schoolmaster. The return for Halloughton had to be completed by Thomas Pawson, the registrar for the Southwell district, and that for Beckingham (in the gift of the prebendary of Beckingham) was signed by John Jebb, a census enumerator. Thomas Coats Cane,[3] non-resident incumbent of Kirklington, signed the return for his parish adding that he 'declines answering voluntary questions.'

George Wilkins commented on the census in his 1854 charge. The official report had only recently been published, and Wilkins devoted virtually the whole of his archidiaconal charge that year to a lengthy criticism of it. He believed that the census was ill considered, and that the interests of the Church of England as the established church had been ignored. He said that if the census

> had been compiled by persons thoroughly conversant with theological and ecclesiastical subjects, the principles of the church and those of the various dissenting communities might have been more clearly and truly defined. When the circulars, requiring answers from every congregation, were issued hesitation was evinced as to the expediency of making written returns to queries not emanating from episcopal authority, and, indeed not emanating from any *legal* authority whatever ... This feeling operated in preventing many connected with the church from giving more than a slight attention to filling up the schedule; and the more so, as the enumerators were desired to state that the replies were not compulsory; compliance with them being left to everyone's sense of their importance to the public.

---

[1]   The return for the Wesleyan chapel in the village was completed by another George Elvidge, evidently his father, who described himself as 'A Wesleyan'. He was a cordwainer, aged 43.

[2]   NAO, PR 20,592: Farnsfield Parish Book', 3 April 1850; *Nottingham Journal*, 12 April 1850.

[3]   Not J.L. Lane, as in Watts.

Thus, in Wilkins's opinion, the statistics were 'far from accurate,' the Anglican returns being based partly on 'conjecture' and 'proportional calculations.' Although there was some justification for these criticisms, nonconformists also had reason to complain. Mann's formula for calculating the number of separate individuals attending gave greater statistical weight to those attending in the morning of 30 March 1851. This disadvantaged nonconformist chapels which tended to have their largest congregations on Sunday evenings. However, Wilkins noted, the statistics were now published and he observed that the 'sectaries' had seized on the findings to 'overstate what would show an increase in their number and influence.'[1] Undoubtedly, the 1851 census provided nonconformity with a useful weapon in its religious and political dispute with all that the Church of England represented.

Wilkins argued that it was not merely partial and inaccurate Anglican statistics or nonconformist deception which accounted for the supposed strength of nonconformity. Census Sunday, he noted, had been a day of 'wind and rain in an unusual degree' which kept people away from church. In their returns many Anglican clergy throughout Nottinghamshire noted that inclement weather accounted for low attendance on 30 March, some recording the storms in detail. Others noted that it was a day on which nonconformist chapels in their parishes had had Sunday school anniversaries or other celebrations (Methodist 'Love Feasts' for example) which members of the congregations of the parish church had attended. Others observed that 30 March that year was mid-Lent Sunday (Mothering Sunday) and that those members of their congregations who were living-in servants were away visiting their parents.

In Southwell and the villages immediately around it adult attendances on 30 March 1851 represented 47.5 per cent of the population of the area. If we add the attendances of Sunday school children, the figure rises 66 per cent. But note that these are *attendances* and do not represent separate individuals. Many people, especially nonconformists, attended twice or more on Sundays. Mann attempted to calculate the number of separate individuals attending by assuming that of the people attending in the morning half would be present in the afternoon, and that a third of those attending an evening service would not have gone to church or chapel earlier in the day. By this formula, together with calculations which attempted to take into account men and women who worked on Sundays in hotels, hospitals or transport, or who were caring for small children, or were too ill or too elderly to attend, or, as members

---

[1] *Nottingham Journal*, 2 June 1854.

**Calverton: church and chapel
adult attendances on 30 March 1851**

Place of worship	Morning Adults	Children	Afternoon Adults	Children	Evening Adults	Total Adults	Children
Parish Church	47	145	132	145	133	312	290
Primitive Methodist	70	—	90	—	150	310	—
Latter Day Saints	—	—	40	—	57	97	—
Particular Baptist	—	—	70	50	100	170	50
Wesleyan Methodist	—	—	—	53	25	25	53
Totals	117	145	332	248	465	914	393

Notes: The return for the Primitive Methodist chapel carries the comment: 'The morning service is occupied by the Reformed Methodists, afternoon and evening by the Primitive Methodists who purchased the chapel [sic] March 1847.' The Latter Day Saints met 'not in a separate building and not used exclusively for worship'. In an apparent reference to the expulsion, in 1849, of three ministers, leading to the formation of the Wesleyan Reformers, the return for the Wesleyan Methodist chapel states: 'The average number attending public worship (for every past lengthened period) cannot be ascertained, the agitation in the connexion having caused a division here.'

of the 'criminal population', could not, or would not, attend, it was assumed that a reasonably accurate percentage of the adult population attending places of worship could be estimated, though Mann produced no evidence to justify these presumptions. Horace Mann's formulae have been much criticised. Michael Watts suggested a more reliable approach. He based his calculations on the figures for the best attended service on census Sunday, and assumed that a third of those attending a less well attended service were not present at another. [1]

Those who went to church were principally from the middle class. Nationally the mass of the labouring poor did not attend church or chapel, particularly in the industrial cities and in the poorer districts of residential towns. The statistics revealed a correlation between non-attendance and social deprivation. Where artisans did attend in any numbers it was mainly at the less prestigious nonconformist chapels, and

[1]   Watts, *Religion*, xii.

the more so where chapel attendance was a form of political protest. The industrial village of Calverton, a centre of Chartist agitation and dissenting militancy, is a case in point. Its returns to the religious census, summarised in the table opposite, are revealing.

In 1851 the population of Calverton, including children, was 1,427 (745 males and 682 females). If we add to the adult attendances of 914 (recorded on the returns as 'General congregation') the 393 'Sunday scholars' who attended, then there were 1,307 attendances at church and chapel on census Sunday. There is some confusion however: it is likely that children were included in the general congregation in the returns for one or two of the chapels. Applying the unreliable formula employed by Thomas Mann, the number of people attending places of worship in Calverton on census Sunday 1851 once, twice or three times was about 880 or over 60 per cent of the population. Although this figure cannot be trusted it seems that a considerable proportion of the population of this centre of nonconformist radicalism went to church or chapel as a mark of their class allegiance. Some went to chapel as a political protest, while others (at least those who could afford to do so) may have attended the parish church as a sign of their commitment to the political and economic status quo or out of fear of not showing that commitment.

This last point is significant. Michael Watts noted the popular appeal of Methodism in the freehold villages south of the Trent. On his formulae 40 per cent of the population of eight villages in the Bingham district (East Bridgford, Scarrington, Whatton, Granby, Cropwell Butler, Colston Bassett, Hickling, and Cotgrave) worshipped in Methodist chapels on 30 March 1851, and only 25 per cent attended Anglican parish churches that day.[1] By contrast, in the Southwell district, where much of the land was in the hands of the Church, the statistics were very different. Using Watts' formulae about 17 per cent of the population attended Methodist chapels and 34 per cent attended Anglican churches.

But the tide was beginning to turn for all denominations. Church and chapel attendances in the Nottingham district on Sunday, 30 March 1851 represented 42.4 per cent of the population. In 1881 it was calculated that only 24.2 per cent attended churches and chapels in the city.[2] Even

[1] Watts, *Religion*, I, xix.

[2] J.M. Golby and A.W. Purdue, *The Civilisation of the Crowd: Popular Culture in England 1750–1900* (1999), 118. When he became bishop of Lincoln, Christopher Wordsworth was 'shocked' to discover that only a fifth of the population of Nottingham attended any place of worship. 'The standard of morality was not high, as in the Bishop's view it could not be when Christianity was so low' (J.H. Overton and Elizabeth Wordsworth, *Christopher Wordsworth, Bishop of Lincoln, 1807–1885* (1888), 300). The 1851 figures for Nottingham exclude the Radford district, where 19.6 per cent of the

allowing for the difficulty of assessing with any accuracy the numbers of those who attended no more than once on Sundays this still represents a considerable decline in actual allegiance. And this despite episcopal encouragement to the clergy to make the services of the church more attractive.

Yet Sunday attendance was, for many of those who occupied appropriated pews, little more than a formal indication of their social class, while the labouring poor did not fill such seats as were made available to them. Church attendance had never been as widespread and as high as some wanted to believe. Chalmers's opinion in 1827 that *'greatly more than* ONE HALF *of the people of sufficient age for church-going* ATTEND NO WHERE' seriously underestimated the extent of non-attendance in the towns and cities. The truth was that as, since the Reformation, the Church of England had never captured the imagination and allegiance of the majority of the people it had never provided a sure bulwark against threats to the integrity of the state. The idea that if more Anglican churches and clergy were provided the less would be the threat of dissenting religion and radical political action was misconceived. This notion had been the primary motivation for the church building programme under the 'Million Act' of 1818[1] and its successors. St Paul's, in the parish of Nottingham St Mary, was built in 1822 under the provisions of the Act.

Two years later the democratic *Nottingham Review* argued that there was no need for the additional sittings that the new church provided, noting that the new church cost St Mary's £400 a year to maintain. Its free seats 'are far from filled ... [and the] Morning congregation does not generally half-fill the church.' The editorial noted the number of sittings in churches and chapels in Nottingham. The five Anglican churches (St Mary, St Peter, St Nicholas and the parochial chapels of St James and St Paul) could accommodate 6,900 people. The five Independent, four Baptist and five Methodist chapels, together with the 'Unitarians, Sandemanians, Catholics, Quakers, Huntingtonians, Jews etc.' provided a further 13,200 seats, making a total of 20,100. These places of worship served a Nottingham population of 'at most' 43,000. Of this population,

population attended a place of worship on 30 March. If these figures are included, there was still a fall of at least a third in church attendance by 1881 (but note the caveat as to the reliability of these statistics).

[1]   The Church Building Act was passed in 1818. £1,000,000 was pledged to build churches in populous areas, ostensibly as a thanksgiving after Waterloo. Subsequent Acts increased this expenditure. A condition of a government grant to build a church under this legislation was that a substantial proportion of the seats should be for the poor.

8,000 were 'children not able to attend a place of worship'; 6,000 were 'old people, sick and invalids'; and there were 10,000 who were 'servants and relatives caring for the sick, together with infidels, vagabonds, and rogues who have no inclination to go.' On this calculation the *Review* held that there were thus 24,000 people in Nottingham 'who cannot or will not go to a place of worship.' Accordingly seats in places of worship were needed for only 19,000 people, against 'a present provision' for 20,100. So 'there is no want of Church or chapel room in Nottingham.'[1] George Wilkins responded to this leader the following week. He argued at length that the population of his parish of St Mary's was some 35,000 and 'likely greatly to increase' and that there was accommodation in his two churches for only 1,200 to 1,300 including seats for only 200 of the poor.[2]

Provision of sittings and attendance had hardly changed ten years later. In 1833 Richard Hopper, a Nottingham cotton spinner, investigated church and chapel attendance in the town.[3] He noted that adult church and chapel congregations totalled 17,800 of which 4,860 had a definite commitment either as Anglican communicants or as registered members of dissenting chapels. Of this total, the majority attended dissenting chapels (12,000, with 4,530 members) while 5,800 (with 330 regular communicants) worshipped with the Church of England. In addition about 1,678 children attended Anglican Sunday schools and 5,048 attended dissenting Sunday schools.[4] The Church of England had five places of worship and Protestant and Roman Catholic dissent had 20. In 1831 the population of Nottingham was 50,680. Assuming the accuracy of these figures just under 50 per cent of the population of Nottingham over, say, five years of age attended the town's Anglican and dissenting churches and chapels in 1833, and would have represented the relatively well-to-do.

Why did so many stay away, and especially from the Church of England? In 1824, the week after the *Review* published George Wilkins's response, it printed a letter from a Newark reader. Under the headline 'The Church in Danger' it posed a number of rhetorical questions:

---

[1]   *Nottingham Review*, 16 April 1824.

[2]   Ibid., 23 April 1824.

[3]   *Nottingham Journal*, 13 Dec. 1833; *Nottingham Review*, 20 Dec. 1833. See also *Nottingham Mercury*, 14 Dec. 1833. Further to this see S.D. Chapman, 'The Evangelical Revival and Education in Nottingham', *Trans. Thoroton Soc. of Notts.* (1962), 35–66.

[4]   In 1834 the Sunday school figures were revised to 1,740 and 4,950 respectively by William Deardon in his *History, Topography and Directory of Nottingham*.

From what is the Church in danger?

Why do numbers secede from the Established Church daily?

Why is there scarce a village without a meeting house of some denomination or another?

Why are there thirty-eight parishes in the hundred of Bassetlaw without a resident Rector or Vicar?

Why should not the Clergy be obliged to reside upon their livings?

Why do not the Clergymen attend to their flocks daily?

Why is it now supposed that doing the duty *once* in the week is quite sufficient?

Why are some Clergymen allowed to hold so many offices of preferment? Some four, and even six?

Why are most livings belonging to cathedrals and collegiate churches (the church in Southwell for instance) only vicarages? I mean that the rectorial tithes are kept by somebody, and the vicarial only given to the working Parson.

Why does the Church of Scotland work better than the Church of England?

Why is there no secession from the Scottish church?

Why do the incumbents in Scotland all reside?

The letter concluded:

The Church is in danger by the NON-RESIDENCE of the clergy, and the want of zeal in those who do reside ... If the clergy desert the Church, surely the people will do the same'.

The mere provision of yet more churches, or even more clergy, would not stem the desertion of people from Anglican services. The fact was that the majority of the common people had never worshipped regularly in their parish churches, at least since the Reformation. Some saw ulterior motives at work behind the drive to provide more churches. In 1841 the *Nottingham Review* published a letter from 'Plain Truth', a Mansfield reader, under the headline 'The "Established" Church again' which opposed the building of a chapel-of-ease at Pleasley Hill. It was not needed, he writer said, as the parish church was 'at most five minutes walk of it' and was 'very little more than half-filled.' In his opinion the only reason why this new church was proposed was 'our vicar's desire ... to get a stipend from a chapel-of-ease in the hamlet (and he has gained his point) and the gentleman who is writing him down, is anxious that he may get some "loaves and fishes" and so *both* have looked for the same object. It is easy for any person to see this.'[1]

Inevitably, church services on weekdays attracted very few. We have noted that in 1836, on George Wilkins's testimony, on average fewer than one person a day attended weekday services in Southwell collegiate church even in the summer. George Wilkins had become vicar of St Mary's, Nottingham in 1817. A letter in 1814 to the *Nottingham Review* from 'An offended but forgiving Churchwarden' tells of weekday services in St Mary's. He went into the church on 22 March merely because he was passing the door at service time. He found the congregation 'to consist of a lady, an elderly gentleman, myself, and THIRTY or FORTY CHARITY BOYS from TEN to FOURTEEN years of age'. The 'Charity Lads' clearly did not count as members of the congregation, for, a few minutes before the service was due to begin, the parish clerk emerged to 'reconnoitre'. The correspondent (who was churchwarden of a church 'not a hundred miles east' of St Mary's) was asked by the clerk whether he was a resident. He replied that, as he was sitting in St Mary's, he was. The clerk asked whether he was resident in the parish. When the churchwarden said that he was not, the clerk replied, 'Then, sir, there will not be any prayers … Our vicar's rule is never to read prayers except there be THREE RESIDENTS of THIS PARISH present'.[2]

The offended but forgiving correspondent noted the better attendance in his parish church. The incumbent of Nottingham St Mary at the time was George Hutchinson who had been vicar since 1810. The democratic *Review* was no supporter of the Church of England, but there is no reason to doubt the accuracy of these reports. They focused attention on the clergy and their ministry.

[1] *Nottingham Review*, 11 June 1841.
[2] Ibid., 1 April 1814.

5

'Nobility, Gentry and Clergy': the social status of the clergy

Throughout this period the aristocracy, the gentry and the clergy of the Church of England were in symbiotic relationship. With few exceptions, to be the squire and principal landowner in a parish was to be a member of the Church of England, to be patron of the benefice and to sit in a pew in a prominent position in the parish church, and perhaps, as at Halloughton, with a private door into the chancel to gain access to it. The landowning class regarded the Church as its spiritual bulwark, and the Church saw the landowning class as its patron and defender. Together, parson and squire exercised, if both were resident, diligent and humane, what Alan Gilbert has called the 'conservative social responsibilities' that were the concomitant of the 'social power of landed property', defined by E.W. Bovill as the 'immense prestige attaching to wealth and acres, the awe which the way of life of the aristocracy inspired, and the respect in which most country squires were held.'[1] As an example, in 1859 when Charles John Myers, vicar of Flintham, was required by the bishop of Lincoln to explain why the collections made at holy communion had not been given to the poor (as the prayer book rubric required) for some ten years, he replied that until the squire went abroad there had been little call on it. When parishioners were unemployed the squire, Thomas Blackborne Thoroton Hildyard, either gave them money or created work on his estate for them.[2] Hildyard felt an obligation to the poor, an obligation which found expression in the notion of 'charity'. Writing of the eighteenth-century gentry, G.E. Mingay observed that for these men 'the ... burden of charity was usually regarded as inescapable, and even proprietors beset by creditors and driven to any expedient to

---

[1]   A.D. Gilbert, *Religion and Society in Industrial England: Church, Chapel and Social Change 1740–1914* (1976), 97, quoting E.W. Bovill, *English Country Life 1780–1830* (Oxford, 1962), 233.

[2]   Penny Gallon, 'Paterfamilias: The Reverend Charles John Myers, vicar of Flintham from 1829–1870', *Nottinghamshire Historian*, no. 49 (1992), 20; and see p. 162 below.

raise cash would not cut down in charities.'[1] In short, inherited money brought with it an inherited obligation always to provide for the relief of distress. These sums, though substantial in absolute terms, were small in relation to the incomes of the donors, and smaller still when compared to the needs of the poor. Nevertheless, for the aristocracy and the gentry, to provide for the poor was an inescapable obligation. This was given theological expression by Bernard Wilson, vicar of Newark from 1719 to his death in 1772. In 1768 he argued that 'the Scripture enjoins us not only to give to the Poor what their Labours demand of us, but even what their Necessities require from us', and that 'Charity to the Distressed is a kind of Debt, which the Almighty Governor of the World has directed us amongst other Duties to discharge', though Wilson, the son of a Newark mercer, added the reassuring caveat that this debt would be honoured from but 'a certain proportion of our Fortune ... according to the Nature of our Circumstances'.[2] For the traditional gentry, their 'Fortune' derived from inherited land. Land alone granted the gentry their status: Sir John Holles could say in Elizabeth I's reign, 'Gentility is nothing but ancient riches.'[3]

It is doubtful whether John Thomas Becher would have had much time for the unquestioning sense of obligation evidently felt by Bernard Wilson in Newark and Thomas Hildyard in Flintham. The idea that property brought with it a moral compulsion to support the poor at the point of need sat uneasily with the notion that men and women in all sections of society were responsible for their own destinies. This was the ethic of the new capitalism that undoubtedly drove Becher's poor law reforms. At just this point the principles of the traditional land-owning gentry, with whom the clergy wished to be identified, could not easily be reconciled with those of their number who came from the new and wealthy entrepreurial class. Becher acknowledged that charity had its place, but it must by no means be arbitrary:

> When Parochial Relief is withdrawn, the measure of public and private benevolence should be proportionately enlarged. Important benefits may be conferred by Individual Charity discreetly distributed, and by Premiums proposed for the encouragement of

---

[1]   G.E. Mingay, *English Landed Society in the Eighteenth Century* (1963), 275.

[2]   Bernard Wilson, *A Discourse addressed to the Inhabitants of Newark against the Misapplication of Public Charities* (1768), 5, 6. I am grateful to Stanley Chapman for this reference.

[3]   Holles's descendants became dukes of Newcastle who were to own a very considerable acreage of north Nottinghamshire.

personal Merit ... But indiscriminate liberality subverts the Morals and deprave the Habits of the Poor, under the specious and misplaced name of Charity. In Southwell these Contributions were formally levied almost Annually, while at the same time the Poor Rates were progressively advancing. But all voluntary Parochial Subscriptions for such purposes have been discountenanced and discontinued for nearly Twenty Years, under a full conviction of their ruinous influence.[1]

Becher created a workhouse system in Southwell in which the able-bodied and improvident poor together with the 'idle and profligate' were 'subject to a system of secluded restraint and salutary discipline which, together with our simple yet sufficient dietary, prove so repugnant to their dissolute habits that they very soon apply for their discharge, and devise means of self-support which nothing short of compulsion could urge them to explore.'[2] For Becher 'self-respect and self-support', compelled by what he himself described as the 'Terror to the Dissolute and Refactory' and the 'degradation'[3] of the workhouse, was vastly preferable to charity – a conviction which clearly reflected the style and attitude of the rising commercial middle class from which Becher, and most of Southwell's leading families, sprang.

Frequently, however, the power of absentee landowners was exercised by agents. Agents had no obligation to the poor. As an example, almost all of the 2,600 acres of the parish of South Muskham (a vicarage in the gift of the prebendary of South Muskham, John Thomas Becher) was owned by Henry Willoughby (1761–1835), 6th Baron Middleton, of Wollaton Hall near Nottingham. In 1831 the non-resident incumbent, employing a resident curate, was Richard Barrow, a vicar choral living in Southwell. In December of that year the *Nottingham and Newark Mercury* published a letter from a correspondent, 'Z', who, having described Lord Middleton as 'an advocate of the religious liberty of the subject' recorded that

On Sunday last, one of his Lordship's stewards being at Newark, sent for one of his tenants from Little Carlton, in the parish of Muskham, to meet him in Newark. The poor woman came, wondering what could be amiss; and knocking at the door of the

[1]   John Thomas Becher, *The Antipauper System* (1828, 1834), 33.
[2]   Ibid., 17–18.
[3]   Ibid., 49, 33.

house where the steward was visiting (in North-gate) was informed he was gone to church. On his return, he told the woman he understood she admitted the Methodists to her house, to hold preachings, &c; that it could not be allowed, and that if she persisted in allowing them to preach she would be discharged. The poor woman, almost broken-hearted, went to a friend's house, exclaiming, 'they could not take her Bible.' If this be religious toleration, I wonder what is persecution — What renders it more oppressive is, the husband of the woman is deaf and dumb, and they have six children, and nothing to depend on but the produce of a few acres of land under his Lordship.[1]

Perhaps 'Z' was exaggerating for effect. That a poor woman, a Methodist, with a large family and a disabled husband should be so treated just before Christmas would have chimed with a growing section of public opinion critical of church and nobility after the rejection of the first reform bill. More important, that the letter was published in a by no means radical newspaper suggests that the traditional rural dependency system was beginning slowly to break down, and, with it, unquestioning deference to squire and parson.

But the parson continued to stand with the squire in defence of the traditional social order, and that required that it was in the parson's interests to vote as the squire voted.

'The objectionable influences of popular opinion': the clergy and political issues

The voting patterns of the clergy show that they were, at least ostensibly and with few exceptions, 'Church and King' Tories. Where clergy voted for reform candidates they did so less from conviction than from considerations of self-interest. This is illustrated from poll books recording votes at the general election of December 1832 which followed the passing of the Reform Act. There is no space here for a detailed analysis of clergy voting but an example illustrates the trend. Three candidates contested the new northern division of Nottinghamshire. They were Richard, Viscount Lumley, John Gilbert Cooper-Gardiner and Thomas Houldsworth. Lumley, with extensive estates at Rufford, was described by the radical Richard Sutton as 'a thorough-paced reformer'

---

[1] *Nottingham and Newark Mercury*, 24 Dec. 1831.

who, as a sitting member, had been 'fully in favour' of the 1831 Reform Bill. Cooper-Gardiner was also known as 'a thorough reformer'. Thomas Houldworth was 'a gentleman of racing notoriety, a decided tory, and a man of long purse.'[1] Of the 29 beneficed clergy who are known to have voted, seven voted for Lumley and Houlsworth, four for Lumley and Cooper-Gardiner, two plumped for Lumley, and 16 plumped for Houldsworth. Few voted against the Tory interest. Those who voted for the reformers Lumley and Cooper-Gardiner were Thomas Cursham, vicar of Mansfield, Charles Fowler, a pluralist living in Southwell but voting on his freehold as vicar of Eaton, John Williams, vicar of North Leverton, and John Hurt Woolley, vicar of Beeston. The two beneficed clergy who plumped for Lumley were Edward Creswell, vicar of Lenton and Thomas Stacye, vicar of Worksop. Although few firm conclusions can be drawn from this evidence it suggests that the clergy believed that their best interests lay in voting for the candidate with local influence. This may explain the Lumley-Houldsworth split. Clergy may have voted for Lumley out of self-interest, and for Houldsworth out of conviction. In a public ballot in front of an often noisy crowd it did not follow that voting for a reform or an anti-reform candidate, even plumping for him, meant that the voter shared the candidate's political views. Nevertheless, over nearly 80 per cent of the beneficed clergy voting in the northern division voted for Houldsworth, with 55 per cent plumping for him. He took the seat, due, Richard Sutton said, to 'the influence of the Dukery [of Newcastle] with their £50 tenants round Retford.'[2]

Another example is the pattern of clergy voting at the bitterly fought by-election in Newark in 1840. Frederic Thesinger, the Conservative candidate representing the very powerful local interest of the duke of Newcastle, stood against Thomas Wilde, the sitting MP who had been required to seek re-election on his appointment as solicitor-general. Wilde polled 541 votes and Thesinger 532. Among the £10-pound householders qualified to vote were five Anglican clergy: Robert Ffarmerie, vicar of Car Colston since 1821, James Foottit, vicar of the chapter benefice of Barnby-in-the-Willows since 1822 and a vicar choral of Southwell, Robert Simpson, who was to become vicar of Newark

[1]   *Poll Book of the Election for the North Division of Nottinghamshire 1832* (Richard Sutton, Nottingham, 1833), iv.

[2]   There appears to be no extant copy of the poll book for the 1832 election for the southern division of Nottinghamshire (which included Southwell), but for the social and political establishment of the constituency in the 1830s see J.R. Fisher, 'The Tory Revival of the 1830s: an uncontested election in South Nottinghamshire' *Midland History*, 6 (1981), 95ff.

Christ Church, John Simpson, and John Garrett Bussell, vicar of the civic church of Newark St Mary Magdelene. Bussell did not vote. The remaining four voted for Thesinger.

An example of compromised loyalties in a confused but highly charged political environment is illustrated by clerical voting patterns at the parliamentary by-election in south Nottinghamshire in February 1846. The sitting member from 1832 had been Henry Pelham Clinton, the earl of Lincoln, of Ranby Hall, Retford. On being appointed chief secretary for Ireland in Robert Peel's second administration he had to resign and seek re-election. Influential landowning constituents had called on Lord Lincoln to resign in 1845 when, in supporting Peel, he had advocated the lowering of corn duties. Peel's policy undermined vested protectionist agricultural interests and increased the strain on the loyalty of the old Tories to Peel. In an election address Lincoln freely acknowledged that his views on protection had 'undergone a great change since the last general election.'[1] This by-election was thus effectively a local battle between traditional aristocratic protectionist Toryism and Peel's new reforming Conservatism. While accepting that Lincoln had served their members well for fourteen years, the pro-corn law Nottinghamshire Agricultural Protection Society put up another Tory, Thomas Blackborne Thoroton Hildyard of Flintham Hall to oppose him.

Ostensibly this was a single-issue contest, but it inevitably engaged with other more powerful, even tribal, concerns. Supporters of Lincoln argued that to oppose him would undermine Peel's administration and let in Lord John Russell who would repeal the corn laws almost immediately and on much less favourable terms,[2] but one of them, a Southwell resident, voiced wider fears. In a series of rhetorical questions he asked:

> Shall ... our sacred institutions be invaded by the destructive policies of Lord John Russell? Shall the Protestant Church in Ireland be overthrown and its resources given to the Romish Priest? Shall our Bishops be expelled from the House of Lords? and a growing debt supplant an overflowing exchequer? Shall slave-grown sugar be again brought to the free shores of England? Shall our amicable relations with all Europe cease? In fine, shall democratic views alone guide the rulers of the state?[3]

---

[1] *The Poll Book: South Nottinghamshire election 1846* (Newark, 1846), 5.

[2] Ibid., 16, letter to electors from 'A Conservative Neighbour'.

[3] Ibid., 24, letter from 'Miles'.

These arguments were employed by both sides. Opposing Lincoln, the author of an unsigned open letter argued that 'yielding to popular clamour' had led to the 'folly' of Roman Catholic emancipation at the hands of the duke of Wellington and Robert Peel.[1] The almost superstitious fear of Roman Catholicism found a focus in Lord Lincoln's position as chief secretary for Ireland. On appointment he became Visitor of Maynooth college in Co. Kildare. The 'Royal Catholic College' had been established by the Irish parliament in 1795 for the education of Roman Catholic clergy for Ireland. Until the disestablishment of the (Anglican) Church of Ireland in 1869 the college was supported by an annual grant from the Westminster parliament. In 1845 this grant, originally for £8,000, had been raised from £9,500 to £26,000 by Robert Peel. Citing Lincoln's appointment as the college's Visitor as evidence of his 'renegade conduct', George Beaumont of Bridgford Hill said that the MP had met with 'marked disgust, except for his friends the Papists and Radicals.' Beaumont called for support for Hildyard, 'the sound Protestant and farmers' friend.'[2] The author of a scurrilous circular, quoting the announcement of Lincoln's Maynooth appointment in the *London Gazette*, claimed that voting for Lincoln would be seen as 'taking thirty pieces of silver, and [a vote] for Papists.'[3]

The hugely influential duke of Newcastle threw his weight behind Hildyard. In an open letter to electors he said that Lord Lincoln had been 'the deluded victim of bad counsel.' For Newcastle, free trade was but one of 'the newly disclosed enormities' of Peel administration.[4]

Lord Lincoln must have that felt that attack to be a particularly bitter blow because he was Newcastle's eldest son and heir. He succeeded his estranged father in 1851 as the 5th duke.

In the event, Hildyard won by 1,736 to 1,049, a substantial majority of 687, and this against the usual charge that Lincoln had bestowed 'benefits' to secure votes. If they were persuaded by the extravagant rhetoric the dilemma facing clergy electors was clear – to support Lord Lincoln and keep out Lord John Russell in defence of the Church of England against 'Papists', 'Radicals', and the 'popular clamour' of 'democratic views', or to put Peel's administration at risk by opposing

---

[1] Ibid., 23.

[2] Ibid., 84.

[3] Ibid., 84. That the question of the Irish church was of importance in the 1846 south Nottinghamshire by-election see correspondence between Lincoln and John Evelyn Denison (later Viscount Ossington): University of Nottingham Dept of Manuscripts and Special Collections, Denison Collection, bundle 27, Os C 347–353).

[4] *Poll Book*, 24.

Lincoln in defence of the vested interests of the landowners on whose patronage they depended and of the farmers who leased their glebe and paid them their tithes. Thirty-seven clergy, resident in Nottinghamshire, can be traced as voting in this by-election, 16 for Lincoln and 21 for Hildyard. The pattern of voting in electoral districts suggests that, as in earlier elections, the clergy were more concerned to safeguard their own personal interests and to maintain local loyalties than to express political principle. Flintham, where Hildyard was squire, was in the Sutton on Trent electoral district. Here the clergy voted 8 to 1 in his favour. In the adjacent East Leake district they voted 7 to 2 for Hildyard. On the other side of the Trent the clergy were more inclined to vote for Lord Lincoln: in the Lowdham electoral district by 3 votes to 1, and in the Newark district (where loyalties to the Clinton family were strong) the clergy voted 4 to 1 in Lincoln's favour, despite the duke of Newcastle's opposition to his son's candidature. The pattern of clergy voting in the Southwell electoral district showed that families and local loyalties were split. Six clergy voted for Lincoln: Charles Fowler, John Thomas Becher, Sherard Becher, Thomas Coats Cane, Robert Hodgson Fowler and George Wilkins. Four voted for Hildyard: Robert Henry Wylde, James Foottit, John Murray Wilkins and John Drake Becher, the last two voting contrary to their fathers. The chapter clerk, Robert Bridgman Barrow, also voted for Hildyard.

After a general election in 1846 Lord John Russell led a minority administration because traditional protectionist Tories would not be reconciled to the anti-corn law Peelites. But bitterly split as the protectionists and Peelites were it was rare for the clergy to vote other than in the conservative interest. As Melville Horne Scott, the vicar of Ockbrook in Derbyshire, noted in his diary in 1868:

> it will usually be a clergyman's best plan to give a silent Conservative vote as the least obtrusive thing that he can do ... A quiet Conservative vote is the best expression of his gratitude to God for England as she is; England as she is to be the clergyman had better leave to be arranged by persons cleverer and otherwise less solemnly occupied than himself.[1]

Most Nottinghamshire clergy would have agreed. Certainly George Wilkins would have done so, though he expressed his political opinions far less unobtrusively than did Scott. The clergy found a ready mouth-

---

[1]   M. Scott, *The Force of Love; memoir of Melville H. Scott* (Derby, 1899), 111.

piece in their archdeacon.

The different but related and equally contentious matters of church rates, 'papal aggression', ritualism, and Sunday observance are but a few of the political issues illustrating the uneasy state of church/state relationships in the middle years of the nineteenth century. Wilkins had much to say about each. For him the Church of England could only be defended by defending the traditional social order to which the Church of England gave religious sanction. By 1856, as he had earlier, he expected little from a government which had 'no leaning to the Church', as he said in his charge that year. In his opinion 'it is vain that we should look to it for that encouragement and support which it ought in these times to expect.' He criticised Palmerston's Whig administration for failing to support Sabbath observance, for not organising and promoting a day of thanksgiving 'for the blessings of peace' at the conclusion of the Crimean war, for its refusal to support the Church of England's request for a 'Sovereign's grant of royal letter' on behalf of the 'charitable institutions of religion', and in particular for its refusal to authorise collections in church for the Church Building Society and to support church schools.[1] These may now seem to be marginal concerns, but they were then regarded by many churchmen as symptomatic of the cavalier attitude of Palmerston's first administration towards the Church of England.[2] In 1851 Wilkins, and many other clergy, had been unhappy when asked by Lord John Russell's Whig administration to provide detailed information about church attendance and, for Anglican parishes, incumbents' benefice incomes, for the census of religious worship – information previously returned only to diocesan bishops and royal commissions.

Wilkins, like most of his clergy, was no scion of a great, or even a landed, family, but he enjoyed aristocratic patronage. He stood for Church and Crown and resisted any attempt to roll back the privileges of the Church of England by law established or to make it in any way subject to government control – least of all subject to parliamentary control and popular opinion. If asked about the further extension of the franchise Wilkins would have opposed it vigorously. For him, to reform

---

[1]   *Nottingham Journal*, 6 June 1856.

[2]   In his two administrations between 1855 and 1865 Palmerston adopted a religious policy which, while securing the pre-eminence of the Church of England as the established church, advocated religious toleration and was unsympathetic to those clergy with ecclesiastical or political ambitions. However, by recommending a number of fine appointments to the episcopate he reformed the Church of England. See John Wolffe, 'Lord Palmerston and Religion: A Reappraisal', *English Historical Review*, cxx (2005), 907–30.

parliamentary representation posed as much a threat to the stability of the Church of England as it did to the integrity of the state. Wilkins would have been all too aware of the strength of the call for reform locally. In 1817, two years after he became resident incumbent of Lowdham, numerous local petitions for the reform of representation had been presented to parliament from Nottingham and adjacent industrial villages, including three, Calverton, Woodborough and Oxton, in the Southwell peculiar.[1]

Wilkins's core conviction, from which all his political opinions flowed, is made very clear in his visitation charge in 1859. In it he speaks with disdain of the 'blending' of 'two *different* motives of *popular* with *public* opinion upon which no dependency can be placed for neither of them represent the joint mature convictions of a preponderance of thinking men.' Indeed, 'popular opinion' is 'too often' constituted 'of the ignorance, passion, and hasty conclusions of the busy, unthinking classes, devoted to what they consider to be progress.' The 'irresponsible masses' sought by their 'interference and citation' to demand of the Church of England that it 'bend' and 'turn its ancient practices and belief to the warrant of the time.' If the Church of England was not defended this 'strength of numbers', this 'aristocracy of numbers', would replace those with 'social position' and 'official qualification' in determining the future of the church. Wilkins added to the list of examples of the power of this new and influential 'aristocracy' that he had given in previous visitation charges. For example, he criticised the proposal to allow a man to marry his deceased wife's sister. For him it rested on two popular assumptions: that 'it is monstrous to attempt to maintain the existing law', and that such a union was 'no longer a question of right or wrong, for public opinion, in defiance of theological conclusions, energetical criticism, or ecclesiastical decrees rules that such matters are not unscriptural, and, whether if so or not, that they are not *expedient,* and are therefore to be insisted upon, to be legalized.'[2] Wilkins also condemned both the 'popular opinion' that 'the

[1] *Nottingham Review*, 28 Feb. 1817: Nottingham, 7,165 signatures; Bulwell, 435; Mansfield, 1,368; Carlton and Basford, 675; Burton, 408; Greasley, 560; Stapleford, 361; Lambley and vicinity, 509; Hucknall, 354; Beeston, 285; Lenton, 183; Chilwell, 161; Calverton, Woodborough and Oxton, 453; Gotham, 137; with additional petitions from Arnold, Sawley and Keyworth.

[2] This question was a cause célèbre in Victorian England, with frequent leaders in *The Times* and the provincial press given to it. The Deceased Wife's Sister Act, introduced in 1835, ruled that all marriages with one's deceased wife's sister contracted before 31 August 1835 were valid (but voidable by an ecclesiastical court) but that all subsequent marriages of a similar nature would be illegal. Matthew Parker's *Table of Kindred and Affinity* of

rite of marriage should be separated from any act of religion, but be legalized by a mere worldly contract',[1] while the 'question of Divorce has been carried in Parliament without any regard to the securities of religion because the public mind has been roused against it.'[2] Further, church rates, 'that most ancient rite', were now threatened to be swept away by 'the violence and influence of popular agitation'[3]. As we will see later Wilkins believed that the integrity of the church's liturgy and even of its scriptures was under threat from the menace of 'popular agitation.'

Wilkins was also greatly concerned that the 'aristocracy of numbers' would influence the appointment of bishops. These appointments, he said, must be made 'in favour of ability, genius and energy, without regard to high birth or political considerations … ' for 'can it be thought that popular opinion is a principle consistent with the influence and character of a great Christian nation – can we doubt but that its application must necessarily operate to the disadvantage both of our Church and country?'

So, for Wilkins, this time of 'trouble' and 'unhappy commotion' had been brought about because 'the objectionable influences of popular opinion has carried us out of the course of those high principles which ought to regulate our feelings and our teaching.'[4] Wilkins returned to this theme in his 1860 visitation charge, again inveighing against 'public

---

1563, given legal force by canon 99 of 1603 and annexed to the *Book of Common Prayer* in 1662, prohibited such unions (17 and 18 in Parker's *Table*). E.B. Pusey made a long defence of the prohibition in his evidence before a government commission to inquire into the state and operation of the laws of marriage as they related to the prohibited degrees (published as *Marriage with a Deceased Wife's Sister Prohibited by Holy Scripture, as understood by the Church for 1500 years* (Oxford 1849)). In 1842 the vicar of Bawtry in Nottinghamshire refused to 'church' a woman after the birth of her child because she had married her deceased sister's husband. The Deceased Wife's Sister's Marriage Act legalised these unions in 1907. This Act removed prohibition 17 from Parker's *Table*. It was followed by a similar Act in 1921 which removed prohibition 18 which forbad the union of a woman with her sister's husband.

[1]   A reference to the provisions of the Marriage Act of 1836 which allowed superintendent registrars to conduct marriages in register offices from 1 July 1837. For the opposition of clergy in Nottingham to the introduction of civil marriage see Francis Knight, *The Nineteenth-century Church and English Society* (1995), 101.

[2]   The Matrimonial Causes Act of 1857 allowed a man to divorce his wife on the ground of adultery, but did not extent the same right to a woman to divorce her unfaithful husband.

[3]   In 1859 Spencer Walpole, home secretary in Peel's second cabinet, introduced a bill to make possible the substitution of a voluntary subscription for church rates. This was refused a second reading by a substantial majority. In 1860 another bill for the abolition of church rates (the first had been introduced in 1841) was passed in the Commons but failed in the Lords.

[4]   Full text in the *Newark Advertiser*, 1 June 1859.

opinion', that is 'the spirit of the world ... now made to operate upon every matter, political, civil and religious ... as a suitable standard of faith'.[1] What was at stake for Wilkins was less the soundness of these reforms than that they were proposed by secular authority and not by the church. This was the case that John Keble had argued in his famous assize sermon on *National Apostasy* delivered in Oxford on 14 July 1833.[2] Provoked by the proposed dissolution by the government of ten clearly unnecessary Irish Anglican bishoprics[3] he said:

> The point really to be considered is, whether, according to the coolest estimate, the fashionable liberality of this generation be not ascribable, in a great measure, to the same temper which led the Jews voluntarily to set about degrading themselves to a level with the idolatrous Gentiles? And, if it be true anywhere, that such enactments are forced on the Legislature by public opinion, is APOSTASY too hard a word to describe the temper of that nation?

A quarter of a century later the power of 'popular opinion' (the 'aristocracy of numbers') to persuade parliament to reform the church was exactly the issue that engaged George Wilkins. As with the suppression of the Irish bishoprics the actual issues in 1859 were far less important than the undermining of the principle that a supposedly Christian nation should be ruled according to the precepts of the Church of England. Keble had argued that 'as a Christian nation, [England] is also a part of Christ's Church, and bound, in all her legislation and policy, by the fundamental rules of that Church ... '. To legislate contrary to this principle was to be apostate. This was Keble's judgment. The whims of a 'fashionable liberality' had been substituted for 'the fundamental rules' of the church. In this he was not only to be supported by those later to be called the Tractarians who believed that the integrity of the church was threatened, but also by evangelicals who saw in the same liberal tendencies a threat to the absolute authority of the Bible. But George Wilkins saw in the power of public opinion another and more immediate danger. It was that the authority of the 'irresponsible masses' was to be substituted for that of those carrying 'social position'

---

[1] Charge delivered in Nottingham St Mary, *Nottingham Journal*, 8 June 1860.

[2] This sermon is considered as marking the beginning of the Oxford Movement.

[3] Local clergy would have read articles in the *Nottingham Journal* in 1845 noting that the probates of wills of eleven 18th-century Irish bishops totalled £3,875,000. This was seen as damning evidence of the worldliness of the Irish bishops and 'reflects disgrace on the church to which they belonged' (6 May 1845, 30 May 1845).

and 'official qualification.'[1]

And they belonged to the social class to which Wilkins aspired and which had provided patronage for him and for the majority of the parish clergy — the gentry and the aristocracy.

The 'gentleman heresy'

The overwhelming majority of incumbents depended on the patronage of aristocratic or gentry families. Their subservience to their patrons was beautifully but bitterly portrayed by Jane Austen and Anthony Trollope, but it was, of course, observed by the radical press. An example of 'CLERICAL COMPLIANCE' was noted in the *Nottingham Review* in 1825:

> In the Church service of thanksgiving of women after childbirth, the Curate of — , afraid of offending his patroness, who was a lady of quality, introduced the word *lady* instead of *woman*; and accordingly said, 'O Lord, save this *lady* thy servant', when the clerk made the answer, 'Who putteth her *ladyship's* trust in *thee.*'[2]

Whether this story is caricature or genuine that it should be published reflects radical opinion at the time. But the parish clergy were now aspiring to their patrons' social class. Nineteenth-century directories listed the 'Nobility, Gentry and Clergy' together. Gentry status was one to which many clergy may have aspired but to which few, other than those from the traditional landowning families, were admitted as equals. Yet it was generally accepted by the mid-nineteenth century that to be a clergyman was to be a gentleman. To be accepted as one of the gentry it was helpful to have a 'seat' and an income to support it. For example, among the holders of the 'Seats of the Nobility, Gentry, and Clergy of Nottinghamshire' in *White's Directory of Nottinghamshire* for 1844 there are only six clergy: Thomas Manners-Sutton (Averham), Robert Lowe (Bingham), George Mason (Norton Cuckney), Christopher Neville (Wickenby, Lincolnshire), John Staunton (Staunton Harold, Leicestershire) and John Storer (Hawkesworth). Of these six, Thomas Manners-Sutton and Robert Lowe held the two wealthiest benefices in the county, but of the six only Thomas Manners-Sutton was a member of the

---

[1]   And this despite his concern that bishops should be appointed on merit and not merely on account of 'high birth'.

[2]   *Nottingham Review*, 2 Sept. 1825.

traditional land-owning class. In Pigot's *Nottinghamshire Directory* for 1835 of the 73 'Nobility, Gentry, and Clergy' in Southwell and its surrounding villages 17 were clergy. With few exceptions they did not possess family seats as squarsons. Inevitably, no nonconformist ministers or Roman Catholic priests are in the list. They were not tainted by the 'gentleman heresy' which Hurrell Froude noted and ridiculed. Commenting on the expectation that clergy should be gentlemen, Anthea Jones says:

> The clergy had never been a homogeneous class. It was probably unfortunate for the Church of England that in the nineteenth century, when an immense effort was made to modernise and to increase provision of parish clergymen, the gentleman heresy was widely and strongly held, particularly by the upper clergy; the result was that much work was directed to providing incomes and houses to attract gentlemen, as well as providing over-grandiose churches. As the *Guardian* wrote on 10 December 1856: 'Is it not extravagant to hamper ourselves with the idea of supplying all England with adequate spiritual ministrations through none but 'resident gentlemen?[1]

What factors led to the relatively recently acquired gentleman status to which many clergy aspired, an aspiration which, by the 1860s, was beginning to lose its reality though not its appeal? In 1865–6 Anthony Trollope published in the *Pall Mall Gazette* his series of ten essays on 'Clergymen of the Church of England'. He wrote of 'The Parson of the Parish' that until 'a few years since'

> [h]e was a man who had lived on equal terms with the highest of the land in point of birth, and hence arose a feeling that was very general in rural parishes, and as salutary as it was general, that the occupant of the parsonage was as good a man as the occupant of the squire's house. It would be interesting to us to trace when this feeling first became common, knowing as we do that for many years after the Reformation, and down even to a comparatively late date, the rural clergyman was anything but highly esteemed.[2]

There is no space here to discuss in detail the causes of this enhancement

---

[1] Anthea Jones, *A Thousand Years of the English Parish Church* (2000), 226.

[2] Anthony Trollope, *Clergymen of the Church of England* (1866), 59.

of social status, but in the main there were three. The first, the effect of
the raising of the level of benefice incomes through increased land
holdings, will be considered later. Secondly, although at the beginning
of the eighteenth century the clergy were generally held in some
contempt by the aristocracy and the gentry, by its end the upper classes
had reason to forge a close relationship with those who, from the pulpit,
could be relied on to stand firm against the threat of a growing spirit of
insubordination (at least, and, at worst, of violent revolution) prompted
by events across the Channel. The old alliance of Church and King,
reasserted in an invigorated establishment, was given eloquent expression
by Edmund Burke. The aristocracy and the gentry who exercised
patronage, and the clergy who sought it, needed each other. So it was
that an increasing number of clergy took their places on magistrates'
benches beside the gentry: the maintenance of law and order, by
increasingly draconian means, finding divine sanction in the church.
Thirdly, and as a result of this close alliance of power, privilege and
church, men of a higher social standing than hitherto were attracted into
ordained ministry at parish level. In particular, the bishops came
increasingly to be drawn from powerful titled families.

Incumbents of wealthy benefices made wealthier still by enclosure,
and those incumbents of poorer benefices who enjoyed ample private
means, built new parsonage houses that rivalled those of the squires.
They had been doing so from the late eighteenth century. Here is one
typical example: in 1838, the year of his institution to Car Colston
(population in 1831, 249), John Chancourt Girardot[1] demolished the
vicarage 'and erected, at a short distance, a handsome building in the
Elizabethan style, with stone mullioned windows and other stone
dressings, with neat grounds around.'[2] The right of patronage of Car
Colston had been purchased for Girardot by his father, making him both
patron and incumbent. It had been sold by the previous patron and
incumbent, Robert Ffarmerie. Girardot had been vicar of nearby
Screveton (population 312 in 1831) since 1824. His gross benefice
income there was £264, but he had employed a curate at £60 a year. The
glebe house there was 'unfit for residence'. His income from Car Colston
was £203, though, in his return to the 1851 census he claimed that it was
then only £150. But Girardot did not seek ordination for financial benefit.

---

[1] John Chancourt Girardot, Eton College, Brasenose College, Oxford, BA 1821, MA
1824. d. 1822, p. 1822 (by the bishop of Chester in St James', Piccadilly), rector of
Screveton, Notts., 1824–79, vicar of Car Colston, Notts., 1838–79. For the Girardots see
Michael Bray, *The Girardot family* (Square One Publications, 1996, 1998).

[2] *White's Directory of Nottinghamshire* (1853).

As a 'rich, sporting parson'[1] educated at Eton and Oxford he could afford to provide for himself a new and substantial parsonage house when he moved to Car Colston.

In 1828 Girardot married Sophia Georgiana, the second daughter of the wealthy, influential and well-connected Robert Chaplin, cousin of Col. John Manners-Sutton, patron of Averham with Kelham. Chaplin had married Ann Georgina Sutton in 1796. He was rector of Averham with Kelham (the second richest benefice in the county) from 1792 to 1837, and also vicar of Tathwell in Lincolnshire. Tathwell, of which Charles Chaplin was the squire, was a Chaplin family benefice. John Sutton[2] of Norwood Park married Sophia Frances Chaplin, Charles Chaplin's daughter. Robert Chaplin was also prebendary of Norwell Secunda in the collegiate church of Southwell. His brother Edward was vicar of Blankney (another Chaplin family benefice) and vicar of Norwell (1797-1833) in the gift of the prebend of Norwell.

Robert Chaplin's other daughters also married clergymen. In 1819 Frances Anne married Henry Houson the younger,[3] who had been appointed a vicar choral of Southwell in 1813. In 1820 he was made rector of the rich benefices of Brant Broughton and of Great Coates in Lincolnshire, the patron of which was Sir Richard Sutton,[4] John Sutton's son. Ann, daughter of the younger Henry Houson, married Richard Sutton[5] of Norwood Park in 1845. In 1832 Georgiana Chaplin married the Revd George William Barrow (1806–57), son of George Hodgkinson Barrow of Southwell. These marriages provide further clerical examples of the cementing of family ties and family fortunes by marriage and patronage within a narrow circle of privileged gentry families in the county.[6]

Girardot moved in the social circle appropriate to his name, connections, education, fortune and status. In 1829 he had been, with John Drake Becher, one of the stewards of the Southwell Ball held in December and which 'was numerously and most respectably attended',

[1] T.C. Blagg, 'Car-Colston', *Trans. Thoroton Soc. of Notts.*, lxxiv (1970), 70.

[2] Son of Sir Richard Sutton, 1st Bt. John died before his father and the baronetcy passed to his son Richard in 1802.

[3] Henry Houson (1789–1873), St John's College, Cambridge; BA 1811, MA 1814; d. 1811, p. 1812, curate of Oxton; rector of Brant Broughton and of Great Coates, Lincolnshire, 1820–73. Houson's sister, the beautiful Anne, bewitched Lord Byron.

[4] 2nd Bt.

[5] Later Sir Richard Sutton, 4th Bt.

[6] Details from successive editions of *Burke's Peerage and Baronetage*, *Burke's Landed Gentry*, parish registers etc.

so the *Nottingham and Newark Mercury* reported,[1] not least by George and Amelia Wilkins, Lady Charlotte Denison, Lady Mary Bentinck, and Ichabod Wright the Nottingham banker (and, in the 1830s, translator of Dante). By 1844, Girardot and John Drake Becher (who had been ordained in 1829) were magistrates sitting at the Newark and Southwell Quarter Sessions under the chairmanship of John Thomas Becher. Chirardot and the Bechers and the clergy scions of other local families were decidedly 'gentlemen', and they lived and conducted themselves as such, living in substantial houses they had built, bought or inherited.

The incumbents of wealthy benefices could live the life of gentlemen on their benefice incomes alone. On his death in 1845 the contents of Robert Lowe's parsonage house at Bingham was sold. Into the first sale went 'highly valuable household furniture, Dairy and Brewing Utensils, Carriage Horses, Pony, Saddlery, live and dead farming stock, including five excellent dairy cows and seven well-bred heifers, quantity of prime old hay, seeds and straw, mangold wurtzel etc.'[2] To the second sale went 'very superior Dining, Drawing and Bedroom furniture, Dairy and Brewing Requisites, Horses, Carriages, Harness and Saddlery, Air Gun and three other Guns, Garden Utensils, Turning Lathe, etc, etc.' The *Nottingham Journal* correctly described Bingham as 'the most valuable [living] in the county'.[3] The average gross benefice income of Bingham in the three years to 1831 was £1,600. Though perhaps not as extensive a property as Blidworth Grange, the contents of which were listed in the *Journal* and which went on sale in the following month,[4] Bingham rectory in Lowe's day was clearly worthy of a gentleman farmer with a considerable income. Farm stock and equipment sold later that year belonging to John James Vaughan, rector of Gotham, was almost as extensive as Lowe's.[5]

But by no means every clergyman could live so well independent of his benefice income.

---

[1]   12 Dec. 1829.

[2]   *Nottingham Journal*, 12 Feb. 1845.

[3]   Ibid., 28 Feb. 1845.

[4]   Ibid., 21 March 1845.

[5]   Ibid., 9 May 1845. John James Vaughan was rector of Gotham and of Ratcliffe-on-Soar, 1836–82. Vaughan was related by marriage to the St Andrew family, lords of the manor of Gotham for 400 years.

'Little or nothing to spare': benefice incomes

In October 1855 the *Newark Advertiser* reported a meeting of diocesan members of the Additional Curates Aid Association. The bishop of Lincoln, John Jackson, argued that to provide adequate pastoral care it was necessary to employ one clergyman for every 1,000 to 1,500 of the population. He said: '[p]robably the largest number that [clergy]men of average strength and ability could properly attend to, if the pastoral work were carried out to its full extent, was 1000 to 1200 souls; 2000 certainly would require not only a man of untiring zeal, but of considerable bodily strength.' Lack of money prevented the employment of more clergy. Jackson noted that the national expenditure on tobacco and snuff was twice as much as 'the whole income of the Church of England, from the archbishops down to the curates.' If the 'whole of the incomes of the Church of England were redistributed and divided equally among all the incumbents throughout the land, the result would be a net average income of only about 200£ a year each.' In fact, Jackson argued, if the total annual income of all incumbents and curates was divided equally among them each would receive only £150 a year, but he maintained that the minimum incumbent's stipend should be at least £300. Twenty years earlier Jackson's predecessor, John Kaye, had argued that an incumbent should receive at least £500 a year if he was to exercise his pastoral ministry adequately. And what of the curates? The church, Jackson said, could no longer rely on clergymen with substantial private incomes paying the stipends of their curates, hence the need for contributions to the Additional Curates Aid Association.[1]

Jackson's calculation that the pooled and redistributed national average benefice income would produce only £200 a year, contrasts with a similar calculation made over 60 years later by Edwyn Hoskyns, bishop of Southwell. In 1918 Hoskyns noted that if his stipend was pooled with that of all incumbents in his diocese and divided equally between them this would have produced £286. In 1832 George Wilkins defined a 'poor' benefice as one worth £200 or less a year. This was Edwyn Hoskyns's bench mark for a poor living in 1918. In purchasing power £200 a year in 1831 was worth over £400 in 1918. These calculations suggest that the real income of the average benefice had been eroded very considerably over the previous 80 years.

The returns to the Ecclesiastical Commission in 1831 show that the national average gross benefice income was £303 a year. The average for

---

[1]   *Newark Advertiser*, 27 Oct. 1855.

the parishes around Southwell was £149, half the national figure. But these calculations derive from information supplied by incumbents and must be treated with caution. For that reason the returns of income of the Southwell deanery benefices made by incumbents to the rural dean in 1855 are of little value for purposes of comparison. For only two of the 20 comparable parishes, North Muskham and South Muskham, is there evidence to suggest a material improvement since 1831, with gross values (in 1831) and 'value returned'[1] (in 1855) of £177 in 1831 and £230 in 1855 for North Muskham, and £65 and £139 for South Muskham – increases of 23 per cent and 53 per cent respectively. In five cases the figures returned varied by only a few pounds over that 25 years, and in 13 cases the 1855 figures were identical to the average for the three years to 31 December 1831. The majority of the local incumbents were evidently as disinclined to reveal their true incomes to rural dean and bishop in 1855 as they had been to the census enumerators in 1851, and perhaps to the Ecclesiastical Commissioners in 1831.

In his letter to Earl Grey in 1832 George Wilkins noted that of the 192 benefices in Nottinghamshire 76 (40 per cent) were valued at under £200. These were 'poor livings'. Of these 76 benefices, 17 (22 per cent) were benefices in the county in the gift of the chapter or of individual prebendaries. They also comprised 46 per cent of the 37 benefices in the gift of the chapter or of prebendaries in Nottinghamshire, Lincolnshire and Yorkshire, and, remarkably, over 77 per cent of their 22 benefices in Nottinghamshire. In fact the average gross income of the 21 chapter livings was £179, and of the 16 prebendal livings it was £153. This was a third of the income that in 1834 John Kaye, bishop of Lincoln, said was necessary. In fact, if the two wealthiest chapter benefices, Barnborough (£640 a year) and Beelsby (£450) are discounted the average gross income of the chapter's benefices reduces to a mere £130 a year. Kaye said: 'The possessor of a living even of £500 a year, with a family and without any private source of income, if he administers as he ought to the temporal wants of his parishioners, has little or nothing to spare.'[2] The caveat 'if he administers as he ought to the temporal wants of his parishioners' is important. Clergy were expected to dispense charity to the needy from their benefice income, which, if this duty was accepted, could be a considerable drain on the net benefice revenues of already

---

[1]   Probably the net value.

[2]   John Kaye, *Charge* (1834); see W.F.J. Kaye (ed.), *The Works of John Kaye* (1888), vii. 143–4.

poor benefices. In fact, in 1831 only one of the 37 chapter and prebendal livings, Barnborough, was worth more than £500 a year gross.

The relative poverty of the majority of the chapter and prebendal livings is measured by two further indicators: the existence or fitness of glebe houses which was considered in some detail earlier, and the level of endowment by the commissioners of Queen Anne's Bounty which was established in 1704 'for the augmentation of the Maintenance of Poor Clergy'.[1]

By 1825, bound by their restrictive rules which they interpreted conservatively, the Queen Anne's Bounty commissioners had augmented by lot or to match benefactions or by parliamentary grant,[2] 68 benefices or 35 per cent of the 192 that the archdeacon of Nottingham had under his jurisdiction. It is a further measure of the low incomes of local benefices that of the parishes which were to constitute the rural deanery of Southwell in 1855, 16, or 70 per cent, had been augmented by the Bounty commissioners by 1825. The first grants had been received in 1715 (Halam, £200 by lot), 1718 (Southwell, £200 to match a benefaction) and Woodborough (£200 by lot). By 1825 these 16 livings had received £9,400 by lot or to meet benefactions or by parliamentary grant. The Bounty's rules and procedures and the lack of local benefactors produced many anomalies. By 1825 Upton (with an average annual benefice income in 1831 of £91) had not been augmented, and neither had six other very poor benefices in the gift of the chapter or of individual prebendaries.

It is difficult to be sure why the average income of local benefices was disproportionately so low. It may be that the Southwell chapter and prebendal estates, and those managed by the archbishop of York's agent, were let at low rents with, as Stanley Chapman has suggested, a small group of local families, with whom several clergy had links by blood or marriage, being particularly 'indulged'. Again, despite late eighteenth- and early nineteenth-century enclosures it may be that local farming practices remained conservative. But there may have been another factor. Evidence from the early twentieth century suggests strongly that farmers had, for many years, taken advantage of naïve clergy to demand low

[1]   Queen Anne's Bounty (QAB) was the fund established by Queen Anne to receive and distribute the first fruits and tenths previously paid by clergy to the Pope and confiscated by Henry VIII. See G.F.A. Best, *Temporal Pillars: Queen Anne's Bounty, the Ecclesiastical Commissioners and the Church of England* (Cambridge, 1964).

[2]   The commissioners distributed their funds in single tranches of £200 either by lot or to match benefactions of the same amount or multiples of it. From 1809 to 1820 they also distributed parliamentary grants totalling over one million pounds.

rents. Glebe lands in the county were generally very poorly managed and produced low returns.[1]

A consequence of poor benefices was, of course, poor incumbents, unless these clergy could subsidise their parochial income by taking pupils or from some other source. One not untypical poor incumbent was John Ison. In 1831 he became vicar of Kneesall and perpetual curate of Boughton, the parish with which Kneesall was united. Both benefices were in the gift of the Southwell chapter. The 1831 commissioners' return gives the benefice income of Kneesall as £60 gross and of Boughton as £300. The copy of Simpson's *The State of the Church in the County of Nottingham* in the Southwell Minster historic library shows an early amendment of Boughton's £300 to a much more realistic £10 a year. The 1851 religious census return gives the permanent endowment of Boughton as £10 with £2 a year from fees. The 1841 census shows Ison, 76, living in Kneesall parsonage with four younger women and a child, evidently relatives. In 1842 George Wilkins reported to Bishop Kaye that Ison had been in debt for years, that he and his sickly relatives were living in poverty often with little or no food and fuel in the house, that neighbouring clergy were taking his services *gratis,* and that a clergy charity contributed £25 a year to support the family. Wilkins gave Ison's benefice income as £90 a year.[2] He died the following year.

Whatever the reason for low benefice incomes, very small populations in many of the villages, and either the absence or unfitness of parsonage houses, compelled many incumbents to be absentee pluralists in the 1830s. In 1831 there were no glebe houses, or houses fit for the residence of a clergyman, in 16 or 73 per cent per cent of the 22 parishes local to Southwell for which information is available. The 1838 Pluralities Act allowed bishops to insist that parsonage houses be built. By 1844 75 per cent of Nottinghamshire benefices possessed a glebe house, of which 73 per cent were occupied by clergy.[3] But these county and national figures somewhat hide the local reality. By 1855, of the 20 Southwell deanery incumbents 16 were resident either in the parsonage house or in their own, or rented, houses in the parishes. This seems a great improvement since 1835. Several lived in houses newly erected by patrons (Bilsthorpe and Maplebeck) or after a QAB mortgage had been

---

[1]   Further to this see M.R. Austin, 'The Many High Proude Ones': the Church of England and the People 1884–1927', in Stanley Chapman and Derek Walker (eds), *Southwell: The Town and its People*, II (Southwell 2006), 178–80.

[2]   LAO, CorB5/8A/11, Wilkins to Kaye, 14 June 1842; T. Sampson to Kaye, 22 June 1842 (see Knight, *Nineteenth-century Church*, 130–31).

[3]   Knight, *Nineteenth-century Church*, 141.

secured (Bleasby, Rolleston and Upton). But other resident incumbents or curates were not well housed. Samuel Oliver of Calverton lived in a 'small – old – not good – rather tumble down' glebe house. There was no glebe house in Caunton, S. Reynolds Hole, the incumbent, living in the family manor house in the parish. James Morris Maxfield, vicar of Norwell, lived in a glebe house described as 'small – Present vicar spent nearly £100 on it out of his own pocket'. The non-resident incumbent of Edingley, Richard Bethell Earle, lived in Southwell as a master of the grammar school because there was no glebe house, though, the rural dean noted, 'a small Farm house and homestead contiguous to the Churchyard recently enfranchised by Ecclesiastical Commissioners on very easy terms ... ought to have been made a Glebe House'. The incumbent of North Muskham, John Winstanley Hull, lived in a rented house in his parish, the glebe house being 'a cottage let to the parish Clerk'. This house was said to be 'an exceedingly small and mean vicarage house ... unfit for ... use'.[1] The vicar of South Muskham, John Drake Becher, lived in considerable style in Hill House in Southwell, his glebe house being no more than 'a cottage let to the Schoolmaster.'[2]

Two incumbents had neighbouring parishes and were each resident in one. Five more were living in Southwell. One incumbent, the non-resident Collingwood Foster Fenwick, had a curate in his parish of Blidworth in a 'bad, small and inconvenient' glebe house, while in Fenwick's parish of Oxton his curate made the best of a 'bad' house.[3] We will meet Collingwood Foster Fenwick again.

In 1853 in Nottinghamshire as a whole, 75 per cent of the parishes had glebe houses. Of these 80 per cent were occupied by clergy. Blatant pluralism was far less rife in the 1850s than it had been in 1831, and it seems that by then, although in most cases benefice incomes may have fallen in real terms, the determination to get rid of scandalous non-residence had succeeded. This was undoubtedly due to the Pluralities Act of 1838 and subsequent legislation and the zealousness of diocesan bishops in securing the building of parsonage houses. During the episcopate of John Kaye, bishop of Lincoln from 1827 to 1853, 214 parsonage houses in his diocese were built, rebuilt, or made fit for the

---

[1] G.Y. Hemingway, 'The History of North Muskham, with Bathley and Holme' (Manuscript, 1973), 54.

[2] In 1851 Becher (aged 44) lived with his wife Elizabeth and their five daughters, a governess, a coachman, a nurse, a ladies maid, a kitchen-maid and three housemaids in the Burgage in Southwell.

[3] Rural dean's visitation, see chapter 9.

residence of a clergyman.[1]

In general, underpinning these advances were agricultural improvements which raised the level of some benefice incomes from increased tithe payments. In addition, from the mid eighteenth century many glebe acreages increased. The very large number of enclosures Acts passed in the century or so after 1740 allotted land in lieu both of glebe rights on commons and of tithes raised benefice incomes, in some cases considerably so.[2] By substituting money payments tied to the price of corn the Tithe Commutation Act of 1836 achieved the same end in those parishes not already subject to an enclosure award. A study of enclosure Acts shows that the rights of the clergy were carefully preserved. W.E. Tate noted that the House of Lords frequently amended bills to the benefit of the clergy.[3] In Derbyshire, in 60 enclosure Acts passed between 1772 and 1832 the allotments of land to the benefices where tithes were extinguished were handsome, and allotments of new enclosure to compensate for loss of right of common relating to existing glebe land were equally generous. Of the enclosure Acts affecting parishes near Southwell, the 1777 Farnsfield award gave 350 acres to the prebends of Normanton, Norwell Overall and Norwell Pallishall, more than 157 acres to the vicar, and five acres to the patrons of the benefice, the Southwell chapter. The 1793 Caunton enclosure Act awarded the impropriator of the benefice 171 acres, and the vicar 124 acres in lieu of tithes. The 1826 enclosure act and subsequent award for Norwell gave the incumbent, Edward Chaplin, substantial allotments totalling 109 acres in lieu of glebe rights on common land and in compensation for tithes.

The economic effect of enclosure for the incumbent could be considerable. The average gross benefice income of the prebendal benefice of Norwell for the three years to 1831 was £342. In the 1790s, Throsby noted that it was 'about £200.'[4] If that latter figure is to be

---

[1]   Knight, *Nineteenth-century Church*, 141.

[2]   Assuming that tithes could be collected. The *Nottingham Review* for 15 January 1841 reported that 'On Saturday last, seven persons were summoned to the Justice Room, Southwell, for non-payment of small tithes due to that parish; only one of the cases was dismissed, the other six were ordered to pay the amount claimed, together with costs. The unpleasantness and ill-feeling which has for a length of time existed in the parish of Southwell respecting the payment of these small tithes will, we hope, for the future, be put a stop to, as the tithe commissioners are now proceeding with the commutation of tithes and will, we think, very shortly be brought to a conclusion ... '.

[3]   W.E. Tate, *Parliamentary Land Enclosures in Nottinghamshire, 1743–1868* (Thoroton Society Record Series, v, 1935), 10–14.

[4]   Robert Thornton, *The Antiquities of Nottinghamshire* (ed. John Throsby), III (1796), 163.

trusted, the value of Norwell rose some 41 per cent within a generation, but many benefice incomes more than doubled within a few years.[1] However, in all rural parishes, even given the effect of enclosure and augmentation by QAB, any rise in benefice income was dependent on the state of agriculture. This may explain why the real value of average net benefice incomes fell, or at best remained steady, during this period. So, as one example of many, when the non-resident incumbent of the prebendal benefice of North Muskham, James Burnell, responded to the QAB commissioners in 1787, fourteen years after the enclosure award in 1773, he returned his gross benefice income as £91 10s. By 1828 the benefice was worth £150, in 1831 it was £177, and by 1855 £230. In 1868 it was returned as £300. In 1884 the gross benefice income of North Muskham was £240, and in 1911 it had fallen to £190.[2] In purchasing power, by 1911 the gross benefice income of North Muskham was what it had been in 1828 and only marginally better than in 1773. Many poor benefice incomes remained low even after augmentation by QAB.

But the enhancement of the social status and aspirations of the parish clergy was not a consequence of the better economic position of the clergy.[3] The doubling of an already low benefice income might still leave it sufficiently poor to qualify for augmentation by Queen Anne's Bounty. The incumbents of these parishes, unless they had other sources of income, could not afford to replace inadequate parsonage houses, or to build them in the many parishes which had none, as required by the 1838 Pluralities Act, even with the help of mortgages. Nor could they afford to pay a pension to a predecessor as they were expected to do. Yet bishops and archdeacons expected clergy to live as gentlemen in houses that befitted gentlemen. This marked the distinction between a glebe house 'fit for residence' and one that was 'unfit' — a critical distinction overlooked by some historians. For the archdeacon of Derby,

---

[1] For a detailed study of evidence from Derbyshire see M.R. Austin, 'The Church of England in the County of Derbyshire 1772–1832' (unpublished Ph.D. thesis, University of London, 1969), 180–93; and M.R. Austin, 'Enclosure and Benefice Incomes in Derbyshire, 1772–1832', *Derbyshire Archaeological Journal*, c (1980), 88–94.

[2] Church of England Record Centre, QAB/7/3/F3390, Lot 29, 7 Jan. 1787; lot 1772, 17 Sept. 1828; returns to the Ecclesiastical Duties and Revenues commissioners, average of the three years to 1831; rural deanery visitation returns, 1855; *Crockford's Clerical Directory* (1868); *Southwell Diocesan Calendar* (1885 and 1912 edns).

[3] The literature touching on this issue is considerable, but for a closely argued analysis of the rise in the social status of the clergy in this period, see Best, *Temporal Pillars*, ch. 2. For the latest study of the clergy in these years see W.M. Jacob, *The Clerical Profession in the Long Eighteenth Century, 1680–1840* (2007).

Samuel Butler, a parish might possess a glebe house, and be so included in the statistics, but it could be 'a small house, fit for a small farmer, but not for a Clergyman' or be a 'bad, old rambling house, occupied by a farmer: will not do for a clergyman'.[1] We have already noted George Wilkins's descriptions of his parsonage houses at Farnsfield ('a mere hut') and at Lowdham, ('a mere hovel') reflecting the low social position of parish clergy of previous generations and the much higher social status to which they now aspired.

'The insufficiency of his income': curates' salaries

Incumbents were generally far better placed financially than the curates they employed. In 1830 it was reported that a national survey revealed a 'melancholy picture' of the incomes of curates. It showed that six were receiving less than £20 a year and 59 under £30. If this report is reliable then one of the six was a curate in Nottinghamshire as were two who received no more than £20. Nationally, of the 4,002 curates, 3,400, or 85 per cent, received less than £110 a year from their incumbents. But, in the main, these curates served in benefices with a low benefice income. Of the 3,719 benefices where incumbents were non-resident, 2,496, or 67 per cent, were valued at under £300 gross. Only 34 curates, or less than one per cent, received £200 or more as year.[2] In some parishes very low salaries continued to be paid to curates. Early in 1857 John Dickinson Bell, curate of Mansfield St Peter, tendered his resignation 'in consequence' so it was reported, of 'the insufficiency of his income.' The churchwardens immediately raised an additional £50 a year for him 'to induce you to stay with us.'[3]

---

[1]   Trusley and Weston-on-Trent. See M.R. Austin (ed.), *The Church in Derbyshire in 1823–4: the parochial visitation of the Rev. Samuel Butler, archdeacon of Derby in the diocese of Lichfield and Coventry* (Derbyshire Archaeological Society Record Series, v, 1972), 172, 177. There are numerous examples which indicate that the size and condition of parsonage houses was indicative of the rising social status of the clergy.

[2]   *Nottingham and Newark Mercury*, 11 Sept. 1830, from the *Sheffield Courant*.

[3]   *Nottinghamshire and Lincolnshire Advertiser*, 7 March 1857. One possible reason for Bell's popularity is suggested by a report in the *Advertiser* for 10 Oct. 1857 which told of a tea party given by him for 25 'aged females'. This was followed by them being offered '*liquids*' of a 'more exhilarating character'. The report added that 'the beaming countenances of the venerable guests gave proof sufficient that the hospitality of the worthy donor was duly appreciated.' More practically, Bell established evening classes for 'operatives, young men and boys' in Clarkson's schools in Mansfield. John Bell was born in St Bees in 1831 and educated at St Bees theological college. He was made deacon in 1852 and ordained priest 1853. He had previously been assistant curate of Church-Kirk, Lancashire.

Curates continued to be poorly paid and housed throughout this period. The Nottinghamshire returns in the 1835 Ecclesiastical Revenues commissioners' report show that 86 curates were employed in the county's parishes in 1831. Almost half of them were either inadequately housed or had to find their own accommodation or were themselves non-resident. Of the 86, 14 served in parishes with no glebe house, and a further 28 in parishes where the glebe house was regarded as 'unfit for residence'.

With few exceptions curates were employed by non-resident pluralists. Some were the well-to-do relatives of their incumbents. For example, Edward Chaplin, pluralist vicar of Norwell 1797–1833, employed Richard Chaplin at £85 a year.[1] In his outspoken report on the state of the Church of England in the county in 1836, Robert Simpson noted the Ecclesiastical Revenues Commissioners' observation that the very many poor livings in the country would not support a clergyman and 'in many of them there *is no glebe house,* nor do the [incumbents] furnish the means of erecting any.' But, Simpson, pointed out, duty was performed in these parishes by curates who had to live somewhere, and

> as for their *support*, God knows that in many cases there is little enough as it is. We have *one* curate returned as receiving from his *pluralist incumbent*, FOUR SHILLINGS A WEEK; *two*, EIGHTT shillings a week; *four* TWELVE shillings a week; *two*, FOURTEEN shillings a week; and taking *all the curates in the county together,* the *average* annual income, does not amount to *thirty shillings* a week!!! Could the 'poor livings' afford *less* support? The average annual income of the 4,224 curates returned as employed by *non-resident* incumbents is, according to the Ecclesiastical Commissioners' Reports only £79 per annum, and yet this sum, small as it is, [is] *greatly beyond the reality*, for very many of the curates *receive nothing at all*, their *title of orders* being deemed by many an equivalent for *two years' servitude.*[2]

Even Simpson's impassioned and justified criticism obscures the full picture. The incumbent paying his curate £10 a year was Thomas Blades,

---

In 1861 he was master of a boys' school for 32 pupils in Wood Street in Chipping Barnet.

[1]   *White's Directory of Nottinghamshire* (1853), gives Richard Chaplin as Edward Chaplin's resident curate. Edward Chaplin, who was resident in his other benefice of Blankney in Lincolnshire, died in 1853.

[2]   Robert Simpson, *The State of the Church in the County of Nottingham* (1836), 92.

perpetual curate of Langford.[1] He seems not to have been a pluralist as Simpson claims. His gross benefice revenue was only £40, so he paid his curate a quarter of his income – though he could not have survived without an additional source of income. There was no glebe house in Langford.

The incumbent (not two) who paid his curate £20 a year was the donative curate of Sibthorpe, Edward Otter. The income from this donative was also £20, so Otter paid his curate what he himself received. Otter was also donative curate of Cotham from which he received an income of £35. This too he paid over entirely to his curate. But Edward Otter could afford to do so. He was a pluralist who held a prebendal stall in York Minster (1808–37) and was also rector of Bothal-with-Hebburn in Northumberland (1810–17). He had held the two donatives, both in the gift of the Duke of Portland, since 1806, when he had also been vicar of Bolsover in Derbyshire (1798–1818). Incidentally, Cotham had been endowed with £400 by Queen Anne's Bounty, though its church was described as dilapidated in the 1835 report.

The four Nottinghamshire curates who were paid 12s. a week (about £30 a year) served Cropwell Bishop (gross benefice income £150), Eaton (£63), Rampton (£176) and Woodborough (£93). Neither Eaton nor Woodborough had glebe houses and the house in Cropwell Bishop was unfit for the residence of a clergyman. Only Rampton had an acceptable house. The vicars of Rampton and of Eaton, Richard Barrow and Charles Fowler, were vicars choral of the Minster and beneficiaries of Southwell chapter and prebendal patronage, Barrow particularly so. They clearly exploited their curates and could well have afforded to pay them more.

The average annual stipend of a Nottinghamshire curate in 1831 was £74 though the range was very considerable, from the £10 paid to the curate of Langford to the £202 paid to the clergyman who served Babworth, where the gross benefice income of the pluralist incumbent, Charles Wasteneys Eyre, was £881. William Goodacre, incumbent of Sutton in Ashfield, Skegby and Mansfield Woodhouse paid his curate, J.R. Unwin,[2] £60 a year, though there was no parsonage house in any of his three parishes.

It would seem that Goldsmith's eighteenth-century curate who was 'passing rich with forty pounds a year' was better paid than many in the

---

[1] Blades had been incumbent since 1802 having previously been curate of North Muskham at £45 a year (CCEd Personal ID 50937).

[2] Curate of Sutton-in-Ashfield in 1827 (G.G. Bonser, *A History of Sutton-in-Ashfield* (1949), 33). This J.R. Unwin was possibly the ill-fated Joseph Rolling Unwin, vicar of Langar, for whom see p. 161.

nineteenth century. In 1764, of the three curates employed by incumbents of the parishes later to form the rural deanery of Southwell, John Holmes received £15 for serving the donative of Winkburn, John Edwards £30 at Rolleston (where he had served for seven years) and only one, Thomas Hurt, the curate of Blidworth, received Goldsmith's £40.[1]

As a consequence of the 'abomination' of pluralism Simpson noted that 'Many of the *curates*, who are employed by pluralists, are themselves *incumbents* of other churches, — and many of the curates are of *much longer standing in the ministry* than their incumbents.'[2] For Simpson, not only did the curates suffer from this injustice, but more importantly the mission of the church was impaired. The commissioners argued in 1835 that only by raising the income of poor benefices could the needs of 'a rapidly increased and increasing population' be served. Simpson claimed that only by abolishing pluralism, increasing incomes of poor benefices, preventing the union of small livings, and requiring that every parish with a population over 500 should have a resident clergyman could the clergy be more efficiently deployed, curates become incumbents, and the church's mission furthered.[3]

As had been the case for at least several generations, evangelical curates had particular difficulty in obtaining preferment.[4] For example, John Conington (1794–1878) had been a stipendary curate for 25 years before becoming the first vicar of Southwell Holy Trinity in 1846. In 1821 he was ordained to a title at Ancaster in Lincolnshire on a salary of £100 a year, together with surplice fees[5]. He remained in Ancaster until 1827 when he was licensed as curate to Navenby with a stipend of £140 'with surplice fees and the use of a house.'[6] There he stayed until 1846 when he became the first incumbent of Trinity Church (as it was then called) in Southwell. This newly established parish was a very poor living. In the parish return to the 1851 census Conington recorded his benefice income as £144 with £32 9s. 8d. derived from endowment income, and £111 10s. 10d. coming from pew rents. When the rural dean

---

[1] Hurt was also curate of the neighbouring Nottinghamshire parishes of Annesley, Lindby and Papplewick.

[2] Bonser, *Sutton-in-Ashfield*, 91.

[3] Ibid., 93–93.

[4] This had prompted Charles Simeon, in 1816, to establish a trust to buy rights of presentation to parishes and to appoint to them clergy of an evangelical persuasion. By 1835 the trust had acquired the patronage of two Nottinghamshire parishes, Clarborough and Ruddington.

[5] That is, fees for the 'occasional offices' of marriages and funerals.

[6] CCEd Person Index ID 8168.

recorded Conington's benefice income in 1855, it was down to £100, the stipend he had received when he first became curate in Ancaster in 1821. Perhaps his economic circumstances were eased by his marriage in 1825 to Sophia Christiana Calcraft, daughter of John Charles Lucas Calcraft of Ancaster Hall,[1] one-time sheriff of Lincolnshire.

The financial situation of curates had not improved at all by the 1850s, at least locally. In 1855 the curate of Southwell collegiate church, Oldfield Kelsall Prescot, was paid a mere £50 and found accommodation in the town. In the same year John Porter, resident curate of the pluralist incumbent of Blidworth, Collingwood Forster Fenwick (who lived in Brooke rectory on the Isle of Wight), was paid £100 and fees. At Oxton, where Fenwick was also the incumbent, the resident curate, Henry Wall Tibbs, was paid £95 with fees. Both curates lived in glebe houses described as 'bad'. Their stipends were far less than the law required or that their predecessors had been prepared to accept. By the 1840s these villages had become local centres of lace weaving and glove making, Oxton with a population of 850 and Blidworth with 1,376 inhabitants. Fenwick employed only one curate to serve both parishes. The 1838 Pluralities Act required that non-resident incumbents of parishes of this size must employ a curate for each at a stipend of £135. Two curates were appointed in 1842, Gilbert Sandbach for Oxton (to 1844),[2] and Martin Roe for Blidworth (to his death in 1849). Fenwick claimed that as he was 'virtually destitute and beggarly' he could not afford to pay his two curates a combined stipend of £270 from the revenue of his two Nottinghamshire benefices from which he received £385 in addition to his benefice income as rector of Brooke.[3] As Sandbach and Roe had independent means they agreed to serve the parishes for £110 each, but Fenwick complained that this was still too heavy a burden.[4] George Wilkins wrote to the bishop of Lincoln, John Kaye, giving him the gross and net incomes for both parishes and implying that Fenwick was in a vulnerable position: 'I do not think that Mr Fenwick holds these two [benefices] by a Dispensation – and if so, one of them is voidable – and

---

[1]   *Burke's Genealogical and Heraldic History of the Landed Gentry* (1847), 173. One of Calcraft's two sons was ordained and became rector of Haceby for 55 years. In 1859 John and Sophia Conington's daughter Caroline married Edward Jonathan Birch, rector of Overstone, Northamptonshire.

[2]   He became rector of Upper Sapey, Herefordshire.

[3]   The 1835 Ecclesiastical and Revenues Commissioners' report gives the gross value of Oxton as £210 and of Blidworth as £210. In 1858 Fenwick's benefice income as rector of Brooke in *The Clergy List* was returned as £250 a year.

[4]   LAO, Cor. B. 5/8/31/5, Fenwick to Kaye, various dates in 1842, cited in Knight, *Nineteenth-century Church*, 126–7.

the *next* presentation of both devolve[s] on your Lordship, by the suppression of the Stall at Southwell, the two Prebendaries of Oxton having alternate presentation.'[1] But Fenwick was still in post in 1855, and still rector of Brooke, paying his then curates Porter and Tibbs considerably less than Sandbach and Roe had been prepared to work for a decade earlier – and notwithstanding the provisions of the Pluralities Act.

Clearly, some incumbents, not least those who could well afford to do so, were ill-disposed to pay curates reasonable stipends if they would employ others for less. In 1845 George Wilkins wrote to the bishop of Lincoln about the curate of the prebendal living of Norwell: 'A very great complaint having been made to me by persons of the greatest respectability and good feeling towards the Church of the manner in which the duties are performed at Norwell and Carlton upon Trent; I went over yesterday to learn the truth of the several particulars.' Wilkins discovered that, 'in a parish of nearly 1000'

> the duties are alternate [between Norwell and Carlton-on-Trent] and they are solely performed by a very aged and infirm man, Mr Herring, now, I believe, in the 80th year of his age – exceedingly – indeed stone deaf – and with an articulation so defective as to make it impossible for any not acquainted with his reading to understand him.

Herring received £70 a year from the vicar of Norwell, Robert Chaplin, 'who, as your Lordship knows, is a wealthy man.' Wilkins urged the bishop of Lincoln to request Chaplin to appoint ' a more efficient person in the parish',[2] and, two years later, he did.[3]

---

[1] LAO, Cor. B. 5/8/36/15, letter from Wilkins to Kaye, 7 June 1842.

[2] LAO, Cor, B. 5/8/20/14, letter from Wilkins to Kaye, 2 Oct. 1845. Edmund Herring (*c*. 1766–1850) married Elizabeth Templeman in Norwell in 1803. Edward Chaplin was vicar of Norwell and also of Blankney in Lincolnshire (where he was resident when he died, and probably from 1833) from 1797 until in death in 1854. Herring, apparently living on the family farm in Norwell, was curate of Norwell 1833–46. He was also curate of Sutton-on-Trent in 1832 (*White's Directory of Nottinghamshire* (1832), 700), receiving £65 a year.

[3] For curates in the diocece of Lincoln at this time see Knight, *Nineteenth-century Church*, 127–30 etc.

The clergy and social order

Throughout much of the nineteenth-century the clergy played a significant role in the pattern of rural social relationships. The parish vestry, usually chaired by the incumbent, retained many of its civil powers until 1894. Many clergy served as surveyors of highways, turnpike trustees and land tax commissioners. They recommended (or declined to recommend) the indigent poor for parish relief at a time when being 'on the parish' was a shameful indication of poverty. Their place in the social hierarchy was secure.

A significant indicator of the civic role of the clergy was their appointment as justices of the peace. In several counties at least 50 per cent of the magistrates were clergy. As Edward Royle points out, to be a conscientious justice of the peace was time-consuming, and many clergy had the time. A largely clerical magistracy also welded the church and the state together at a local level, and this was politically advantageous in the years after 1790 when the perceived threat of subversion was at its height. A local bench could be dominated by clergy. In 1818 a letter in the radical *Nottingham Review* from 'A Constant Reader', evidently referring to the Nottingham justices, noted that 'Clergymen are not eligible to sit on a Jury, and yet act as Judges at Quarter Sessions &; ... A few years ago, there was generally nine Reverends to Six Gentlemen.'[1] In the same year, of the 43 county magistrates in Nottinghamshire 12, or 28 per cent, were clergy.[2] In 1832 it was reported that there were 5,371 magistrates serving on county benches in England and Wales of whom 1,354, or 25 per cent, were clergy. There was a wide discrepancy nationally: Derbyshire and Sussex had no clergy magistrates at this time, while 50 per cent of the magistrates in Cornwall, Herefordshire, Lincolnshire, Norfolk, Somerset, Brecon, Denbigh and Glamorgan were clergy.[3]

The number of clergy magistrates declined as the years passed. In

---

[1] *Nottingham Review*, 27 Nov. 1818.

[2] *Sutton's Directory of Nottingham* (1818), 99.

[3] *Nottingham and Newark Mercury*, 11 Feb. 1832, quoted from *The Morning Chronicle*. Edward Royle cites slightly different figures. He suggests that by 1831 over 20 per cent of all magistrates in England were clergy. In counties where enclosure had been recent, the proportion was much higher: 47 per cent of magistrates in Lincolnshire were magistrates in 1831, 45 per cent in Cambridgeshire, and 41 per cent in Bedfordshire (*Modern Britain: a Social History 1750–1997* (1997), 294). That counties with recent enclosure should have more clergy magistrates may be accounted for by the fact that enclosure Acts gave many benefices large allotments of former commons or open fields, fenced at the expense other landowners, and thus, within a very few years, achieved incomes which enabled some incumbents to enjoy, or to appear to enjoy, the lifestyle and status of the gentry, though note the caveats already entered.

1864 some 15 per cent (11 out of 81), of the Nottinghamshire magistrates were clergy, though well before this time there had been no
clergymen sitting on the Nottingham bench. By the end of the nineteenth
century, it had become accepted that the direct association of the clergy
with local government and the maintenance of law and order was to be
avoided. In 1900 in Nottinghamshire there were 128 county magistrates.
Of these only two were clergymen, and both of these lived well outside
the county — one in Bridlington and the other in Blackheath.[1] Yet from
at least the end of the eighteenth century and for much of the nineteenth
just as their social aspirations identified the clergy with the gentry so the
legal and administrative functions of the magistracy had increasingly
identified them with the forces of social control. This identification
undoubtedly had a lasting negative effect on public perceptions of
Anglican clergy even at a time when few, if any, clergy served as
justices. To pray for sinners from the pulpit on Sundays but to pass harsh
judgement on them from the bench on Mondays inevitably alienated the
poor from the clergy. Joseph Arch noted that 'it is a matter of common
knowledge that clerical magistrates are always the hardest and most
severe, and yet they call themselves ministers of One Who always
tempered justice with mercy.'[2]

However, although justices of the peace continued to exercise a major
judicial role, from the 1830s much of their administrative responsibility
was taken out of their hands. In 1834 the new poor law removed from
the local justices a significant financial responsibility. The Factory Act
of 1833 provided for independent inspection of cotton manufacturers, and
the 1835 Prisons Act placed prison administration under Home Office
inspection and control. Magistrates lost their responsibilities for highways
in 1835, and, gradually, their control of the police and of licensing. But
with the loss of administrative power there was no loss of the social
prestige and influence that went with the office of magistrate. To be a
justice of the peace was to be recognised as a 'gentleman'. In 1833 a
letter to the *Nottingham and Newark Mercury* called for justices of the
peace to be salaried owing to the 'arrogance' of a magistracy based on
'aristocratical government'. Local government was 'completely at the
disposal' of the aristocracy. The writer concluded: 'In short we are at the

---

[1]   *Kelly's Directory of Nottinghamshire* (1900), 9. The Newark and Southwell bench was
still chaired by a Becher – John Henry Becher Esq., the son of John Drake Becher and
grandson of John Thomas Becher. John Henry Becher lived in South Muskham Prebend
in Southwell, formerly the town house of the prebendary of South Muskham, the stall once
occupied by John Thomas Becher.

[2]   Joseph Arch, *The Story of His Life, Told by Himself* (1898), 144.

mercy of those few gentlemen whom some proud Lord may think proper to set over us to dictate justice.' Later in the same year this question was addressed in a leading article in the same newspaper. While denying that a magistracy composed of the squirearchy necessarily acted in 'an oppressive illegal manner' it nevertheless argued for the need for magistrates to be kept under close scrutiny. It told its readers that it had appointed a court reporter to exercise that role.[1]

John Thomas Becher, chairman of quarter sessions for 20 years, would have dismissed out of hand the notion that the magistracy should be monitored. For him the poor were the 'inferior classes' who had to be kept in their place. If they were allowed to rise above their station they would become dangerous (the bishop of Lincoln, John Jackson, was later to agree with those who described the urban poor as the 'dangerous classes'). But Becher was but an energetic and able representative of those whom George Wilkins described as enjoying 'social position' and 'official qualification' and who opposed, as a matter of theological as well as political principle, government by 'popular opinion' and the 'aristocracy of numbers.' The theological principle was the dictum that as God ordered the estate of rich and poor so this was the divinely ordered structure of a Christian society. The consequent political principle was that the hierarchy of those with 'social position' was headed by a monarch appointed by divine right. That being so aristocracy by birth or by crown appointment alone secured the integrity of the state. Was it not for this reason that the Litany in the Church of England's *Book of Common Prayer* prays that it might please God 'to endue the Lords of the Council, and all the Nobility, with grace, wisdom and understanding' and, in the next petition, that he should 'bless and keep the Magistrates, giving them grace to execute justice, and to maintain truth'? For most clergy these principles determined the nature of their relationship with the labouring classes.

'The labours of this toilsome day': a pastoral ministry

When candidates for holy orders were made deacon they were reminded that it is of 'the office of a Deacon ... to search for the sick, poor, and impotent people of the Parish, to intimate their estates, names and places where they dwell, unto the Curate, that by his exhortation they may be

---

[1]   16 Feb. and 26 October 1833.

relieved with the alms of the Parishioners, or others.' On their ordination to priesthood, candidates were exhorted *inter alia* 'to seek for Christ's sheep that are dispersed abroad, and for his children that are in the midst of this naughty world, that they may be saved through Christ for ever.'

The importance of pastoral ministry could hardly have been given greater emphasis, yet it is difficult to assess its practice or its effect at this or most periods of history. Neither those men who neglected their parishes nor those who were dedicated to their ministry paraded the fact. Few recorded their day-to-day work in journals still in existence.[1] One who did was William Goodacre (1783–1859), usher and under-master of Mansfield grammar school and in 1820 perpetual curate of Mansfield Woodhouse and of Skegby. That year he also became vicar of Sutton in Ashfield, though he was not instituted until much later.[2]

He was born in Long Clawson, Leicestershire, in 1783. When the 1851 census was taken he was living with his three unmarried daughters and a servant in his own house, the White House, Coxmoor Road, in Sutton. This was within easy reach of his three parishes. He died in office in 1859. In his journal for 8 October 1851 (he was then 68) he recorded a typical day:

> Rose at 6.30. Morning Devotion. Breakfast at eight. Rode to Sutton and called on Sarah Housley; found her much better so did not stay. Called at the Post Office, found letters to be answered. Rode towards Huthwaite calling at Butterworths [churchwarden] on business. Went to Hucknall Coal Pit and found Mr Mellors very ill, so spent an hour with him in reading and prayer. Visited Ann Ellis who is in decline, prayed with her. Took some refreshment at Benjamin Burton's and left my horse. Visited Amy Allsop, a great sufferer and declining, talked and prayed. A clear prospect of bliss has Lavinia Allsop whom I next visited and prayed with. Visited and prayed with Sarah Massey, much better and in a pleasing frame of mind. Next visited and prayed with Amelia Hardy who is nearly gone but is prepared. Visited and prayed with Allen's wife. It will still prove a decline, though Dr Lomas thinks not. Visited and prayed with William Stendall's wife. Went to Burton's for my horse and took an early tea with the family. Then went to see John Cheetham, much better so did not stay. Called

---

[1] For a useful summary of material see W.M. Jacob, *The Clerical Profession in the Long Eighteenth Century, 1680–1840* (Oxford, 2007), 205–35.

[2] Ecclesiastical Duties and Revenues Commission, *Report* (1835) gives 1831 as the date of institution. Bonser, *Sutton-in-Ashfield*, 35, gives 1827.

upon Mary Ward, aged 95, but now recovering. Indeed a humble Christian. Rode from Hucknall to Sutton.

Called upon Mr Placer to pay my Poor Rate and drank a cup of coffee. Rode to Eastfield Side and visited Cupit's wife, found her better. Visited and read at length with Charles Keeling's wife, a most distressing case of body and soul. Ordered some arrowroot sent by a friend in such cases. Visited and prayed with Thomas Hall and wife, both ill. Found Herbert Parker much better. Visited and prayed with Mary Hooly, a poor but worthy old woman. She affords a strong testimony that those who serve God in youth are not deserted in old age. Visited and prayed with John Hudson and family. The old man now ill, and son and daughter both in decline. Visited and prayed with John Askew, a real comfort to see his happiness weekly increase, being confined to his bed for four year with paralysis. Visited John Boot's wife, better. At half past nine pm. I returned home.

If we can accept his word, William Goodacre seems always to have been assiduous in exercising his pastoral ministry. Twenty-five years earlier, in appealing to the archbishop of York to appoint an assistant curate to Sutton in Ashfield, he described, this time in verse, 'the labours of this toilsome day', 8 May 1825. It began when he left home at 8.30 and did not finish until

> This scrawl complete, the hour of twelve,
> Brings my day's labours to a close;
> The past fatigue secures my rest,
> To you I wish a sound repose.[1]

Independent and unbiased contemporary commentary on the pastoral ministry of the clergy is very difficult to find. Thomas Mozley wrote of the clergy of nearby Derby in the 1820s and 1830s. Of Charles Stead Hope, vicar of both All Saints and St Alkmund's, Mozley says that 'he was always in the presence of his people ... He could not walk ten yards without exchanging greetings, or fifty yards without being stopped for a talk.' But Hope was 'a High Churchman after the fashion of the day and a Tory of course' and Mozley was bound to be sympathetic. Another

---

[1]   Quoted in W. Clay-Dove, '"Around the Parish": memories of a 19th-century vicar of Sutton-in-Ashfield', *Nottinghamshire Historian*, no. 23 (1979), 6–7, and Bonser, *Sutton-in-Ashfield*, 33. Goodacre employed, successively, eight curates every two years between 1822 and 1837.

writer, Joseph Tilley, had a very different opinion. For him Hope was

> Divine, politician, huntsman ... How many times he graced the
> hustings in the Cavendish interest, or how many years he followed
> the Meynell hounds is of no great moment. There are those living
> who say that this divine added a picturesque feature to many of the
> interments at which he officiated by wearing beneath his surplice
> a coat of scarlet hue, and that he read the burial service in hessian
> boots with spurs and a skull cap with a velvet peak.

Mozley had no time for the evangelical clergy of his childhood. He
asserted that their theology 'was held to relieve the clergyman of his
pastoral duties altogether. All he had to do was to declare his message
every Sunday. They who accepted it were saved; they who did not were
damned. That concluded the matter.' Hope's contemporary at Derby St
Werburgh was the evangelical Edward Unwin, who, says Mozley,
'resided in a pretty villa ... a good step out of town. I am certain that
neither I nor anyone else ever saw him in his parish except when he
drove in to take part in the Sunday service ... He knew absolutely
nothing about his parishioners.' Mozley recorded these opinions in his
Reminiscences chiefly of Oriel College and the Oxford Movement. When
this was published in 1882 John Wakefield, who had been Unwin's
curate in the 1830s (and a fierce opponent of Thomas Mozley's father
Henry, churchwarden of St Werburgh's) wrote to *The Record* of Unwin's
'quiet visits of duty, his religious and other occupations and the extent
of his knowledge of the persons and events of his parish.'[1] Even
allowing for Mozley's theological, and Tilley's political, bias the picture
they present of Anglican pastoral ministry in a midlands town in the
1820s and 1830s is not an attractive one and is hardly relieved by
Wakefield's defence of Unwin. Candid friends and radical opponents
alike were always ready to publish evidence of pastoral neglect resulting
from non-residence.

By the middle years of the nineteenth century the position had
changed for the better. Owen Chadwick puts the improvement of pastoral
standards down to 'public opinion, press, nonconformist rivalry and
nonconformist conscience, moral fibre of the middle classes, evangelical
gospel and Puseyite sacramentalism, alarm at French Revolution and

---

[1]   Mozley, *Reminiscences*, i. 194, 195, 196; J. Tilley, 'Short Biographies of Seventy Derby
Clergymen of the Church of England' (MS, *c.* 1880), 61; letter from Wakefield, *The
Record*, 25 Aug. 1882.

English slums', of which the most potent was the change in public opinion which demanded higher standards from the professions.[1] For bishops this required greater discipline from their clergy.

[1]   Owen Chadwick, *The Victorian Church*, i (1966), 127.

6

'The rule of common practice': the clergy, theology, and tradition

Deeply rural though the rural deanery parishes were they felt the touch of national events. The bishop of Lincoln, John Kaye,[1] conducted a triennial visitation of the diocese in 1843. He delivered his charge in two centres in the archdeaconry. The first was Nottingham St Mary in July 1843.[2] The *Nottingham Journal* admitted that it did not have the space to report the bishop fully as his charge was, it said, 'exceedingly voluminous'. However, the *Journal* did note that Kaye dealt at length with the then very contentious issue of the contrasting claims of Anglican doctrinal authority and of the Council of Trent. It recorded the bishop's 'disapprobation of some of the writings of the Tractarians, and more particularly of Tract 90.'[3] Initially sympathetic to the Tractarians, Kaye was later to oppose the ritual and liturgical innovations of their successors, and in 1841 he prohibited Bernard Smith, vicar of Leadenhall, from placing a cross and candlesticks on the communion table of his parish church. Smith was received into the Roman Catholic church the following year. In his visitation charge in 1846 Kaye accused the Tractarians of betraying the English Reformation.

Many saw these years as a disturbing time for the Church of England. In 1843 the *Nottingham Journal* quoted at length an article from the *Christian Rembrancer* which expressed the widely held view among

---

[1] 1783–1853, bishop of Lincoln 1827–53; see *Oxford DNB*.

[2] On the second occasion, in Southwell Minster on 8 July, the young rector, John Murray Wilkins, preached a sermon on *Unity and Love Essential to the 'Making Increase of the Body of Christ'*.

[3] The famous *Tract XC* was the last of the series of *Tracts for the Times* published between 1833 and 1841 by the leaders of what was later to become known as the Anglo-Catholic movement in the Church of England. The leading authors of the tracts included John Henry Newman, E.B. Pusey, John Keble, R.H. Froude and Isaac Wlliams. The first *Tract*, written by Newman, was a four-page pamphlet which defended the doctrine of apostolic succession as establishing the integrity of Anglican ordination. The last, *Tract XC*, also written by Newman, was a substantial booklet which proposed a Catholic interpretation of the Thirty-Nine Articles, the central Anglican doctrinal statement. Its publication created such a storm that the series came to an end.

evangelicals that England was 'Un-Christian and Anti-Christian'.[1] The 1851 census revealed that the nation was by no means as faithful in its public Christian profession – and certainly not as Anglican – as its more complacent citizens had believed. As the Church of England began to feel itself beleaguered, so its bishops determined to impose discipline, the more so because the pope had re-established a hierarchy in England posing a further threat to the supremacy of the Church of England.

As the relation of church and state was discussed in the rural deanery, occasionally heatedly, so was the associated question of the relationship between the denominations. The most significant issue was the restoration of the Roman Catholic hierarchy. This had been carefully planned and stage-managed. The pope required that, to minimise English antagonism, formal promulgation of the restoration be made when a Whig government was in power in England, at a time of year when Parliament was not sitting, and that the bishoprics established should not bear the names of any Anglican diocesan or suffragan see. The appropriate moment came in September 1850. On 29 September Pius IX issued the bull *Universalis Ecclesiae*. By this edict the archdiocese of Westminster was established together with twelve suffragan sees, of which Nottingham was one. The bull declared that the occupant of the see of Westminster was the lawful successor to the Catholic archbishops of Canterbury, a succession extinct since the last of Mary's bishops died in 1582. On 30 September Nicholas Wiseman became archbishop of Westminster and a cardinal. Very well-attended public meetings sponsored by the Anglican and dissenting churches in major population centres, not least in Nottingham, showed how great the threat to Protestant supremacy this papal initiative was perceived.

These were not easy years for the Church of England. Demands for its disestablishment were becoming more strident as political opposition grew. In 1845 John Henry Newman, the best known of the leaders of the Tractarian movement, was received into the Roman Catholic church. The Tractarians were opposed both to the subjugation of the Church of England to an increasingly secular (or at least non-Anglican) state and also to what they saw as the liberalising and undermining from within of their church's traditional Catholic doctrine and practice. Newman's departure was followed by that of other notable Anglicans. One of them was Henry Wilberforce. When, following his conversion, Wilberforce lectured in Nottingham, he was condemned as a 'pervert' by the

---

[1]   *Nottingham Journal*, 16 June 1843. The article was published in the May edition of the *Christian Remembrancer*.

Nottingham Journal. Many parish clergy, remaining loyal to the Church of England, interpreted the rubrics of the *Book of Common Prayer* in ways sympathetic to ancient practice and introduced into their services such notionally inconsequential details as coloured stoles, and adding rich adornments to their churches. In many places, as the *Book of Common Prayer* provided, they introduced a daily service.[1] The 1855 visitation returns show that in the Southwell deanery S. Reynolds Hole, rector of Caunton, followed this practice. That some clergy held a high doctrine of the sacraments well before this time is suggested in William Goodacre's letter to the archbishop of York. He recorded that during the 'toilsome day' of 8 May 1825,

> I mounted steed to Skegby rode
>   Imparted to a female ill
> The Holy Eucharist, as before
>   She had to me expressed her will.[2]

The bishops and archdeacons of the Church of England felt threatened by these developments. In 1850 there were 587 Roman Catholic churches in England and Wales served by 168 priests. By 1870 there were 1,152 churches and 1,528 priests. By 1900 there were 1,529 churches and 2,812 priests serving a Roman Catholic community of one and half million, more than twice the number half a century earlier. In the 1850s many believed that the Tractarians were leading the Church of England into the arms of an 'aggressive' Church of Rome. In a public lecture in the Exchange Hall in Nottingham in September 1859 arranged by the Nottingham Protestant Alliance, James Aitken Wylie, one of the leading Protestant polemicists against Roman Catholicism, argued that the 'fundamental principles of Popery' had been advocated in *Tracts for the Times* and by the 'Romanizing priests' occupying 'certain chairs of Oxford'.[3]

In a very lengthy visitation address in the spring of 1851 George Wilkins inveighed against the 'papal aggression – long entertained but now formally put forth by the Bishop of Rome – to enslave the souls of

---

[1] Of Morning and Evening Prayer.

[2] W. Clay-Dove, '"Around the Parish": memories of a 19th-century vicar of Sutton-in-Ashfield', *Nottinghamshire Historian*, no. 23 (1979), 7.

[3] *Nottingham Free Press*, 10 Sept. 1859. The vicar of Nottingham St Mary, J.W. Brooks, opened the meeting.

our people and to infringe the prerogative of our Sovereign.'[1] Although
ten years earlier Wilkins had admired the scholarship and piety of the
writers of *Tracts for the Times*, he had no time for Anglican liturgical
practices which, so he and many now believed, aped those of the Church
of Rome. His diocesan bishop would have applauded him for this at
least.

On 29 March 1851, in a long and measured statement given full
coverage in the *Nottingham Journal*, 24 diocesan bishops, including the
bishop of Lincoln, John Kaye, and led by the archbishops, expressed
their 'deepest anxiety' at the 'troubles, suspicions, and discontents which
have, of late, in some parishes accompanied the introduction of ritual
observances exceeding those in common amongst us', due to clergy
interpreting the Prayer Book rubrics in ways which infringed the 'rule of
common practice.' This was clearly directed at the more radical of the
Tractarians' successors[2] who had, the bishops believed, encouraged the
'distinct and serious evil' of allowing 'the obvious corruptions abolished
by the Reformation' to be introduced into Anglican worship on the
assumption that 'whatever form or usage [which] existed in the Church
before the Reformation may now be freely introduced and observed'
unless there was an existing formal prohibition. After all, the bishops
pointed out, the English Reformation 'intended to establish one uniform
ritual.'

The bishops showed a concern for the congregations, and their acceptance or otherwise of infringements of 'the rule of common practice.'
They asked the clergy to consider the following: firstly that 'any change
of usages with which the religious feelings of a congregation have
become associated is in itself so likely to do harm that it is not to be
introduced without the greatest caution'; secondly, 'that ... any change
which makes it more difficult for the congregation at large to join in the
service, is still more to be avoided,' and, thirdly, 'that any change which
suggests the fear of still further alterations is most injurious.' As the
'universal practice of the Catholic Church' had never given to 'the
officiating ministers of separate congregations any such large discretion
in the selection of ritual observances', the bishops required that the *Book
of Common Prayer* be adhered to, and that all 'doubted and diversely
taken' questions should be referred to them.[3] A few months later the

---

[1]   *Nottingham Journal*, 23 May 1851.
[2]   Edward Bouverie Pusey (1800–82) pleaded for simplicity of worship and holiness of
life as the supreme catholic virtues.
[3]   *Nottingham Journal*, 4 April 1851.

archbishop of Canterbury himself proceeded against parish clergy in his diocese who had 'persisted in performing the services of their Churches in a manner opposed to his Grace's wishes.'[1]

Yet, in the opinion of many clergy, the establishment of the Roman Catholic hierarchy in England in 1850 was not evidence of a Church of Rome intent on enslaving the souls of the English but rather of the neglect of those souls by the Church of England. In May 1851 the *Nottingham Journal* reported that 24 parish clergy in the diocese of Gloucester and Bristol had presented an address to their bishop, James Henry Monk, one of the signatories of the bishops' declaration on ritual observances. They argued that 'the real causes of the papal aggression' were due not to 'Romanizing tendencies' in the Church of England, or to concessions made to Rome by successive governments, but were to be found in the fact that 'the Episcopate and parochial clergy have lost that hold on the affections and respect of the people which they ought to have, and which they once possessed.' Reasons for this included

> a lamentable indifference, during almost a century and a half, on the part of the parochial clergy, to the sacred trust committed to them; the mercenary views and simoniacal disposal of Church preferment; laxity in regard to letters testimonial; the decay of ecclesiastical discipline; a want of distinctive education for the clerical office; the consequent inefficacy of public teaching; formality in the performance of Divine service; the decay of Cathedral institutions, and the anomalous position of the Cathedral Clergy; the vicious principle of Government appointments to the Episcopate, and the suppression of the powers of Episcopal confirmation; the infrequency of parochial confirmation; the facility of admission to Holy Communion; the divisions in the Episcopate itself; the want of uniformity in the determination of rubrical questions. [2]

This was a comprehensive condemnation of the state of the Church of England. Although the signatories acknowledged that, in harbouring these 'evils', the Church of England was no worse than other churches, they clearly believed that the resurgence of Roman Catholicism was due primarily to Anglican complacency. These reports would have been read by many local Anglican clergy.

---

[1] Ibid., 8 Oct. 1851.

[2] Ibid., 9 May 1851.

It is worth noting here the concern about 'the infrequency of parochial confirmation.' For the signatories this was evidence of the lack of episcopal contact with the parishes. Although bishops argued that the size of their dioceses prevented this it also suggests a somewhat complacent attitude to confirmation by some clergy. We have noted evidence that, a generation earlier, children of the well-to-do were rarely prepared for confirmation: their parents merely applied for tickets. The practice of confirmation by ticket seems to have continued. In July 1855 the proprietor of the *Newark Advertiser* thought that 'it may be useful to remind some of our readers that the Bishop of Lincoln will hold a confirmation at the Parish Church [Newark] on Tuesday morning next.'[1] The bishop was John Jackson who insisted that candidates be adequately prepared,[2] as did his predecessor, John Kaye. Kaye conducted confirmations every three years. Between 12 June and 8 August 1850 he visited sixteen centres in Nottinghamshire confirming twice each day in all but two. He felt it necessary to instruct his clergy 'to preach sermons setting forth the nature and importance of confirmation' and to 'impress upon all parents, guardians, masters and mistresses, the obligation under which they are placed not only to bring such children as are living under their care ... to be confirmed but also to assist in preparing them for the due reception of the rite ... [3] Inevitably large numbers of candidates were confirmed on these occasions. In September 1841 Kaye confirmed 473 candidates in Newark St Mary Magdalene. It was noted that this number was 'considerably larger than in former occasions.' Of this total 288 (61 per cent) were females and 185 (39 per cent) were males.[4]

'Some very unpleasant proceedings'

Not that archdeacons did not attempt to impose discipline when they had an opportunity. When in 1854 Wilkins refused to admit to office a

---

[1]   *Newark Advertiser and Farmers' Journal for Nottinghamshire*, 28 July 1855.

[2]   *Charge* (1855), 26.

[3]   *Nottingham Journal*, 19 April 1850.

[4]   The ratio of females to males remained, on average each year, within around 60:40 nationally and regionally until at least the end of the 20th century despite a drastic fall in the number of candidates (about 79 per cent nationally between 1928 and 1999). Further to this see M.R. Austin, *A Stage or Two Beyond Christendom: a Social History of the Church of England in Derbyshire* (Cromford 2001), 295. However, of the 204 confirmed in Newark St Mary Magdalene in March 1859, 137 were males (67%) and 67 (33%) were females (*Nottingham Review*, 11 March 1859), the reverse of what was to be the trend.

churchwarden at Calverton whom he believed had been improperly elected it was not to be the last time he exercised his judicial authority in this very public way. On 5 June 1857 Wilkins held his visitation in Newark. The *Nottingham Review* reported that there were 'some very unpleasant proceedings' on that occasion when the churchwardens of Balderton (in the parish of Farndon cum Balderton) complained to the archdeacon about the conduct of their vicar who, they alleged, had not properly administered the sacraments. The *Review* noted that 'the archdeacon expressed himself very warmly upon the matter, and in terms very strong against the churchwardens, who, it is believed, are not generally to blame.' In fact, as the *Nottinghamshire and Lincolnshire Advertiser* noted, the 'strong complaints' made by the Balderton churchwardens had concerned 'the manner in which the Vicar's duties were discharged during his absence', though this was not specified.

The Balderton and Farndon wardens had complained about their incumbent in 1849, though the nature of the complaint is again difficult to determine.[1] As to the 'very unpleasant proceedings' in 1857 this may be a reference to the request made a few months earlier by the church-wardens of Farndon on behalf of the parishioners to the vicar, R.S. Walpole, that he preach wearing a surplice rather than a gown as was his custom.[2] If he was consulted, Wilkins would probably have supported the incumbent. In Elizabethan England the wearing of the surplice was a bitterly controversial issue, but under canon 58 of 1604 the surplice was ordered to be worn during divine service and when administering the sacraments. Yet by the 1840s the wearing of a black gown had become commonplace, certainly when preaching. When the Tractarians, in accordance with canon 58, revived the use of the surplice it became a badge of that movement. In 1845, at St Sidwell's in Exeter, its use was met with violent public protest.[3] In the same year, Bishop Kaye evidently asked his archdeacons to monitor the wearing of the surplice. George Wilkins reported that 'the only Clergyman that has held out in adhering to the surplice and to various other attachments not of popular approval, in this County — is Mr Woolley of Beeston.' Wilkins visited the parish and advised the incumbent 'to fall in with the recommenda-tions of the Archbishop of Canterbury' which, concerned at the reaction

---

[1]   LAO, Cor.B.5/8/40/1/7a, Wilkins to Kaye, 9 June 1849.

[2]   *Nottingham Review*, 21 Nov. 1856. It was customary in many churches for the clergyman to wear a surplice when conducting the service and to change into a black gown before preaching the sermon.

[3]   For the 'Surplice Riots' see O. Chadwick, *The Victorian Church*, i (1966), 219–21.

of his congregation, he very readily agreed to do.[1] As Owen Chadwick notes, 'The surplice riots at Exeter were the symptom of distrust growing between ordinary layman and high churchman'[2] but twelve years later in Balderton and Farndon it was the parishioners who had requested the incumbent to preach wearing a surplice rather than a black gown.

The incumbent in question was Robert Seymour Walpole, vicar of Farndon cum Balderton 1852–78. A first reading of the report in the *Review* would suggest that in 1856, Walpole, by wearing a gown when he preached, wished to indicate his opposition to any tendency to make the Church of England more Catholic in its theology and practice. If so, then Walpole was subsequently to experience a conversion. During his incumbency Balderton become a ritualist centre, and Walpole was elected a member of the Anglo-Catholic Society of the Holy Cross (the SSC) at its May synod in 1873. Before his ordination training at St Bees theological college Walpole had been an army officer. It was later said of him that when he came to Balderton the parish had within it 'many rough, lawless characters' and that 'the situation demanded the application of a very plain and practical muscular Christianity in which he did not hesitate. In his church, too, he was a martinet. He had been described by a contemporary as an "ultra-ritualist", who offered the people an advanced ritual whether they liked it or not.'[3] It seems that the Farndon wardens had some reason to object to their incumbent's behaviour. In its report of Wilkins's visitation in 1857, the *Nottinghamshire and Lincolnshire Advertiser* referred to 'a similar unpleasantness with the Farndon churchwardens' which had occurred at the archdeacon's visitation the previous year. The *Advertiser* observed that 'it is much lamentable that such an unsatisfactory state of things should exist in church matters and it would be well if the authorities would take steps to bring about a better state of feeling between the churchwardens and the Vicar or those officiating for him.'[4] Walpole was to resign Farndon (in 1853 it was reported that 'the vicarage house is an old thatched building, now

---

[1]   LAO, Cor.8.5/8/20/13, Wilkins to Kaye, 23 May 1845. The incumbent of Beeston St John Baptist was John Hurt Woolley (1796–1877), vicar of Beeston 1822–54.

[2]   Chadwick, *Victorian Church*, i. 220.

[3]   W. Margetson, *G.H.S. Walpole, Bishop of Edinburgh* (1930), 4. Robert Walpole was not alone in Nottinghamshire in promoting 'ritualistic' practices at this time, though he was probably more advanced than others. In 1858 the vicar of Radcliffe-on-Trent was criticised by the *Nottingham Review* for his 'recently acquired Puseyistical tendences'. By 1867 he had increased the number of services of holy communion in his parish from three or four a year to 26, though this was reduced to once a month in 1869 (Pamela Priestland (ed.), *Radcliffe-on-Trent 1837–1920* (1989), 47).

[4]   *Nottingham and Lincolnshire Advertiser*, 6 June 1857.

occupied by poor people')[1] but retained Balderton.

Generally, George Wilkins would have supported the bishops in opposing 'the introduction of ritual observances exceeding those in common amongst us' but he was sanguine about minor departures from common practice. At his visitation in Southwell in May 1865 he indicated that while he regretted that the Lord Chancellor had been unsuccessful in persuading the House of Lords to accept the Clerical Discipline Bill as this would have strengthened the hand of the church in proceeding against clergy guilty of serious moral offences, he was not only relaxed about minor deviations from established liturgical practice but also appreciated the motives of innovators. He said that

> with regard to cases coming under the cognisance of the bishop, or his Consistory Court, at which offence is taken against things indifferent, or non-essential, involving decorations, ornaments and vestments, it is to be regretted that these should have been carried so far, in so few churches, as to have incurred what is absurdly termed the censure of 'public opinion', where it is evident that only respect and reverence are intended in things pertaining to the service of God, or where, at most, over zeal may have marked those who, labouring amongst the negligent and indifferent, seek to instil into them higher and better sentiments by the adjunct of external worship in aid of inward devotion.

Public opinion, for Wilkins, was 'too often nothing but the clamour of a multitude.'

These seem to be the only occasions in the archdeaconry in this period when questions 'involving decorations, ornaments and vestments' were at issue. In 1877 the Newark and Southwell branch of the English Church Union, under the chairmanship of S. Reynolds Hole, vicar of Caunton, resolved that any court hearing a case brought under the provisions of the 1874 Public Worship Regulations Act was 'spiritually null and void' and expressed support and sympathy for any priest suspended or inhibited under the Act. In a letter to Hole, Christopher Wordsworth, the bishop of Lincoln, listed fourteen reasons why he could not support this resolution. Hole accepted his bishop's judgment which, he said, would 'settle many a doubtful mind.'[2] The diocese of Lincoln

---

[1] *White's Directory of Nottinghamshire* (1853).

[2] J.H. Overton and Elizabeth Wordsworth, *Christopher Wordsworth, Bishop of Lincoln, 1908–1885* (1888), 260–1.

was significantly low church, and no cases were brought under the 1874 Act during Wordsworth's episcopate. Wordsworth's successor was to be Edward King who, in 1888, was famously accused by the Church Association of ritual acts contrary to the rubrics of the *Book of Common Prayer*.

In his visitation charges George Wilkins was occasionally concerned with less weighty matters. When addressing the Nottingham clergy and churchwardens in May 1852, so the *Nottingham Review* reported, he referred to the practice in some parishes of allowing grass to grow in churchyards: 'In one of these parishes, which he himself was visiting a short time since, he was perfectly wet through owing entirely to his being obliged to walk through the long grass.'[1]

It seems that at times George Wilkins was less than careful about his own conduct. In May 1857 he admitted churchwardens and delivered his charge in the chapter house in Southwell where, it was reported, he was 'listened to with much attention.' Clergy and churchwardens then crossed to road to dine together at 'Mr Richardson's, the Saracen's Head Inn.'[2] It seems that on these occasions George Wilkins provided the hospitality because, a year later, James Frederick Richardson of the Saracen's Head in Southwell proceeded against George Wilkins in Newark Court for non-payment of a bill for £8 12s. The county court judge, Richard Wildman, declared the case against Wilkins a nonsuit as there 'was no proof to show the agency of the plaintiff in the transaction'.[3] One may assume that relations between the collegiate church and the Saracen's Head were somewhat soured as a result.

Despite his own financial indiscretions Wilkins was concerned to maintain probity in the financial dealings of his clergy. One notable example involved simony relating to advowsons, that is the right to present a clergyman to a benefice. These were regarded as property and could be freely bought and sold. Clearly, the richer the benefice, the greater was the monetary value of the advowson. For example the very valuable benefice of Averham with Kelham had a gross worth of £1,435 a year in 1858. It had been in the patronage of the Sutton and Manners-Sutton family for over a century. The right to the next presentation was sold in 1855 for £16,000 to Joseph Need Walker of Rotherham, whose family had made its fortune from lead manufacture, in order that his third son, Joseph Walker, could become the incumbent. The Revd Joseph

---

[1]   *Nottingham Review*, 28 May 1852.
[2]   Ibid., 29 May 1857.
[3]   Ibid., 18 June 1858.

Walker eventually bought the patronage from the Manners-Sutton family.[1] This is one of many examples of rich manufacturers in the nineteenth century buying the right of benefice patronage from long-established landed families, thereby advancing their own families' social standing and, by not residing in the parishes in their gift, changing the nature of the relationship between church and people.

Trafficking in advowsons could be readily abused. In 1834 the rector of Langar, Joseph Rolling Unwin (who had become incumbent in 1824), was forced to vacate his living on being accused of simony in that he had allegedly entered into an agreement with the patron of the benefice, the Revd William Bowerbank,[2] and a farmer, John Wright, to lease 324 acres of benefice land to Wright at a fraction of its market value. As Unwin resigned the benefice (valued at £210 gross in 1831) the case never went to full trial.[3] However, Bowerbank was evidently held to be guilty because the right of presentation to the living passed from him to the Crown at least for the next turn. An account published at the time claimed that Bowerbank had purchased the patronage with the intention of his son becoming rector once he had graduated and been ordained. In the interim he gave the benefice to his friend Unwin presumably on the condition that he would vacate it in favour of Bowerbank's son. When the time came Unwin refused to go and, it was said, 'a law suit has ensued which we should think will terminate in his [Unwin's] favour, though he may have committed a breach of friendship.' It was not to be, and it was later reported that, on 13 May 1837, Unwin, 'without a penny', walked to Nottingham where he pawned his spoons for £3 and the following morning was found drowned in the Nottingham Canal near Sneinton. For this tragedy George Wilkins, described as a 'venerable

---

[1]   Brian Robinson, *Three Nottinghamshire Parishes Revisited: Historical Highlights of Averham, Kelham and Staythorpe* (2006), 9–18.

[2]   The *Nottingham and Newark Mercury*, 12 Feb. 1831, reported that a letter, bearing a Mansfield postmark, signed 'Swing' had been received by John Coke, high sheriff of Nottinghamshire. It had supposedly been traced to 'the Revd W. Bowerbank, a clergyman of the Established Church, and, we believe, is or was, Head Master of the Grammar School [in Mansfield]'. Bowerbank was tried and acquitted of issuing a threat. J.R. Unwin had, in 1827, been appointed curate of nearby Sutton in Ashfield, the incumbent of which was William Goodacre, Bowerbank's undermaster at Mansfield free grammar school 1813–30. Bowerbank resigned the headmastership in 1830.

[3]   See Sandford Neville (ed.), *Report of cases argued and determined in the Court of King's Bench in Michaelmas, Hilary and Easter terms in the third [– sixth] year[s] of William IV.*

pluralist and panter after prebends,' was held responsible.[1] Trafficking in advowsons was not abolished until 1924.

The vicar of Flintham, Charles John Myers, caused Wilkins to exercise his authority over a very different financial matter. At the archdeacon's visitation in Newark in May 1859, so the *Newark Advertiser* reported:

> In calling over the names, the archdeacon ... on coming to the name of Revd Charles Myers ... received no answer, upon which he called upon the churchwarden of that parish and asked him what had been done with the sacrament money of late. The churchwarden replied that it had been accumulating for the last nine years, and now amounted to about twenty pounds. The archdeacon read a portion from the prayer book which points out what must be done with the sacrament money, and expressed himself strongly against this accumulation, instructing the church-warden to inform the vicar that the case had been brought before him and that it would be his duty to represent it to the bishop of the diocese.[2]

Myers was incensed, and wrote to Wilkins that he was 'surprised that you so far forgot yourself as to attack me publicly in this insulting manner behind my back' for no other reason than 'for the sake of a little cheap popularity.' Myers claimed that as the squire supported the poor there had been no call on the communion alms. Nevertheless the bishop of Lincoln required Myers to account for income and expenditure for the previous ten years, and to explain why he had not attended the visitation.[3]

In a letter to ruridecanal chapters two years earlier the bishop, writing about 'a subject of some delicacy', called the clergy of the diocese to task for another widespread financial irregularity:

> A custom of long standing prevails in many parts of the Diocese

---

[1]   *An account of the Conduct of the Reverend Dr Wilkins, Archdeacon of Nottingham, towards the late Rev. J.R. Unwin* (n.d). This pamphlet was printed in Nottingham by Herbert Ingram of 17 Chapel Bar, who was later to establish the *Illustrated London News* and to become MP for Boston: John T. Godfrey, *Notes on the Churches of Nottinghamshire: Hundred of Bingham* (1907), 291.

[2]   *Newark Advertiser*, 1 June 1859.

[3]   See Penny Gallon, '"Paterfamilias": the Reverend Charles John Myers, vicar of Flintham from 1829–1870', *Nottinghamshire Historian*, no. 49 (1992), 20.

of taking the whole marriage fee at the time when the Banns are put up, so that, when the parties reside in different Parishes, the Marriage Fee is paid twice over, and the expense of a Banns wedding is raised, in some cases, to as much as £1. There is reason to believe that many Churchpeople have been driven unwillingly to the cheaper marriage at the Registrar's Office or the Dissenting Chapel.

Bishop Jackson reminded his clergy that this practice was illegal, though his letter gives the impression that he was rather less anxious about the illegal charging of double fees and more concerned that couples were being married by registrars and nonconformist ministers. When the Southwell chapter clergy discussed this letter at their meeting in December 1857 it was noted that the practice of double charging was followed in several parishes in the deanery 'whilst in others it is customary to charge 1s for the publication of Banns and an additional fee of 2s. 6d. for a certificate of such publication this being the sum allowed by Act of Parliament for a Baptismal or Burial Certificate.'[1]

The bishop of Lincoln could have added that the double charging of the whole marriage fee inevitably bore hardest on the poor: doubling even the cheaper 5s offered in many parishes would be equal to a week's wages for farm labourers. We now turn to them, and the place of the church in their lives.

---

[1]   Bishop's letter dated 12 Dec., chapter meeting 15 Dec. 1857 (SMHL 699)

7

Church and Society

The church and the poor

The 1851 census showed how few of the poor attended church or chapel in either town or country. By the end of the decade socially aware urban clergy were attempting to address the problem. In Derby, John Erskine Clarke had rebuilt St Michael's, insisting that all its seats were free, and, with other clergy in the town, had established reading rooms, penny banks, sick and funeral aid societies, clothing clubs and cocoa houses for artisans. In Nottingham a similar range of clubs and societies and parish working-men's associations had been formed. Notably, in 1859 Thomas Mosse Macdonald, vicar of Holy Trinity since 1851, built a 'working men's free church' in the slums of his parish. It held 550 and cost £1,200. It was consecrated by the bishop of Lincoln in December 1859. Reporting the event the *Nottingham Free Press* noted that 'the church was crowded to excess, every part being occupied by the class for whom the building was specially erected'.[1] These urban initiatives were well-meaning, if eventually unsuccessful, attempts to win the hearts of the labouring poor. Few similar initiatives were undertaken in rural parishes. There they were considered at best unnecessary and even subversive of the established social order.

In his *Village Politics: Addresses and Sermons on the Labour Question* published in three volumes in 1878, Charles William Stubbs, then dean of Ely, held the clergy responsible in part for 'creating [a] class of men, the stolid helplessness of whose ignorance has become proverbial.'[2] In his view this was due to the sad fact that 'popular reforms in all ages and all countries, from the Prophet Amos down to Joseph Arch, have rarely met with much favour from the established

---

[1] *Nottingham Free Press*, 10 Dec. 1859.

[2] Quoted in Mark Freeman, 'The agricultural labourer and the Hodge stereotype c.1850–1914', *Agricultural History Review*, xlix (2001), 180. Charles William Stubbs (1843–1912) was a member of the Christian Social Union and had been a rural incumbent when rector of Wavertree in Lancashire. See also his *The Land and the Labourers: facts and experiments in cottage farming and co-operative agriculture* (1890).

authorities in either Church or State.'[1] In 1892 another rural incumbent, Arnold Turner, vicar of Churchstanton in Devon, also blamed the clergy for having 'a determination at all costs to keep things as they are, to oppose all reform, and especially to oppose all efforts on the part of Hodge himself to obtain a voice in the management of parish affairs.'[2] Stubbs and Taylor were late to the battle for better conditions for farm labourers and for the breaking down of class prejudices. As we will see, Frederick William Naylor of Upton and S. Reynolds Hole of Caunton had been arguing the labourers' case locally, and courting controversy, many years earlier. Nationally, James Fraser had been outspoken about working and housing conditions of farm labourers. It was not that the Church of England was unaware of the poor – it had advocated philanthropy, and had been educating the children of the poor for generations – it was rather that social distinctions destroyed in all classes any notion that the Church of England was a church for the poor.

'Like a mine at the base of society'

Particularly in periods of actual or feared social unrest, the church was apprehensive of the poor. In 1855 at a meeting of the Additional Curates Aid Association in his diocese, the bishop of Lincoln, John Jackson, noting the 'necessary neglect' of the population by over-worked clergy, said that this had far-reaching consequences:

> He would not say that there was not much vice and much irreligion in the rural districts, because to say so would be to say that human nature had ceased to be corrupt; but he had no hesitation in asserting that the greatness of the vice, irreligion, and infidelity which existed in our country, was to be found in those large overgrown parishes where the Church had long ceased to reach the great part of the population. Either in the wide suburbs, where there were long rows of small and ill-built houses, or in the hearts of cities, where the number of bells at the side of the door, one above the other, told that the house, which was a large and

---

[1]   Stubbs, *Village Politics*, quoted by Frances Evelyn, countess of Warwick in her preface to Joseph Arch, *The Story of His Life, Told by Himself* (1898), xvii.

[2]   Arnold Taylor, 'Hodge and his parson', *Nineteenth Century*, xxxi (1892), 361, quoted in Freeman, 'Agricultural Labourer'. 'Hodge' was a general term signifying the typical English agricultural labourer (the word is said to derive from an abbreviated form of the Christian name Roger).

well-looking one, was inhabited from its garrets down to its damp cellars – each single room lodging a whole family – they would find the places for the most part of vice, infidelity and irreligion, though he did not deny that in such places were frequently to be found persons whose Christian graces might well shame those who possessed much more extended advantages. They would find that not one in ten or twenty went regularly to any place of worship whatever. They would find a large proportion of persons professing unbelief in that Bible which most of them had never read, or of which their knowledge was gleaned only from irreligious publications; and would also find that the degrading sin of drunkenness prevailed to an alarming extent among the men and the women, and, he might almost add, the children. This was a state of things which it was impossible to contemplate without grief, whether it was looked at politically, economically, or religiously. Looking at it politically, these were the classes which writers on political economy had termed the dangerous classes.[1] They were those who, having no stake in the welfare of the country – nothing, as they fancied, to lose – and no religious principles to deter them from what they might think would be to their advantage, though wrong, and apt to suppose that any change would be for their good, were ready to listen to any demagogue who would propose to them what seemed to be to them a plan for their amelioration in the social scale; and, though kept quiet perhaps by fear or by the general prosperity of the country, were ready, like a mine at the base of society, to explode and dash the state to atoms.

On the basis of this political analysis, Jackson then produced a socio-economic argument for employing more Anglican clergy. He said that the cost of keeping 'a single criminal while in prison would support a clergyman for a similar period.' Jackson argued that poverty caused crime, and that by increasing the number of clergy 'the redeeming knowledge of Christianity' would be brought to these 'benighted' and 'dangerous' classes and violent revolution would be prevented.[2] It was to provide the finance to provide additional clergy in poor areas that cathedrals and collegiate churches, the Southwell foundation among

---

[1]   The term 'les classes dangereuses' was coined in 1840 by H.A. Frégier. 'Frégier's term was rapidly anglicised and taken over by British men of property as much to define their fears as any social group lurking in the city slums' (Clive Emsley, *Crime and Society in England 1750–1900* (1996), 37).

[2]   *Newark Advertiser*, 27 Oct. 1855.

them, had been reformed in the late 1830s. But Jackson had no word to say about the economic and social conditions that caused poverty and which kept so many 'wretched creatures' in such degrading conditions. There is little doubt that Jackson reflected the opinion of very many of his clergy. Little wonder that labourers, and so many in the rising middle class, did not count the clergy among their friends.

'The dead hand of the Church'

In 1872 Joseph Arch (1826–1919) created the National Agricultural Labourers Union by bringing together into one organisation the county unions that he had established. In her preface to Arch's autobiography, Frances Evelyn, countess of Warwick,[1] one of several powerful supporters of Joseph Arch, wrote of ' … the dead hand of the Church in those days' and that 'sympathy with the people was certainly not a strong point with the clergy.'[2] Arch himself observed that 'the Church of England gentry have too often trampled ruthlessly on the labourer in the past; but we had our own Union now, and they would trample on us no longer.'[3] As an example of this lack of sympathy for the rural poor, in October 1855, so the *Newark Advertiser* reported, the earl of Leicester, residing on his Norfolk estate, addressed a meeting of 'gentry and clergy'. He told them that 'I believe that the giving of largess has a most injurious effect upon our labourers; in many cases I think it is the first introduction to the beershop.' He added that although he provided cottages for his many labourers they were made available at as little expense to himself as possible.[4]

The lack of adequate housing and secure tenancies for rural abourers

---

[1]   Francis Evelyn 'Daisy' Greville (1861–1938), mistress of Edward VII and of Lord Charles Beresford, founded a needlework school at Easton in Essex and also Studley Agricultural College for Women. She hosted meetings of trade unionists at Easton Lodge.

[2]   Arch, *Story of his Life*, xvii.

[3]   Ibid.

[4]   *Newark Advertiser*, 13 Oct. 1855. For conditions in Norfolk see also Alan Howkins, *Poor Labouring Men: rural radicalism in Norfolk, 1870–1923* (1985), and Nicola Verdon, 'The employment of women and children in agriculture: a reassessment of agricultural gangs in nineteenth-century Norfolk', *Agricultural History Review*, xl (2001), 41–55. However, the *Oxford DNB* says of Thomas William Coke, second earl of Leicester from 1842, that 'Leicester was a patron of agricultural causes and a member of the Royal Agricultural Society of England. He was responsible for building more than 200 new cottages on the estate from the 1860s onwards, and he was not prepared to join with other landowners against trade unions. Although many were singled out for abuse from union platforms, Lord Leicester escaped.'

was a key measure of neglect. The earl of Leicester was not alone in providing no more than minimum accommodation for his workers. In 1867, in the report of the royal commission on the employment of children, young persons and women in agriculture, James Fraser,[1] an Anglican priest and an assistant commissioner, had been passionate in his condemnation of the state of rural cottages. He described their condition at length. He concluded that they were 'deficient in almost every requisite that should constitute a home for a Christian family in a civilised community.' They were the cause of disease and immorality, for 'the whole atmosphere is sensual, and human nature degraded into something below the level of the swine. It is a hideous picture, and the picture is drawn from life.'[2] It is clear that, in this part of Nottinghamshire, the conditions in which many labourers lived were generally very poor. In 1873 S. Reynolds Hole, vicar and squire of Caunton, said that 'the stables of the rich' were, in many cases, far more spacious and better constructed than the 'habitations of the poor.'[3] Although in 1892 William E. Bear was to report to the royal commission on labour that 'the standard of cottage accommodation is higher in the Southwell Union than in any district which I have previously visited' with cottages 'comfortably furnished, and cheerfully decorated with pictures',[4] the clergy did not share this opinion. In 1889 the Southwell ruridecanal conference discussed the housing of the poor. The rector of Eakring and rural dean of Southwell, W.L.B. Cator, noted that among 'the causes of uncomfortableness of the Poor in their homes' was 'the temptation on the part of contractors to build houses to pay [i.e. for profit] rather than consider the benefit of those who inhabit them'. In 1909 the county medical officer, Dr Henry Handford, addressing the Southwell ruridecanal conference, attributed 'mischief' to the bad housing, insanitary conditions and overcrowding in labourers' cottages. As late as 1919 the vicar of Farnsfield and rural dean, R. A. McKee, echoing Samuel Reynolds Hole nearly fifty years earlier, said that 'the well-built sheds for cattle [were] in some cases preferable to the places that sheltered human beings.'[5]

---

[1]   In 1870 James Fraser (1818–85) was made bishop of Manchester on the recommendation of W.E. Gladstone.

[2]   Quoted in Richard Heath, *The Victorian Peasant* (1989), 29–30.

[3]   Samuel Reynolds Hole, *The Cry of the Labourer against Landlord, Farmer and Priest: a Sermon* (1873), 9.

[4]   Royal Commission on Labour, *The Agricultural Labourer* (1892), 109–10.

[5]   SMHL, 699: Southwell ruridecanal conference minute book, 15 Feb. 1889, 8 June 1909, 23 Sept. 1919.

But these criticisms came late in the day. With few exceptions rural clergy in the 1850s were less concerned for the material welfare of the poor than with their immorality and that they remain content in their stations. The general attitude of local 'gentry and clergy' to the poor can be assessed from a variety of disparate sources. For example, in March 1850 the Southwell Association for the Prosecution of Felons met in the George and Dragon Inn in the town. It was attended by 80 'gentlemen' out of 166 members, the greatest number since the association was formed in 1775, witnessing to the fear that if the criminal poor were not pursued vigorously the social status quo would be threatened.[1] Yet these men would have known well that the felons they pursued were poor ill-educated men, and that many were driven to crime.[2] In April 1846, the *Nottingham Journal* reported, the Southwell Quarter Sessions calendar contained the names 'of 99 prisoners of whom 2 can read and write well, 66 can read and write imperfectly, and 31 can neither read [n]or write. The number of prisoners at the [current] sessions amounted to 17 of whom not one could read or write well, 10 read and write imperfectly, and 7 can neither read [n]or write.'[3]

These men and women were the parents of the children who attended parish Sunday schools condescendingly referred to in a report of Norwell parish church Sunday School anniversary in June 1855: 'The contribution of one small girl was a small wooden cross, chastely ornamented with leaves and blossoms, the spontaneous act of a cottage family ... We happen to know that no parties were more gratified than the vicar and his family, in thus being able to provide for the sons and daughters of toil, who are to be the men and women of the next generation.'[4] Children from 'cottage families' were taught to know their place. In 1855 the Blidworth National and Sunday Schools' annual sermon was preached by Robert Money Weale, the curate of Mansfield Woodhouse, on Psalm 43:11: 'Come ye children, hearken unto me, I will teach you the fear of the Lord'. The sermon was deemed 'excellent and appropriate' by the

---

[1] *Nottingham Journal*, 28 March 1850.

[2] For example, of 13 sentences handed down at the Nottinghamshire Michaelmas Quarter Sessions in 1829 and served in Southwell House of Correction only one was for the theft of money and valuables (and this from a relative). Apart from the theft of three donkeys, all the others were for the theft of animals (either live or dead weight, probably for food), or of clothing. 1829 was a year marked, not least in Nottinghamshire, by high food and coal prices (the latter kept artificially high by a cartel), depressed trade and low wages, and depressed agriculture.

[3] *Nottingham Journal*, 10 April 1846.

[4] *Newark Advertiser*, 23 June 1855.

Newark Advertiser.[1] Beneath the surface of these reports lay what S. Reynolds Hole was to call 'one of the saddest sorrows of our time', the 'estrangement … of the classes of society.[2] The middle and upper classes were distant, emotionally and physically, from the culture of the common people — the culture of the crowd.

'Sources of boundless evil': the statutes

In the middle years of the nineteenth century there were regular references in the Nottinghamshire press to the annual 'statutes'[3], or hiring fairs, causing considerable concern to the comfortable classes and to the clergy in particular. These were the occasions, once or twice a year, when agricultural labourers and domestic servants were hired. The Martinmas statutes in Southwell in November 1856 were 'well attended by servants, and, during the early part of the day, a fair amount of hiring was done. The wages asked, particularly by female servants, were very high. All passed off peacefully and quiet.'[4] In the same month Martinmas was celebrated in Farnsfield with tea parties in the Plough and the Wheatsheaf inns: 'dancing was also indulged in in the different public houses'.[5] No reference is made to the hiring of servants, but this would probably have taken place earlier in the day. In the larger centres the statutes could become rowdy, if generally good-natured, occasions with many more than the labourers coming into town. At Retford in November 1855

---

[1] *Newark Advertiser*, 13 Oct. 1855.

[2] Hole, *The Cry*, 13.

[3] 'Statutes' refers to the *Statute of Labourers* of 1351. Following the Black Death (1347–9) there was a shortage of labour and, so the *Statute* said, wages were demanded up to three times the pre-plague levels. In an unsuccessful attempt to regulate wages, labourers were required to accept offers of work at 1346 wage levels. Farm labourers were to be 'allowed to serve by a whole year, or by other usual terms, and not by the day', hence the annual hirings. The system was to be regulated by 'sheriffs and bailiffs of our lord the king', stewards and parish constables. Eventually it was controlled by justices of the peace in quarter sessions. Up to the late nineteenth century Nottinghamshire farm and domestic servants went to the statutes in search of new jobs, and employers were in the market for good workpeople. In periods of agricultural depression, or merely on the whim of a farmer, labourers were not re-hired: on this see Thomas Hardy, *Tess of the D'Urbervilles* (Penguin edn, 1994), 449ff. Over the years the holiday accompanying the hiring fair developed into a few days of 'frivolous, if not vicious, pursuits', as H.R. Wilkins put it.

[4] *Nottingham Review*, 14 Nov. 1856.

[5] Ibid., 28 Nov. 1856.

there was larger influx than usual of itinerants, nut vendors, 'cheap jacks', street musicians etc. ... The mayor permitted shows to take their stand as in former years in the Market-square, and throughout the day five or six paltry exhibitions proved the centre of attraction for the lads and lasses, who could not possibly resist the temptation of having their fortunes told by a diminutive specimen of the equine species, and of beholding the downfall of 'Sebastopol' as 'natural as life.' The light-fingered artistes were busily engaged in their nefarious vocation and we heard of several instances in which cash was abstracted from the person. The police, however, were on the alert, and though nothing very serious occurred, the police-station was rather thickly populated during Saturday night and Sunday.[1]

To those living in towns, a leader in the *Nottingham Free Press* said in 1859, the rural 'Statty' fairs were thought of as 'humorous Arcadian spectacles' with 'plenty of nut brown ale, and rustic courting, and dancing "Sir Roger de Coverley" on the greensward when the hiring is concluded; and all is very pretty and pastoral.' In reality, plenty of nut brown ale 'leads too often to bestial drunkenness and brutal violence; and the rustic courtship is only preliminary to the coarsest profligacy ... Statute fairs ... are, too frequently, but turbulent assemblies of young people, ready through mere ignorance to drift into depravity.' A long letter from 'Veritas' in the same edition of the newspaper plaintively complained that 'statutes are rapidly degenerating into a positive nuisance.' The following week 'Excelsior', another correspondent, went further: during the statute-fairs, he wrote, 'I believe more farmers' servant girls lose their chastity than at any other season of the year.'[2]

The Southwell ruridecanal chapter, meeting on 30 May 1856, discussed 'The Hiring of Farm Servants' at the request of the bishop, John Jackson. No record of this discussion was recorded but the chapter returned to the subject on 16 December 1856, when it discussed the annual report of an association established in Bingham 'for the better regulation of the hiring of farm servants and the abolition of Statutes and their consequent evils'. On 15 December 1857 a letter from the bishop of Lincoln on the subject of 'Statute Hiring' was read to the chapter. Jackson wrote that

---

[1] *Newark Advertiser*, 10 Nov. 1855.

[2] *Nottingham Free Press*, 19 and 26 Nov. 1859.

> While it is no doubt desirable that the Clergy should avoid taking
> so prominent a part in the Movement [to abolish annual statutes]
> as to cause among the Farmers any jealousy of their interference,
> it is thought that their influence may be beneficially used with the
> Magistrates, or as Magistrates themselves, to obtain from the
> Quarter Sessions ... a resolution no longer to direct the Statutes to
> be called. It is to be hoped that these sources of boundless evil to
> our young people may thus at least gradually fall into disuse.

On this occasion members of the chapter signed a declaration opposing
the prevailing practice of hiring servants, be they agricultural or
domestic, as 'highly detrimental to the interests of the employers, as well
as injurious to the morals of the employed' and urged the registration by
employment offices of men and women seeking work. This was a
forward-thinking proposal. Although a registry office for labourers was
established in Gloucestershire in the late 1850s, little came of the idea
nationally until labour exchanges were established in 1909. Not only
farmers but also the labourers themselves had an interest in maintaining
the statute fairs. Irrespective of economic conditions farmers could
bargain with labourers on rates of pay, and for the labourers the annual
statutes offered one of the few holidays they had. As the *Nottingham
Free Press* noted, 'the well meaning promoters of Agrarian reform must
remember that our peasantry have far too few holidays as it is.'

The chapter returned to the subject on 18 December 1860. That the
statutes were 'injurious to the morals of the employed' was again the
principal concern of at least some members of the chapter. Henry Robert
Wilkins, vicar of Farnsfield, described the efforts that he and others had
made at the last statute hiring in Mansfield 'to counteract in some degree
the mischief which arises on these occasions.' The minute recorded:

> With a view of obviating the necessity of Servants who attended
> the Statutes having recourse to Beer Shops etc to obtain refresh-
> ment, tea, coffee, etc was provided at a cheap cost in the Town
> Hall, and in the evening an amusing Lecture was given in order to
> afford some rational entertainment which might induce them to
> pass their holiday in other than frivolous, if not vicious, pursuits.
> These endeavours met with considerable success. Very many
> Servants, both male and female, availed themselves of the
> opportunities thus presented to them, and on leaving for their
> respective homes expressed their warm gratitude to Mr Wilkins
> and the other Clergymen who had taken so much trouble and
> interest on their behalf.

The chapter again urged that registry offices be established to remove altogether the need for statutes and hiring fairs.[1]

A concern for farm labourers engaged members of the ruridecanal chapter in another way. On 30 May 1856, on the proposal of James Morris Maxfield, vicar of Norwell, the chapter petitioned parliament that the so-called 'Half Time Act'[2] be extended to agricultural districts 'so that children throughout the kingdom may be enabled to attend School during one half of each week, thus affording them the advantage of combining intellectual and religious with industrial training.' John Drake Becher, vicar of South Muskham, and Thomas Coats Cane, perpetual curate of Halloughton, objected to the petition 'as not being sufficiently explicit and practical in its suggestions.' That these two refused to sign the petition suggests that they represented the conservative gentry and farming interest in the chapter. The majority of the chapter signed, and the petition was sent. These were clergy resident in their parishes. T.C. Cane, J.M. Wilkins noted in his visitation return for Halloughton, resided in the parish of Southwell. He did, but at his 'modern seat' of Brackenhurst, as *White's Directory of Nottinghamshire* for 1853 notes. J.D. Becher was also a non-resident, living at Hill House in Southwell. Both Cane and Becher were also prominent magistrates. For four members of the chapter, J.M. Maxfield, F.W. Naylor, J.W. Marsh and S. Reynolds Hole, the concerns of the labourers and their families were more important than those of the landed interest.

Social initiatives: sick clubs and clothing clubs

By the 1850s attempts had made in a few parishes in the Southwell rural deanery to meet the material needs of poor families by establishing benefit clubs, if not by the churches at least by those with some religious affiliation. These clubs were often established in public houses. For example, in Southwell a sick club met at the Wheatsheaf Inn. On Whit Monday 1859 it held its anniversary dinner, preceded by a service in Holy Trinity parish church. The sick club meeting at the Old Reindeer

---

[1] Southwell ruridecanal chapter minute book, 1855–71 (SMHL, 699). The need for 'a respectable registry office' to replace the 'slave market' of the annual statutes was argued in the letter from Veritas on 'Statutes and their Abominations' in the *Nottingham Free Press*, 19 Nov. 1859.

[2] This was the Factory Act (Mills) of 1844. It applied only to the textile industry and limited the hours of work of children aged between eight and 13 to 6½ a day, which was considered to be half time.

Inn held its dinner on the same day. Its members first went to the Baptist chapel for a service. The Baptist and Methodist chapels in Southwell had their own sick clubs and held their anniversaries on the same day. The funds of each of these clubs were said to be 'in a very prosperous condtion.' At Edingley, the parish sick club met at 'the house of Mr Hallam'.[1] A clothing club was established by the vicar of Farnsfield, Henry Wilkins, in the 1850s. In November 1859 The *Nottingham Free Press* reported that

> on Monday last the annual distribution of clothing tickets took place at the house of the worthy vicar. All families who have to work for their living are allowed to become members of this club by paying 1d and 2d every week, and at the end of the year 3d is added to every shilling. They are allowed to go to any shop they please in the village for their clothing.[2]

Yet other than discussing, on one or two occasions, F.W. Naylor's cottage gardens scheme and his proposals for village libraries and night schools, and petitioning Parliament that the half-time legislation be extended to farm labourers, the Southwell rural deanery clergy seem rarely to have discussed the conditions in which farm labourers in their parishes lived and worked. But for two members of the rural deanery chapter, Frederick William Naylor and Samuel Reynolds Hole, the immediate welfare of farm labourers and their families was of primary concern.

Frederick William Naylor:
'Education belongs to the whole of life'

Throughout the 1850s and 1860s the chapter discussed village libraries and night schools for labourers, undoubtedly led by F.W. Naylor. By the 1850s a few clergy were no longer sanguine about the relationship of the Church of England to the poor. The publication in 1854 of the analysis of the 1851 census showed that the church was far from being the church

---

[1] *Nottingham Review*, 17 and 24 June 1859. When the 1861 census was taken a William Hallam was a licensed victualler in Edingley. This indicates that 'the house of Mr Hallam' was licensed premises.

[2] *Nottingham Free Press*, 26 Nov. 1859. The *Free Press* was established as 'A Family Newspaper to Advocate the Rights and Promote the Moral, Social and Political elevation of the People'.

of the poor. No doubt informed by this, but fired by his own vision of what the encouragement of the poor could achieve, Frederick William Naylor, vicar of Upton 1840-58, not only promoted the cultivation of cottage gardens, but developed 'a reformatory experiment in the shape of a cricket club for the young men of this village whose whole time is employed in agriculture and whose mental condition assimilates too nearly to the nature of the soil they are so familiar with.'[1] Naylor also addressed this earthy 'mental condition' more directly. In 1855 he published *Popular Libraries in Rural Districts, their availability to meet one of the social necessities of the times, with remarks on the advantages of general reading to all classes, and suggestions for the establishment of popular libraries in rural districts, on a self-supporting and inexpensive plan*,[2] following this in 1858 (the year of his death) with *Continuous Education: or practical suggestions about Libraries, Discussion-meetings, Lectures, and other means of promoting self-culture, with special reference to rural and suburban districts, To which are added remarks upon the half-time system on farms, tea-festivals, suitable books, working men's associations, village cricket clubs, etc.*[3] In his *Popular Libraries* Naylor argued the case for continuous adult education primarily on moral grounds. He held that 'the person who can read is better qualified for discriminating and appreciating the good'. However, as 'the immense sale obtained by pernicious publications in districts where there are facilities for disseminating this demoralizing intellectual supply' illustrates, the 'best way to expel the darkness of ignorance is to admit freely the light of truth and knowledge … in the cheapest and most abundant manner.' Naylor suggested that those living in large towns were well aware of this,[4] but for those in rural parishes 'hardly any facility is afforded, and little encouragement given, to seek for further information from the sources now open to them', for 'the labouring population of our villages are almost entirely without books for general reading.' That the 'permeation of knowledge amongst the adult population of the lower classes is almost a social necessity' was illustrated, in Naylor's view, by the fact that 'to a certain extent crime and ignorance go hand in hand.' He noted that 'crime advances by a sudden and

---

[1] George Lillywhite, www.upton150.co.uk/index; also NAO.

[2] London, Simkins, Marshall & Co.; Nottingham, W. Dearden; Southwell, J. Whittingham (1855).

[3] London, Bull, Hunton & Co.; Nottingham, W. Dearden; Southwell, J. Whittingham (1858).

[4] This is clearly a reference to public libraries, but these were closed on Sundays, the only day when the working poor could use them.

precocious maturity between the ages of 14 and 20 – commencing just at that period when the forced constraint of school is taken off, and when the young are left to follow their own devices, and to choose their own companions and pursuits.' As a final argument for providing libraries for the rural poor Naylor returned to his initial theme: 'Knowledge disperses superstition, prejudice and pride', and 'despotism and oppression are best kept in check by a liberal diffusion of knowledge.'[1]

The full title of Naylor's *Continuous Education* summaries the breadth of his approach. In this book he developed his concept of 'self-culture'. He fully recognised that 'literary means alone are of small power to school the heart or to modify the character' but he argued that 'knowledge, without having the power to impart and fix a religious principle, is a most valuable auxiliary to the enlightened appreciation of religious truth', for

> It qualifies the mind by tracing out with distinctness the evidences of the doctrines that religion teaches, and it helps to give an insight into the mysteries of the Book of God, far more grand and illustrative than can be arrived at by those whose minds are uninformed about the matters of circumstance and figure, which form, as it were, the framework of the teaching that book contains.[2]

That last comment is arresting. It shows that Naylor was, at the very least, aware of what later came to be called the 'higher criticism' of the Bible which emphasised the importance of understanding the historical contexts (the 'circumstance') and the literary forms (the 'figure') of the biblical text. Naylor believed that the educated, critically aware mind of the poor man gave him an understanding of religion that mere instruction by rote learning could not. In the 1850s this was a radical and controversial position to hold.

Naylor was a farsighted rural incumbent and a pioneer of adult continuous education.[3] He formed a book club in Upton which became

---

[1]   Naylor, *Popular Libraries*, 2, 3, 5, 8, 15, 19.

[2]   *Continuous Education*, 6, 8.

[3]   See also Thomas Kelly, 'Continuous Education: a nineteenth-century pioneer', *Journal of Librarianship and Information Science*, i (1969), 62–7, and John C. Crawford, 'Advocacy for rural library provision in central and southern England in the late nineteenth century' in ibid., xvii (1985), 225–43. Crawford notes that the contribution of amateur advocates to rural library provision 'was marred by a lack of technical expertise and by over-enthusiastic propaganda. The professionals failed to develop a comprehensive theory of rural library provision and were indebted to the most able amateurs, F.W. Naylor and

a subscription library. This was open to all, with no fines, and with no restriction on the length of time that books could be borrowed. The Upton library was non-sectarian with the choice of books left to the secretary subject only to the right of members to protest against his selection. It was also very liberal in the types of books on its shelves. Naylor argued that many existing village libraries were unsuccessful because the books were quite unsuitable:

> They are often provided at the expense of the wealthy for the use of their poorer neighbours, and so, if used at all, are used only by the poor; they are frequently only sectarian expedients, established with a view of giving expression of a particular modification of the outward church; they are sometimes exclusively religious libraries, circulating books of only a decidedly religious character, and not admitting of the introduction of works relating to ordinary life, or that appeal to the imagination; and many are merely stores of old books, into which persons, who desire credit for liberality, are encouraged to pour the refuse of their shelves, without regard to their actual suitability or attractiveness.[1]

A well-resourced village library should, in Naylor's view, have

> histories, biographies, enterprises, the principles of social and political economy, moral philosophy, governments, themes relating to the use of opportunities, the formation of opinion, the responsibility of position in society, individual character, personal influence, mutual dependence, common sympathies, universal brotherhood, and the thousand matters of general interest which are comprehended under the designation of social subjects.

This was a proposal far distant from the belief that the poor should be taught only that which would enable them the better to serve their masters and who should never be exposed to material of a specious nature as this would foster expectations that would make them resentful and potentially rebellious. A generation earlier (and admittedly at a time of social unrest) Henry Robert Crewe, vicar of Breadsall in Derbyshire,

---

the Verneys.' Note also that Naylor took preparation for confirmation seriously, and in 1853 published two sermons on the subject.

[1] *Continuous Education*, 9–10.

had pleaded for a Christian education which taught a poor man only how to live and how to die, for to give a poor man 'general knowledge on worldly principles would be to bestow upon him no greater curse'. Crewe blamed those who made a god of education for creating the 'waste howling wilderness wherein infidelity, blasphemy and confusion and every evil work doth abound.'[1] Very many clergy at the time shared Crewe's fear. By the 1850s those turbulent days were over, but many of Naylor's contemporaries would have looked askance at his advocacy of making freely available to the poor the principles of social and political economy and of government, and particularly arguments about 'the responsibility of position in society', for this would encourage and develop a capacity to criticise the established social order and to hold those with 'social position' and 'official qualification' (as George Wilkins, Naylor's archdeacon, described them) to account.

A village library should contain books which appealed to children and young people – and Naylor recommended a number that could be included. It should also be a centre for 'discussion meetings' for the 'testing of ideas and principles by conference and comparison', a process 'in constant ... exercise in those grades of society that possess frequent opportunities of refined and intellectual intercourse' but denied to those who 'receive but a small proportion of moral, and less of literary advantage, from their ordinary communications with each other.'[2]

Naylor believed that the poor could best be helped by encouraging their continuous, life-time, learning. At least one local incumbent, the evangelical John Conington of Southwell Holy Trinity, also saw the need for adult education, though he did not share Naylor's breadth of vision. In January 1860 the *Nottingham Review* reported that 40 males attended 'the evening school' in the parish. As we have noted, John Dickinson Bell, curate of Mansfield, also established evening classes for 'operatives' in his parish in the 1850s.

Frederick Naylor's advocacy of village libraries, adult education, village cricket and cottage gardens was far more than a well-meaning attempt to provide an alternative to the public house and the bowling alley. The clergy who lacked Naylor's broader vision might have made available what the archbishop of Canterbury, Charles Thomas Longley, described in 1864 as 'wholesome and edifying literature where immoral and irreligious publications might otherwise find their way.'[3] The

---

[1]   H.R. Crewe, *Sermon in Dartmouth Chapel* (1832), 3, 10.

[2]   Naylor, *Continuous Education*, 30.

[3]   *Primary Charge* (1864). 12.

Church of England Book-hawking Association sold this material, published mainly by the Religious Tract Society, through its diocesan auxiliaries. In 1857 the bishop of Lincoln, John Jackson, urged his rural deans 'to take measures for establishing Book-Hawking in the County of Nottinghamshire' and the Southwell deanery chapter discussed this topic at its meetings on 3 March and 9 June.

But for S. Reynolds Hole, over a decade later, the poor had to be protected from greater dangers than immoral and irreligious publications.

Samuel Reynolds Hole:
'A poor man is Christ's stamp'

S. Reynolds Hole, was vicar of Caunton from 1850 to 1887 and, succeeding his father, was squire of Caunton from 1868.[1] In 1873 he published his sermon *The Cry of the Labourer against Landlord, Farmer and Priest* preached on James 5:4: 'Behold, the hire of the labourers who have reaped down your fields, which is of you kept back by fraud, crieth: and the cries of them which have reaped are entered into the ears of the Lord of sabaoth.' This sermon was an outspoken and sharply focused attack on those who oppressed farm labourers. Its background was the deep depression which struck British agriculture after the harvest of 1872 and the establishment by Joseph Arch in the same year of a national union for agricultural labourers. Hole could not have known how serious and long-lasting the depression was to be. Wheat prices fell to below 50s. a quarter in 1875, below 40s. after 1883, and below 30s. after 1893. Farm incomes fell by 40 per cent in this period. Inevitably this collapse hit farm labourers and their families and made worse their already very poor living and working conditions.

The long-term consequences of the depression were in the future when Hole published his sermon. His theological basis was straightforward enough: 'Man is God's image, but a poor man is Christ's stamp to boot, and if we turn away from the meanest of His servants, we turn away from the Master.'[2] This being so, the 'cries of them which have reaped' must be listened to, even though (and here he challenges Arch) 'we may condemn the arbitrary dictatorial tone in which demands are made ... '. Acting as their self-appointed spokesman Hole sets out complaints raised by labourers against landlords, farmers and clergy.

---

[1] See entry in *Oxford DNB*.

[2] *The Cry*, 7.

Against landlords Hole raises three grievances. first, the quality of labourers' cottages was very poor. 'In many instances', Hole said, 'the stables of the rich are far more carefully, commodiously, and expensively constructed than the habitations of the poor ... '. A cottage is often so small that 'if [the labourer] had wife and children, they are crowded like sheep together, with bad ventilation, feeble light, and probably bad drainage.' Second, labourers complained that landlords showed little or no interest in them. This, for Hole, was primarily a question of social class: 'The isolation, I might almost say the estrangement, of the different classes of society, is one of the saddest sorrows of our time'. In a shrewd observation Hole noted that there was little opportunity, or inclination, for the classes to meet: 'our enjoyments are class enjoyments ... we have so few set times and seasons of mutual rejoicing.'[1] Third, labourers complained that landlords gave 'no encouragement ... to industry, honesty and sobriety among the labourers, but that all are regarded with a like indifference, and, whatever their way of life has been, may end it in the workhouse.'[2]

Labourers' complaints about farmers, Hole reported, focused mainly on wages and hours of work, but behind these complaints lay 'an entire neglect and indifference as to the work which [the labourers] do' with too many farmers making 'the poor-rate, paid grudgingly and of necessity, an excuse for lack of real charity.'

But Hole kept his sharpest invective for the lack of concern for the poor labourer shown by his fellow clergy. The leaders of the county agricultural labourers' unions 'have reviled the clergy as refusing to take the poor man's part, and to help him in his hour of need.'[3] In particular, the labourers complain about the priest because 'he declines to take their side against the farmers in the matter of wages', though, 'with far more justice ... they have complained of a careless and neglectful treatment within and without the Church' and 'that the Church of England was more the rich man's than the poor man's Church.' Questions 'full of bitter truth' and directed by labourers against the church were these:

> Why should we work, daily and all day, and the parsons for two hours in the week? How comes the house, which they tell us is God's, to be bolted and barred for six days out of seven, and to be not only deserted, but defiled by dust, and damp, and decay? Why

[1]   Ibid., 13, 14.
[2]   Ibid., 15.
[3]   Ibid., 6.

should the shepherds live away from the sheep? Why are they not continually with the lambs, and with the lame, as we are? And why, when Sundays come, are services so feeble and so few? Why is there not more life, more reality, more love, more beauty of holiness, more hope, and heart, and faith, in the worship of Almighty God?[1]

Hole spoke more passionately about the neglect of the poor by the priest than he did of the neglect by landlord and farmer because he knew the shortcomings of the clergy better. The clergy he knew best were his neighbours in the Southwell rural deanery. Nationally, a few clergy stood even more resolutely with the labourers. On 29 May 1872, in Leamington, Joseph Arch convened a general congress of delegates from the county agricultural labourers' unions to establish the National Agricultural Labourers' Union. On the platform at that congress were four clergymen. They included James John Trebeck who was later to succeed J.M. Wilkins as rector of Southwell, and, in 1884, to become sub-dean of the new cathedral (to the titular dean, the bishop of Southwell, George Ridding) when the diocese of Southwell was created. Also on the platform was the magistrate and wealthy radical John Charles Cox, later to be ordained an Anglican clergyman (and to be a prolific historian, not least of the churches of Derbyshire and Nottinghamshire) who was a friend of Joseph Arch and a strong supporter of the new union. On one occasion he was summoned before magistrates because of his active support during a union demonstration.[2]

However, local clergy were, in the main, less concerned with poverty than with sin. They may well have believed, as did John Thomas Becher, that sin caused poverty – and the two most public sins were Sabbath-breaking and intemperance.

'The desecration of the Lord's Day'

On 12 February 1856, at its second meeting after the re-establishment of the rural deanery, the Southwell ruridecanal chapter, on the proposition of John Conington, the evangelical incumbent of Southwell Holy Trinity, agreed to petition parliament 'against the desecration of the Lord's Day'. Of the 14 clergy present 13 signed the petition. The exception was

[1]   Ibid., 21, 22.

[2]   Arch, *Story of His Life*, 109, 135, 235. For further evidence of Cox's radical opinions see *Oxford DNB*.

Frederick William Naylor, vicar of Upton. The minutes do not record the reason for his refusal, but it is not difficult to deduce what they were. Naylor was, the chapter minutes of its meeting on 16 December 1856 noted, the secretary 'of a Society extending its operations in a circuit of five miles round the Village of Upton and having for its object the Encouragement of Farm Servants and the better cultivation of Cottage Gardens.' A similar society had been established in Bingham, and Naylor urged that another be established in Southwell. He hoped that district societies would be established throughout Nottinghamshire. As farm labourers were employed for long hours six days a week they had no opportunity to tend their gardens other than on Sundays. This infringed Conington's strict sabbatarianism. To tend a garden on a Sunday would be 'desecration' – hence Frederick Naylor's refusal to sign the chapter's petition.

Throughout the period Sabbath-breaking, at least by the poor, was frequently condemned. For example, in April 1840 the *Nottingham Review* ran an article on 'Effects of Gypsying on the Sabbath':

> On Sunday Richard Palmer of Old Radford, with three other 'bottle' companions, who had been spending the night at a public house, adjourned to a field, near to Boot's lane, and under a bank which sheltered them from a keen north wind, made a fire; and having a plentiful supply of ale, enjoyed themselves (as they termed it) in the true gypsy style. At length, overcome with drink and want of sleep, this *temperate* lot fell asleep; some time had elapsed when one of the party was awaked by a strong smell of burning and he discovered that Palmer's clothes were on fire. The miserable man was still fast asleep, although dreadfully burned. He was conveyed to the infirmary, where upon examination it appeared that his left hip and the flesh on the spine for about twelve inches was almost calcined, particularly the hip.[1]

What engaged the *Review* was less the horror of the incident than the fact that it had been fuelled by alcohol and, to make it worse, had taken place on a Sunday. Men of all classes, or at least the middle and working classes, defended Sunday observance, though for different reasons. In April 1850 the *Nottingham Mercury* published the names and occupations of 1,200 men of Nottingham who had signed a petition against 'the desecration of the Lord's Day'. There existed, the *Mercury* noted

---

[1]   *Nottingham Review*, 3 April 1840.

THE CHURCH AND SOCIETY 183

a strong party, not only in our community but everywhere else, who are always labouring to instil into the public mind that the advocates of a due and sacred observance of the Lord's Day are a sickly, sentimental class of religionists, who, having no particular call upon their mental and moral energies at any time, either on the Sabbath day or working day, take up the advocacy of questions like this as a relief to the ennui of which they would otherwise be the inevitable victims.

On the contrary, the list showed that very many of the signatories were labourers and skilled manual workers – painters, builders, cork-cutters, saw-makers, joiners, cordwainers, plasterers, braziers, leather cutters, sinker-makers, plane-makers, and sackcloth weavers, as well as clerks, librarians, surgeons and clergy.[1]

For the *Mercury* thee men were no 'sickly, sentimental class of religionists' with nothing to do other than complain about the breaking of the Sabbath. Yet, despite this evidence that working men supported legislation enforcing Sunday observance, no doubt primarily as a protection against employers, throughout this period the arguments of the sabbatarians were rejected as at best hypocritical. Nearly forty years later, in March 1888, the *Nottinghamshire Weekly Express* ran an article by 'Verax' on 'The Sunday Question.' It is worth quoting at length. On Sundays, he wrote, the rich 'can manage to pull through the day somehow' with 'their comfortable seats to sit on, books to read, pictures to look at, good wine to drink, good music to hear. They have horses to ride or drive, pleasant gardens or grounds to stroll in; something with which to fight the demon of *ennui*.' It is the poor who are to be pitied, for

> On Sunday there is, as a rule, no place for a working man to go except to church or chapel, or the public house. If he have the good luck to live in a town which owns a free library, it is provided that on the Sabbath he shall be debarred access to the works of reference, to magazines, to newspapers. This, we understand, is done in the interests of religion and virtue. If he chance to live in a town in which there is a picture gallery, it is, as a rule, provided that on the Sabbath he shall have no opportunity afforded him of looking at the pictures which he, as a ratepayer, has helped to get together or to pay for. He may listen

---

[1] *Nottingham Mercury*, 12 April 1850.

to the dispiriting strains of a Salvation Army band, but that is all the music he is ever likely to hear out of doors. If the working man chooses to take a walk in the fields, accompanied by his faithful dog, it is true that he may exhilarate himself with some ratting on the sly. But the wisdom of the community takes very good care that he shall not improve his Sunday's leisure by consulting books he cannot afford to buy, or by looking at good pictures, the masterpieces of great artists. That would be a 'desecration of the Sabbath'. The rich can 'desecrate the Sabbath' to their hearts' content: there is no one to say them nay. They can go out driving in drags[1] on Sunday, can have dinner parties, can have all the pleasures of the senses – need not go to church or chapel. The poor man is told that it would be a 'desecration of the Sabbath' if he set foot inside the walls of a free library on a Sunday, and a sin not to be thought of without horror if he were given permission to look at his own pictures contained in a building put up partly at his own expense, on the Lord's Day. It seems to many persons, not naturally fools, that there is much hateful, contemptible hypocrisy in such a state of things. Why, for instance, should we do all we can on the Sunday to drive the working man, not to church or chapel – thousands on thousands will not go to either – but to the public-house? ... Why should we make Sunday a sort of fetish which all Englishmen must worship whether they like or no? ... Of course, we shall be told that the man who spends a summer Sunday with a terrier behind a ditch, driving rats into a sack, is not a man to whom the blessings of literature and art, of books and pictures, will appeal. That is very true; but that the rat-hunter does not care for books or pictures, or what intellectual and well-meaning persons may deem to be rational amusement and instruction, is that any reason why those who do *not* hunt rats on Sunday should be treated as if they were mere children whose wants and wishes were not worth a moment's consideration?[2]

Well before libraries, galleries and recreation grounds were established by local authorities, only to be closed on Sundays, it was clear to many that sabbatarian legislation restricted the poor but not the rich.

[1] A four-horsed private vehicle, similar to a stage-coach.

[2] *Nottinghamshire Weekly Express*, 16 March 1888.

The Temperance Question

So it was, too, with the 'Temperance Question' with which sabbath observance was often closely related. Teetotallers were usually assiduous Sabbath observers. Surprisingly, the first Southwell deanery chapter minute book, covering the years 1855 to 1870, does not record discussions about temperance, although the ruridecanal conference in April 1891 'strongly deprecate[d] ... the encouragement or assistance in any way of "Friendly Societies" of any kind that are not enrolled, and urges the importance of transacting their business and holding their anniversaries away from the public house.' In June 1887 the clergy of the rural deanery resolved 'to do their best to influence the farmers in their different Parishes to substitute money for Beer in the Harvest Field' and to distribute 'Harvest Temperance Literature' to promote the temperance message.[1] Nearly seventy years earlier, in 1823, in the preface to his *Rules and Regulations of Southwell Friendly Institution*, John Thomas Becher had asserted that 'Foresight, habitual Temperance and early Industry can never be too forcibly or too frequently impressed on the minds of the Labouring Classes. — DEATH is the punishment imposed upon wilful transgression. Let it however be remembered, that "the Sting of Death is Sin".'

The consumption of alcohol and the observance of Sunday were frequently linked in the local press. As two of several examples, in 1854 the *Nottinghamshire Advertiser* reported the sending of a petition to Parliament in favour of closing Newark public houses 'on the Sabbath day' signed by the vicar, mayor and more than 1,100 inhabitants of the town,[2] and in 1856 James Whitworth, licensed victualler of Eakring, was fined £1 and costs 'for keeping his house open during divine service on 31st ult.'[3] As with the Radford 'gypsying' incident in 1840, for many people intemperance on the Sabbath was doubly sinful. In 1859 a public meeting in the Exchange Hall in Nottingham considered 'the prevalence, causes, and remedies of intemperance, as it affects Sabbath schools.' There was 'a large attendance, the hall being filled.'[4] But many linked strict teetotalism with hard-heartedness: in 1855 the Nottingham *Stevenson's Penny Times*, in an article on 'Our Starving Poor', bitterly

[1] Southwell rural deanery chapter minute book, 30 June 1887 (SMHL 699).

[2] *Nottinghamshire Advertiser and Newark Monthly Railway Intelligence*, no. 88, April 1854.

[3] *Nottingham Review*, 12 Sept. 1856.

[4] *Nottingham Free Press*, 12 Nov. 1859.

criticised a London magistrate, Sir William Carden, 'citizen and teetotaller', for punishing begging by those who were 'literally starving.'[1] For Thomas Stevenson teetotalism and mercilessness were synonymous.

Together with their supposed indifference to Sabbath observance, the excessive drinking of the poor remained a major social question for the middle classes throughout the period. It surprised some observers that the poor could possibly support the temperance movement, least of all harddrinking navvies; so, for example, in January 1850 the *Nottingham Mercury* reported 'crowded audiences' in the town hall in East Retford to hear Jabez Inwards lecture on the virtues of teetotalism. 'It is worth recording to their praise', the *Mercury* said. 'that a considerable part of the expense attendant on the lecturer's visit has been contributed by the railway-labourers in the employ of Messrs Potts and Betts, in this vicinity.'[2]

The temperance movement had developed in response to the passing of the Beerhouse Act in 1830. This abolished the tax on beer and allowed licensed premises to be open for 18 hours a day. It also introduced a free market in the brewing and selling of beer. Any ratepayer, by paying a licence fee of two guineas, could brew beer and sell it from his own house. By 1833 there were 35,000 so-called 'Tom and Jerry' beershops in England and Wales. The figure rose to 46,000 in 1838, doubling the number of licensed premises and resulting in a rapid rise in beer consumption, drunkenness and disturbance. Whereas inns, taverns and alehouses were supervised by justices of the peace, the beerhouses were, until 1869, virtually unsupervised. Beerhouse beer was cheap and easily available in unregulated premises, and the poor took advantage of this.

Whether they themselves were teetotal or opted for a less rigorous temperance, most members of the church-going middle class believed that alcohol and the labourer should be kept apart. As we have noted, in 1832, soon after the passing of the Beerhouse Act, George Wilkins condemned the spread of beerhouses as 'this growing evil, THIS *souldestructive* plague, — THIS *pestilence,* — THIS *deadly curse*' and in 1855 the earl of Leicester condemning the giving of 'largess' to labourers as 'most injurious' and leading to 'the first introduction to the beershop.' In 1860 Henry Wilkins told the deanery clergy that he had tempted labourers away from the attraction of the beerhouse during the annual

---

[1] *Stevenson's Penny Times*, 1 Dec. 1855.

[2] *Nottingham Review*, 11 Jan. 1850.

statutes in Mansfield. Yet to condemn beershops was to condemn something that made life bearable for the common people. Francis Place, the social reformer, said in 1834 that the attraction of alcohol was that it was 'the sole means such men have of getting away from themselves, and the pleasure of drinking to excess is beyond all comparison greater to such men than to any other class of persons.'[1] In 1835 Frederick von Raumer noted that in England most working men drank because they 'have generally no means of excitement or amusement at command during the week.'[2] In a remarkable letter published in 1858 in the Nottingham newspaper *Stevenson's Weekly Times*, giving a detailed and balanced account of their economic and social condition, the 'Labourers of Nottingham' described how the underfed urban labourer, with his muscular strength decreased, his mental powers injured and his vivacity of spirit lost, 'seeks for something in the shape of stimulant to exhilarate him, and often leaves his home and family to drown the cares that oppress him in the public-house. His hard lot works upon his mind in such a manner as to produce a sort of hardened carelessness, which in some instances ripens into crime of the worst character.'[3] In the country parish, Joseph Arch wrote, 'the village lad had two kinds of recreation open to him, he could take his choice between lounging and boozing in the public house or playing bowls in the bowling alley. That was all.'[4] But arguments which stressed poverty as the cause and not the consequence of excessive drinking would not have appealed to the majority of the clergy in the Southwell rural deanery.

Popular culture

Although the clergy were well aware of the existence of popular culture, the way of life which was 'largely made by the people, their appetites, demands and aspirations',[5] it was one with which the clergy rarely had direct contact. They engaged with it only when it broke their sabbatarian

[1]   Quoted in B. Harrison, 'Two roads to social reform: Francis Place and the "Drunken Committee" of 1834', *Historical Journal*, xi (1968), 283.

[2]   Frederick von Raumer, *England in 1835: being a series of letters written to friends in German* (1836), ii. 122.

[3]   *Stevenson's Weekly Times*, 6 Feb. 1858.

[4]   Quoted in Brian Harrison, *Drink and the Victorians* (1971), 32; see also J.M. Golby and A.W. Purdue, *The Civilisation of the Crowd: popular culture in England 1750–1900* (1999), 117ff.

[5]   Golby and Purdue, *Popular Culture*, 7.

and temperance taboos, or when a desire to lift the poor out of it led them to promote village libraries and night schools or sell them tracts, or when 'turbulent assembles' during the statute weeks led them to offer wholesome alternatives to the beershops, or when its excesses led them, as magistrates, to pass judgment on it from the bench. Other than on these occasions the clergy of the Southwell rural deanery had nothing to say about the way that the common people lived their lives.

What we know of popular culture shows an ethos and style of living alien to the clergy. Early in this period the combat sports in which poor men were involved, brutal bare-knuckle fighting and cudgelling, were sports that attracted 'gentlemen' who wagered large sums on their outcome and could hardly be said to be enjoyed by the men who were paid to provide the spectacle. The beer-house drinking which was the principal escape from the drudgery of life for many working men met only with condemnation. Pastimes like ratting and dog-fighting were beyond the experience or comprehension of the comfortable classes.

Locally, we can only catch glimpses of working-class culture. In July 1856 the *Nottingham Review* reported on the annual feast at Morton near Gainsborough which extended over two days. It commented: 'A fact deserves to be recorded: On nearly all former occasions, the feast time was selected for the settlement of all grievances by resort to fisticuffs; but on this occasion, with one or two slight exceptions, this barbarous and savage custom was abandoned; and, with these exceptions, everything passed off in a manner highly creditable and satisfactory.'[1] What took place on these 'former occasions' suggests a culture virtually outside the law and certainly outside middle-class social norms. A few years earlier S. Reynolds Hole, vicar of Caunton, officiated at a gypsy wedding in his parish. The *Nottingham Mercury and Midland Advertiser* described the subsequent celebrations in some detail. The travellers were allowed to camp by permission of George Radford, a Winkburn farmer, in his Home Close. The wedding was of Samuel Holmes, son of Gipsy Holmes, 'of horse dealing notoriety', and Lucy Lacy of Walesby. 'Holmes provided an 18-gallon barrel of ale and a liberal supply of gin for his friends.' John Rickett, publican of Winkburn, attended 'and sold a great quantity of ale during the day. A fiddler being in attendance, dancing was the order of the day, which was kept up with great spirit in the open air until completely dark when the company returned to their respective homes, highly delighted with their day's recreation at a gipsy

---

[1]   25 July 1856.

wedding.'[1]

The contrast between the culture illustrated here and that represented by the Church of England, its parish churches, with their rented and few free seats and their forms of worship, could hardly be sharper. In the 1850s the majority of the clergy of the rural parishes of central Nottinghamshire were more concerned to maintain the church's distinctiveness and to protect its traditions than to make the church's worship more accessible to the poor. In his 1859 visitation charge George Wilkins, in opposing the destructive influence of the 'popular opinion' of 'the aristocracy of numbers' urged resistance to 'agitation in favour of alterations in our Book of Common Prayer', and 'restless commotion among some' to produce an amended version of the Bible

> which, if conceded, would hazard the peace of our Israel; for the voice of popular opinion would foment disagreement rather than concord in such an enterprise. [The Bible] would become like a picture that pleased everyone provided each might rub out what he judged to be an imperfection, and therefore become unsatisfactory to all.

In resisting changes to the liturgy, Wilkins chimed with local opinion. At its meeting on 28 February 1858 the Southwell rural deanery chapter drafted a petition 'to the Lords Spiritual and Temporal through the hands of the Lord Bishop of the Diocese praying them to resist any attempt to alter the Liturgy of the Church of England.' John William Marsh, vicar of Bleasby, and Frederick William Naylor, vicar of Upton, did not sign the petition. Naylor, for one, with his declared concern for the material well-being and further education of field labourers, may well have believed that the church's public worship should be made much more accessible to them. By the 1860s 'it was almost an axiom that only a more elaborate service fitted the needs of the urban poor,'[2] though it became clear by the 1880s and 1890s that if the urban poor were attracted to the Church of England's services it was due far less to an elaborate and colourful ritual than to the sacrificial lives of the priests who performed it.

But if the town labourer was attracted by light and colour in worship why not the field labourer also? Naylor and Marsh were not ritualists. They were undoubtedly concerned to make the church's services more

---

[1]   16 April 1852.

[2]   Chadwick, *Victorian Church*, ii (1972), 313.

attractive and accessible to the poor. For all his resistance to any change driven by popular 'agitation' George Wilkins, when he remarked in 1836 that the majority of the inhabitants of Southwell were 'averse to *choral* services', recognised that many people were not attracted to the church's services. John Murray Wilkins, too, appealed for more 'natural' services. In 1870 the recently enthroned bishop of Lincoln, Christopher Words-worth,[1] asked his rural deans to discuss with their chapters not only how the public services of the church could be made 'more interesting and attractive to our people', but also the ways 'for maintaining and advancing the study of Holy Scripture', how to achieve 'the proper management of the Parish Choir', 'greater uniformity in our musical services', and generally how 'to awaken in our people a more lively sense of their religious responsibilities.'[2] But who were 'our people'? Evidently Wordsworth was concerned to make the church's services more readily accessible, yet, though he strongly opposed the Public Worship Regulation Act of 1874, he opposed the new lectionary of 1871 and denounced the *Revised Version* of the New Testament when it was published in 1881. When, in 1870, the proposal was made to revise the King James version of 1611 in the light of advances in scholarship Wordsworth warned Convocation to 'beware lest by altering the text of the authorised version of the Bible, you shake the faith of many', and above all of the poor.[3] Perhaps Wordsworth, nephew of the poet, was aware that the poor were moved more by the beauty of the language of the 1611 version of the Bible and less by its notional meaning.

Reformist clergy in the diocese of Lincoln might have regarded their bishop's position as somewhat ambivalent but the law was against them. For most clergy the *Book of Common Prayer* possessed virtually the authority and status of the Bible, and the law reinforced this belief. The Prayer Book (Table of Lessons) Act of 1871 merely achieved what its title indicates, and, in 1872, although the Act of Uniformity Amendment Act of 1872 made provision for services not in the *Book of Common Prayer* it did so only where they consisted of readings from the Bible and the prayer book and of anthems or hymns. This, together with permission to use shortened forms of morning and evening services, were hardly the changes that forward-thinking clergy sought. But a church for the people from which the poor felt excluded, and not least, as we will

---

[1]   1807–85, bishop of Lincoln 1869–85.

[2]   Southwell rural deanery chapter minute book, 15 March 1870 (SMHL 699).

[3]   *Chronicle of the Convocation of Canterbury* (1870), 222, quoted in Chadwick, *Victorian Church*, ii. 44.

see in chapter 9, the miserable physical condition of many of its churches, would hardly have attracted them however accessible its forms of worship. The culture of the church was alien to the culture of the majority of the people. But did not the two cultures meet in the church school?

'Not sufficient means': educating the children of the poor

The nineteenth-century Church of England might take much credit for serving the social emancipation of poor labourers by educating their children. It would be unwarranted because emancipation was far from its purpose. The purpose of teaching the children of the poor to read, write and cast accounts was to equip them the better to serve their masters, but socially necessary knowledge easily elided into specious and politically dangerous knowledge. Working-class leaders were to say that in teaching them to read the Bible the church equipped them to read the radical tracts.

In the first of a series of reports beginning in 1819 the select committee of the House of Commons on the education of the poor (set up on Henry Brougham's initiative) received national data on the number of children attending school. In that year it was reported that only about 7 per cent of the total population of England and Wales were attending day schools – and this without reference to the actual length of attendance, which might be measured in months or even only in weeks. The evidence for Nottinghamshire is revealing. Other than through government grants made available from 1833 to the Church of England's National Society and the dissenters' British and Foreign Schools Society[1] (and only to those of their schools that qualified, after inspection, for state aid) the education of the poor was funded by charitable endowment, donation, and, when it could be afforded, children's pence. As with all parochial charity its provision and quality, if it existed at all, was entirely a matter of chance. Only if historic endowments provided a free school, or local landowners and clergy actively supported it, were the children of the poor offered free education. In the 1819, of the 211 parishes in Nottinghamshire (including 'consolidated' parishes and chapelries), 136, or almost two thirds, lacked endowed, free, schools for

---

[1]   The National Society for Promoting the Education of the Poor in the Principles of the Established Church and the British and Foreign Schools Society received, between them, a first grant of £20,000.

the children of the poor. Thirty-nine parishes, or 18 per cent, had no educational provision at all, free or by payment – not even a Sunday school. In several parishes the poor taught their children themselves, but only for payment: in Averham, the rector, Robert Chaplin, reported that 'a poor woman teaches about 18 children, and those who have not the means of sending them are assisted by their friends', and in Bleasby, the vicar, Henry Houson, noted that three small schools were 'taught by labourers wives, containing upon an average of 8 children in each', but, Houson added, 'one of the teachers of the above schools is a Calvinist.' Of other unendowed schools in the county many were dame schools where children would have been educated by women often barely more literate than the children they taught.

Of the 37 parishes in the patronage of the Southwell chapter collectively or of individual prebendaries, ten had endowed schools, 22 had unendowed schools, and 12 (32 per cent) had no educational provision at all. Many of these parishes were very small. Of Hawerby in Lincolnshire, in the gift of the chapter, Richard Powley noted that, with a population of only 56 people, 'there are very few children in this parish.' Yet in the chapter benefice of Ravensdale, with a population of 54, there was a Sunday school attended by eleven children, 'supported by a small gratuity from the minister', John Parkinson. At Kneesall (population 367) 70 children were taught in a Sunday school the master of which 'is paid 2s. 6d. per Sunday by the parish.' This compensated for the poor state of an unendowed day school which 30 or 40 children had once attended 'but from the bad conduct of the master it has decreased to 10 or 12.'

In many parishes the incumbents or curates signing the returns noted that, for example, 'the poorer classes are desirous of possessing more sufficient means of education' (Bleasby) or 'the poorer classes have often lamented the want of a school for the education of their children (Barnby in the Willows). In Kirklington (population 237) the curate, Thomas Wilson Morley, reported that the parish had no endowed school but that there was 'one school, to which the principal farmers send their children, but the poor are debarred from the benefit, on account of expense … The poor cannot afford to educate their children, and are desirous of possessing the means'. There were no schools in Upton (population 325), though the curate, William Bristoe, noted that 'the poorer classes have not sufficient means of educating their children, nor do they seem desirous of it, as a school was begun a few years ago, chiefly supported by subscription, but the master not finding it worth his attendance, soon resigned.' In other places the clergy decided for themselves whether there was adequate educational provision for the poor. In the unsigned return for Edingley, a parish of 286, the endowed school attended by 20 or 30 children was deemed sufficient as 'the poorer classes have the means of educating their children', while at Farnsfield (population 637) William Barrow noted that in his parish an endowed school offered free education to 12 children ('besides others who pay') and a Sunday school attended by 70, yet 'the poor are indifferent to the improvement of their children'.

The Nottinghamshire data in the 1819 report deserves closer analysis that there is space for here, but the strong impression it gives is that education for the poor was piecemeal, that the overwhelming majority of children received no education at all, and that those who did receive it were often taught by teachers whose level of education was barely above that of their pupils. In that year in the 21 parishes in the Southwell rural deanery that was to exist in 1855, eleven had some form of day school, and ten had Sunday schools. In these parishes some 730 children attended day schools (345 in Southwell alone) and 820 might be found in Sunday schools, though comparatively few of these were free places in schools maintained by endowment or donation.

A generation later the provision of education for the poor in most parishes in the then rural deanery of Southwell had improved only marginally. When John Murray Wilkins conducted his visitation in 1855 he found that in the 21 comparable parishes 19 possessed Sunday schools and 13 had day schools. Some 1,077 children attended the former and 766 the latter, although day-school children were usually required to attend on Sundays also. Boys and girls were taught in each school, in most cases (where figures are available) in approximately equal numbers. On Sundays, attendances varied between the 'very few' in Farnsfield to 156 (84 boys and 72 girls) in Calverton, and, in the day schools, between 150 (80 boys and 70 girls) in Southwell National school to 'not half a score' in the school in Farnsfield (population in 1851: 1,149).

Educational provision in Farnsfield was particularly dire when Wilkins visited on 11 May 1855. He found that the parish had a school well endowed with 'a good House, garden, orchard and homestead' and with 'two acres of valuable land bringing in £10 pr. annum.' The school was further supported by a Mr Houldsworth (probably the elderly William Houldsworth who lived on the road to Blidworth) who subscribed £14 a year. It seems that no boys attended either the Sunday or the day school. Wilkins noted that although the master of this school was 'totally unfit for his office', the newly appointed trustees refused to dismiss him and that the vicar, Henry Robert Wilkins (a cousin of John Murray Wilkins), 'not being put into the Trust Deed, is powerless.' As a result 'the children that were at the School have been taken away & sent to the

Dissenting School'. Perhaps owing to the rural dean's visit the trustees dismissed the schoolmaster and within a year new schools had been built. Provision in nearby Blidworth was altogether better. In that parish 'good and large' school buildings costing £1600 had been erected 'through the exertions of the late Curate, Rev. M. Roe'.[1] This school, unlike most schools in the rural deanery, was under government inspection and grant-aided. Its two teachers, though uncertificated, were 'good'. In Calverton the vicar, Samuel Oliver, 'disliking the conditions', had refused government grants for the large school in his parish. The two schools in Norwell were described by Wilkins as 'not very good' and were taught by 'inefficient' teachers. The school at Upton was in an unsatisfactory condition, and its two teachers were 'old & inefficient'. This is surprisingly given Frederick William Naylor's conviction that education was 'for the whole of life' and his pioneering development of substantial and well resourced adult education in his parish.

John Murray Wilkins had a genuine interest in primary education, and his observations carry some weight. In the 1850s, other than the few schools in the rural deanery that may have qualified for government aid, most were financed (and that barely) by local landowners, public subscription, collections in church following an annual sermon, and the pennies that poor parents paid each week. The condition of school premises inevitably varied widely. In Maplebeck and South Muskham there were no day schools and, as they had been for generations, the Sunday school children were taught in church. In Morton a school had been 'lately' built by subscription at a cost of £40. New schools had been erected at substantial cost in both Blidworth and the new parish of Southwell Holy Trinity. Educational provision was therefore still very piecemeal, and depended almost entirely on the presence or absence of charity and local leadership. It was to remain so for many years to come.

'Caution to the Benevolent': the dispensing of charity

As with the provision of education the relief of poverty by local charitable donation was never to match the need. Beneficent landowners and the charitably disposed well-to-do made contributions as they always had, and the church was frequently, but by no means exclusively, to the fore. There are many examples. Taking a few as representative of others:

---

[1]   Martin Roe was curate of Blidworth from 1842 to his death in 1849. In 1851 Sarah Roe (34) 'widow of a Clergyman' was still living in Blidworth with her daughter Harriet Martha (2) and a servant. Martin Roe had married Sarah Potts at Blidworth on 5 June 1845.

in 1811 in Warsop parish church the Revd Samuel Martin appealed for the fund for the relief of British prisoners of war in France. He raised £7 15s. 9d.[1] At Kegworth in 1827 'at his last rent-day, the Rev. Dr. Parkinson ... made a reduction of 20 per cent to his poorer tenants, and has since been letting them have hay at one half the price at which it is now selling in the neighbourhood.'[2] In January 1852 in Southwell William Leacroft[3] 'contributed to the wants of his poorer neighbours by giving to each poor family residing in Burgage two cwt of coals, the number of families being nearly fifty',[4] and in the same month in Calverton 'according to annual custom, Lady Sherbrooke is causing to be given a quantity of coal to each poor family in this parish.'[5]

In urban areas, while appeals were made to relieve need, particularly in periods of severe hardship, to show concern for the poor could be viewed either as politically charged, or at least as encouraging lack of thrift by the poor. In a 'Caution to the Benevolent' in the *Nottingham Journal* for 24 April 1846 it was reported that twist-hands in the depressed Nottingham lace industry had received support from Joshua William Brooks, vicar of St Mary's. Brooks promptly denied this, but when he had been vicar of Clarborough in 1830 he had played a leading part in relieving widespread distress in and around Retford. This is an interesting case-study. A committee of well-to-do Retford inhabitants surveyed the area and noted that in the town and adjoining hamlets there were 348 families containing 1,413 individuals 'whose means of existence were exceedingly precarious' and who were in urgent need of relief. On its establishment the committee (which was chaired by the 'Senior Bailiff') had been addressed by Brooks. The area had been divided into seven districts and relief made available proportionate to need. By February £163 had been raised and disbursed in coal and food and other necessities.[6] By the end of February 1830 the Retford Relief

[1] *Nottingham Review*, 26 April 1811.

[2] *Nottingham and Newark Mercury*, 24 March 1827.

[3] In 1841 Leacroft, of independent means, lived in the Burgage in Southwell as a near neighbour of John Thomas Becher. He had served as a poor law guardian for Southwell.

[4] *Nottingham Review*, 9 Jan. 1852.

[5] Ibid., 23 Jan. 1852.

[6] *Nottingham and Newark Mercury*, 20 Feb. 1830. J.W. Brooks succeeded George Wilkins as vicar of Nottingham St Mary. Ordained deacon 1820, curate of East Retford 1821–7, domestic chaplain to Viscount Galway; vicar of Clarborough 1827–43; rector of Grove 1837–43; domestic chaplain to William Vesey-FitzGerald, 2nd Baron FitzGerald and Vesey c. 1840; vicar of Nottingham St Mary 1843–64; prebendary of Lincoln 1858–82; rector of Great Ponton, Lincolnshire 1864–82. Brooks was a leader of a movement which reasserted the premillennial coming again of Jesus Christ. From 1831 to 1836 he edited *The*

Committee had distributed the equivalent of £200, and 1,500 inhabitants were being relieved weekly. Food was gratis, but coal was no longer distributed 'in consequence of the breaking up of the frost'.[1]

It was a widely held (and conveniently morally justifying) belief that offering indiscriminate charity to the poor would encourage their improvidence. This was certainly the view of John Thomas Becher. Early in February 1830 a public meeting in Nottingham, chaired by the mayor, the evangelical Octavius Thomas Oldknow, was called 'to take into consideration the propriety or impropriety of raising a subscription for the relief of the poor in this inclement season'. A prominent Independent minister, Richard Alliott[2] asked 'whether there was anything at the present moment of an extraordinary nature in the state and condition of the poor'. He argued that the meeting should 'bear in mind not only the wants of the poor, but the condition of those likely to be called upon to contribute relief'. This contribution, he said, 'was a species of extraordinary taxation [which] laid its burthen principally upon persons of a middling class.' He held that

> an extraordinary subscription, unless there was extraordinary distress, might be productive of evil … for the poor would rely upon it, and it would operate to a considerable degree like the poor laws, which encourage persons to marry, knowing that they can have recourse to the parish when all other resources fail.

Alliott, somewhat grudgingly, eventually supported the proposal. C. N. Wright noted that distress was felt principally among those not receiving parish relief, which, a Mr Callow[3] pointed out, were pit workers, canal workers and stocking-makers. A Mr Herbert[4] said that distress was acute, with families without employment, clothing, bedding, furniture or

---

Investigator, a publication devoted to proclaiming the imminent second coming. In its last volume Brooks listed over 2,100 books on prophetic topics together with some 500 biblical commentaries in *A Dictionary of Writers on the Prophecies*. He also published *Abdiel's Essays on the Advent and Kingdom of Christ* (1834) and *Elements of Prophetical Interpretation* (1836).

[1]   The 1831 census return for East Retford (compiled by the local overseers of the poor) was 2,491 in 546 houses (*Nottingham and Newark Mercury*, 18 June 1831). If West Retford (as part of the town) is included (593) this gives 3,084. An estimate for the unnamed adjoining hamlets might raise the total to a maximum of 3,200. The 1,413 'exceedingly precarious' poor would thus constitute 44 per cent of the population.

[2]   Richard Alliott (1769–1840), minister of Castle Gate chapel from 1794.

[3]   Possibly of Callow & Leavers, framesmiths and twist-machine makers.

[4]   Possibly Thomas Herbert, a benevolent lace manufacturer.

food. He said that 'if any gentleman present would accompany him into Narrow Marsh, Millstone-lane and some other places he would show them what they had never seen before with their eyes'. By the end of February, the committee had raised over £1,720.[1] Alliott's misgivings would have been shared by many Anglican clergy and were representative of those who believed that they were supporting the poor more than adequately through the poor rate.

Yet when faced with distress some clergy appealed for aid. In November 1865 Samuel Rogers, in the unlikely setting of North Muskham parish church, appealed on behalf of distressed workers in the cotton manufacturing districts, hard hit by the loss of trade caused by the curtailing of cotton imports from the Confederacy states during the American civil war. It was a very successful appeal: £14 was collected for the Lord Mayor of London's relief fund. Rogers had been successively curate of Nottingham St James, Bulwell and Sutton on Trent. Other clergy contributed as need arose. In 1832 the poor of West Bridgford 'return their best thanks to the Rev. R. Pocklington, rector, for his liberal donation of blankets, flannel and other clothing.'[2] He, as his bishop, John Kaye, was to say two years later, may well have acknowledged that serving 'the temporal wants of his parishioners' was an obligation of his beneficed status. For Kaye a minimum benefice income of £500 a year was necessary to meet this obligation. Pockington's gross income at West Bridgford was £600.[3] Similarly, it was reported in 1832 that the Revd Thomas Beever[4] had given to the poor in Barnby in the Willows 'his usual handsome present of counterpanes, blankets, cloaks, shoes etc'.[5] The parish was a chapter benefice, and Beevor was the curate of the non-resident incumbent James Foottit, who paid him £50 a year. There was no parsonage house.[6] Two years earlier, across the border in Derbyshire, the Revd John Hancock Hall of Risley 'in compassion for the wants of the numerous poor in Breaston had directed a large quantity

[1] *Nottingham and Newark Mercury*, 6 and 27 Feb. 1830.

[2] *Nottingham and Newark Mercury*, 17 March 1832. Roger Pockington became rector of West Bridgford in 1831.

[3] *Ecclesiastical Duties and Revenues Commission Report* (1835).

[4] Thomas Beevor (1786–1868), Queens' College, Cambridge, MA 1812, BD 1821, Fellow 1810–65; d. 1810, p. 1811, curate of Claypole, Lincs, 1814–20, curate of Barnby in the Willows, 1814–37. Beevor, the son of John Beevor (rector of Claypole 1779–1820), was born in Claypole. By 1851 he was living in Wilson Street in Newark with his sister and three servants. In the census he styled himself 'Clergyman, B.D. (without Cure of Souls)'.

[5] *Nottingham and Newark Mercury*, 6 Jan. 1832.

[6] *Ecclesiastical Duties and Revenues Commission Report* (1835).

of soup to be made, which is doled out twice a week to those who apply for it [at] a half-penny a quart.'[1]

There are many similar examples, though appeals for aid frequently fell on deaf ears. A correspondent to the *Nottingham Review* in March 1814 lamented that a meeting called a few weeks previously to raise funds for the relief of the poor in Nottingham had produced very little: 'Thousands will be collected to send to the distressed of a distant country, while a few hundreds cannot be raised for the needy poor at home, many of whom [are] pining through want, occasioned by the severity of winter's piercing blast.' He had a point: a week later the *Review* noted that a subscription list for the 'Relief of Suffering Germans' already stood at over £800[2] although, two years later, the *Review* was to note the apathy of the 'British Church Establishment' to the suffering of French Protestants.[3] By the 1820s the economic causes of distress were more widely acknowledged, though the churches were less in the forefront of relief than were other agencies. For example, in February 1826, Nottingham's theatres raised money in aid of a fund for the Relief of Distressed Tradesmen, who, 'through the great depression of Trade, have been reduced to Want and Poverty'. By mid March the fund had reached £2,000.[4]

While their own poor might not elicit relief and have their needs ignored because to meet them might be 'productive of evil', parishes readily contributed to the 'relief and benefit' of the families of men killed at Waterloo. In October 1815 the *Review* listed 21 parishes in and around Nottingham that had donated via their clergy, Basford giving a total of £32 7s. 6d. and West Bridgford £20 5s. 0d. By 6 October £1,562 had been collected.[5] Similarly, those who suffered at home through no perceived fault of their own could expect some support. In 1831 a committee set up to relieve those affected by a thunderstorm in Mansfield received a number of donations from church and chapel, the congregation of the parish church giving £13 9s. 3d., the Unitarian chapel £4 0s. 6d., the Primitive Methodist chapel £1 1s., and the Quakers £1. About 13 poor people received between 5s. and 12s. each.[6] Of course, churchmen were only a few of many who contributed to charities

---

[1] *Nottingham and Newark Mercury*, 20 Feb. 1830.

[2] Letter from 'A True Born Englishman', *Nottingham Review*, 11 and 18 March 1814.

[3] Ibid., 16 Jan. 1816.

[4] Ibid., 3 Feb. 1826, 17 March 1826.

[5] Ibid., 15 Sept., 6 Oct. 1815.

[6] *Nottingham and Newark Mercury*, 1 Oct. 1831.

for the poor. In 1830, over 3,500 penny loaves were distributed in Newark 'to such of the inhabitants who choose to accept them' under the will of Hercules Clay.[1]

Of wider concern than immediate and local economic distress was the great evangelical *cause célèbre*, the abolition of slavery. A meeting of the Nottingham Anti-Slavery Society was held in December 1832. It was chaired by the mayor, the Congregationalist minister Joseph Gilbert.[2] Gilbert was reported as saying that 'it was plain [that] the planters had no ideas of conferring liberty upon the slaves, but perverted the ways and word of God to their own designs, and he could only think of slavery as the very excrement of hell.' The evangelical Anglican Philip Gell (vicar of Derby St John) 'spoke of the blessings of liberty' illustrated by Paul's address before Festus.[3] At its conference in May 1830 the Society for the Mitigation and Gradual Abolition of Slavery voted to drop the words 'Gradual Abolition' from its title. In the same month anti-slavery petitions were presented to Parliament by twelve parishes in and around Nottingham, women being the majority of the signatories.[4] In October petitions were sent from the parishes of Pinxton and South Normanton in Derbyshire. In November women in Derby signed a petition to the Queen supporting the abolition of slavery.[5]

In the early 1830s, a period in Nottinghamshire of depression of trade, low wages, high unemployment, high food and coal prices, and social unrest, there was, despite the caveats we have noted, no lack of goodwill by the liberally minded, well-to-do for the distressed poor. What were not addressed critically and theologically by the Church of England were the political and economic causes of widespread distress, yet the Bible, which was called in support of the abolition of slavery, could more pertinently have been cited to justify radical political action to address the sources of poverty. Other than by a few prophetic and courageous voices, it rarely was throughout the period covered by this study.

[1]   Ibid., 13 March 1830.

[2]   Gilbert was minister of Friargate Independent chapel 1826–52.

[3]   *Nottingham and Newark Mercury*, 8 Dec. 1832.

[4]   Ibid., 11 May 1833. The women's petition from Nottingham attracted 15,000 signatures, the men's 5,300.

[5]   Ibid., 30 Oct. 1830, 27 Nov. 1830.

The wider social and critical debate

Generally, most clergy in the rural deanery of Southwell were less concerned for the welfare of the poor than with other, professional, interests: revisions of the liturgy, the abolition of church rates (at its meeting on 29 December 1859 members were unanimously in favour of maintaining rates and petitioned Parliament accordingly), the much debated issue of marriage with a deceased wife's sister, church schools, the diminution in the number of marriages solemnised in church, the subdivision of the diocese (at its meeting on 16 March 1869 the chapter discussed a letter from the bishop, Christopher Wordsworth, who noted that should he wish to spend a Sunday in every church in the diocese it would take him 15 years 'to make the circuit'), as well as 'how the services of the church be rendered more interesting and attractive to our people'. Very occasionally the rural deanery clergy discussed international affairs. No sooner had the Government of India Act been passed in 1858[1] than the chapter discussed the religious significance of British rule. At its meeting on 14 September 1858 John Fuller Humfrys Mills, rector of Hockerton, presented for consideration a draft petition to the House of Lords praying

> That Government aid in support of Mission schools be continued.
> That in Government schools the Holy Scriptures be admitted.
> That neither Caste nor Creed be an obstacle to Government appointments.
> That Government grants in support of Hindoo Worship and Ceremonies be discontinued.

John Murray Wilkins, the rural dean, read what the chapter minute book describes as 'a very interesting statement bearing upon the several points which, at his request, had been prepared by his Brother Dashwood Wilkins Esq., who, from a long residence in India, was enabled to throw considerable light on the subjects under consideration, and to clear away several misconceptions which have arisen concerning them.'[2] After

---

[1] 21 and 22 Vict. c. 106. Following the first war of Indian independence (the Indian Mutiny), this Act formally transferred the government of India from the East India Company to the British government (initiating the period of the British Raj, 1858–1947).

[2] George Dashwood Wilkins (1813–85) served with the East India Company. At the time of the 1851 census he was staying with his parents at the Residence in Southwell, and gave as his occupation 'Govt. Service Bengal (on leave)'. He was then 37. He was baptised 28 Sept. 1813 at Hadleigh, Suffolk. In the 1881 census he was living in Cheltenham, aged 67, with his wife Emma Maria (59) who had been born in 'East India', as had two of their

'much deliberation' the chapter agreed to postpone further discussion until its next meeting. This took place on 14 December when, apparently without amendment, the petition was sent. Although the chapter agreed on the apparently liberal stance that 'neither Caste nor Creed' should be an obstacle to government appointments, the clergy, together with the majority of British middle- and upper-class opinion, clearly wished India to remain a bastion of western, and specifically English, Christian values, as the antithesis of the last two of the chapter's 'prayers' indicates. The religions and cultures of the sub-continent were to be ignored. As Llewellyn Woodward put it, 'the weight of opinion inclined to Macaulay's cocksure judgement that "a single shelf of a good European library was worth the whole native literature of India and Arabia." '[1]

Other international events engaged the clergy. The end of the Crimean war excited interest locally as it did elsewhere. At Caunton, S. Reynolds Hole preached 'a very appropriate sermon' on the restoration of peace and raised a collection of £5 'for the erection of a church in Constantinople', while in the collegiate church in Southwell George Wilkins preached 'an excellent sermon' on the same subject. The congregation raised a collection of £15 10s. for the erection of the same 'memorial church'. At Holy Trinity the evangelical John Conington preached no more than 'an appropriate sermon'. His congregation contributed a collection amounting to £11 11s., not for the 'memorial church' but for the Turkish Missions Aid Society. Reporting these sermons, the *Nottingham Review* noted that 'the whole of the services were well and respectably attended.' Again, the need to assert English Christian values is very evident.

What is missing from the deanery chapter minute book is evidence of any sustained engagement with the pressing intellectual challenges to orthodox faith. The clergy would have known of the large number of widely advertised and reported public lectures for and against Christian belief and practice. In January 1860 the *Nottingham Review* carried an account of a lecture delivered by the Revd T. Cartwright[2] in the Mechanics' Hall in Nottingham on 'British Heathenism'. Cartwright maintained 'with painful vividness; that heathenism was responsible for the social disorders and moral pollution of the country, the Sabbath-breaking, the drunkenness, the prostitution, and the other crimes which

---

grandchildren, Kathleen Maria (9) and Cecil Bird (6).

[1]   Llewellyn Woodward, *The Age of Reform 1815–1870* (Oxford, 1962), 407.

[2]   Probably Thomas Cartwright, a Methodist New Connexion minister, who published *The Age of the Church, or the Church called to Action* (1852) and *England's Shame and England's Hope: an Essay on the Social and Moral Condition of the People* (1862).

disgrace us as a nation and a Christian people'.[1] Much less likely to
have been attended by Anglican clergy was another meeting two months
later addressed by a Baptist minister, J. Martin, though the topic was
congenial. Martin lectured in Nottingham YMCA on 'The Biblical
History not a Myth'. He drew, it was reported, on recent archaeological
evidence, and may well have been engaging with the radical agenda of
the Tübingen school. Mary Ann Evans (George Eliot) published her
English translation of the fourth edition of David Friedrich Strauss's
revolutionary *Life of Jesus* in 1860. Martin was the minister of the
Particular Baptist chapel in Derby Road, Nottingham. He also spoke at
a meeting of the anti-church rate society, the Society for the Liberation
of Religion from State Control, held in Friar Lane Independent Chapel
in the same month.[2] The clergy would also have been well aware of
three lectures delivered in May 1860 in the Assembly Rooms in
Nottingham by 'an iconoclast ... [an] individual well known as an infidel
of the ultramontane kind', denouncing 'What the Bible has done for
England's sons and daughters'. The lectures were very well attended and
fully reported. The 'iconoclast' was Charles Bradlaugh.[3]

This wider critical debate seems to have been ignored by the deanery
chapter, although F.W. Naylor would have been sympathetic to the line
adopted by J.A. Baynes in a lecture in Nottingham Mechanics' Institute
on 15 January 1850 on 'The Study of History'. Baynes argued that the
mere knowledge of historical facts does not equip us to understand their
significance. Rather, the *Nottingham Journal* reported, 'the necessity of
a higher harmonizing principle was asserted, that the signification of
historical teaching may be attained. This is to be sought, chiefly, by the
wise use of the imagination, as the power of insight working beyond the
fact to its spirit and meaning.'[4] That approach keyed with Naylor's
contention that, in approaching the text of the Bible, the reader must be
conscious of the 'circumstance', the historical context of the writer, and
the 'figure', the literary forms employed by him. Naylor would also have
noted in 1855 that John Garrett Bussell, vicar of Newark St Mary
Magadalene, had given the first of a series of lectures on 'The Figurative
Language of Scripture.'[5] He would also have been sympathetic to the
theme of a letter published in the *Nottingham Journal* for 22 March

[1] *Nottingham Review*, 20 Jan. 1860.
[2] Ibid., 3 and 23 March 1860.
[3] *Nottingham Journal*, 18 May 1860.
[4] Ibid., 18 Jan. 1850.
[5] *Newark Advertiser*, 20 Oct. 1855.

1850. Commenting on the Gorham judgment,[1] 'A Constant Reader' quoted Cicero's aphorism, *verboram controversice torquent homines* ('human beings have perpetual misunderstandings about words').

The debate about the nature and authority of the Bible had begun, but there is no evidence that the clergy of Southwell and its surrounding parishes (or in fact elsewhere) engaged with it. The revolutionary theories of Charles Darwin seem to have passed them by. There is no indication that the clergy recognised the urgent need for 'a free handling, in a becoming spirit, of subjects peculiarly liable to suffer by the repetition of conventional language and from traditional methods of treatment' as the authors of the controversial *Essays and Reviews* said in 1860, or were aware that a growing number of thoughtful and open-minded men and women no longer believed what the clergy thought that they believed. By 1870, although so much had changed in the previous fifty years (and was now changing more rapidly) in the public's perception of the theological claims of the Christian religion and the social and moral authority of the Church of England, there is little evidence that the majority of the rural clergy in this part of Nottingham-shire engaged theologically and pastorally in constructive and creative ways with the issues that these changes raised. The consequences of this neglect were to be profound.

---

[1] In 1847 G.C. Gorham, a Calvinistic evangelical, was presented to the benefice of Brampford Speke in the diocese of Exeter. Henry Phillpots, the high church bishop of Exeter, rightly suspecting Gorham's orthodoxy on the question of baptismal regeneration, refused to institute him, and was upheld by the Court of Arches. Gorham appealed to the judicial committee of the Privy Council. Although the committee found in Gorham's favour, Phillpots still refused to institute him, and Gorham was eventually instituted by John Bird Sumner, the archbishop of Canterbury. The case caused huge controversy.

8

The Rural Deanery of Southwell in 1855

In their second report the Ecclesiastical Revenues commissioners encouraged bishops to revive the post of rural dean. The bishops of London (Charles James Blomfield), Lincoln (John Kaye) and Peterborough (Herbert Marsh) were among the first to do so. The commissioners recommended further that if rural deans were to be 'efficient officers' there should be 'some small annual payments, sufficient to defray the expenses incurred by them in their visitations.' In quoting the commissioners Robert Simpson proposed in 1836 that the Nottingham archdeaconry's four rural deaneries (Nottingham, Bingham, Newark and Retford) should become five by making the peculiar of Southwell subject to the bishop and his archdeacon.[1] In Simpson's opinion only by this reform 'can proper discipline be maintained, and the laws of the church be enforced.' This is what happened once the Southwell college of canons had been dissolved, and with it the peculiar jurisdiction, although the new rural deanery of Southwell, with its 23 parishes[2] was not coterminous with the 28 parishes in the peculiar. By 1842 other Nottinghamshire parishes not previously within the archdeaconry came within its jurisdiction with a consequent re-ordering of deanery boundaries.

The first minute book of the reconstituted Southwell rural deanery records that at its initial meeting on 30 November 1855,[3] with John Murray Wilkins, the rural dean, in the chair, the chapter agreed to meet on the Tuesday of the four Ember weeks each year, though at its next meeting on 12 February 1856 it agreed that the meeting after Pentecost be transferred to the Tuesday after Trinity Sunday.

[1] Simpson, *Satte of the Church*, 55, 61.

[2] Excluding Winkbourne. This was a donative, and although included among the parishes in both the 1835 (1831) and the 1855 lists, was outside the jurisdiction of bishop and archdeacon. In 1835 the return for the donative merely records the name of the donative curate (T.C. Cane), its population (134 in 1831), and, under church accommodation, 'sufficient'.

[3] The last entry in this minute book records the chapter's meeting on 20 May 1871.

The first visitation of the deanery parishes was conducted in 1855 by John Murray Wilkins. An additional date at the head of the manuscript returns, and amendments to the text, indicate that he conducted a further visitation to some parishes in 1860.

The rural dean:
John Murray Wilkins (1816–1881)

John Murray Wilkins was born in 1816 in Hoveringham and baptised on 28 February 1816 in Lowdham St Mary. Lowdham was one of several parishes and other ecclesiastical benefices that his father George held in plurality. After attending Trinity College, Cambridge, he was made deacon by the bishop of Rochester in 1839 and ordained priest by the bishop of Lincoln in 1840 serving his title as his father's assistant curate at Nottingham St Mary before being presented by him to the newly established rectory of Southwell in December of the same year.

As prebendary of Normanton in Southwell collegiate church George Wilkins was patron of the rectory. It is hardly likely that his 24-year-old son, only very recently ordained priest, would exercise much authority in the Minster. He would, as the successor of the vicar of the parish under the previous constitution, be responsible for the day-to-day conduct of worship and for the Minster's pastoral ministry but probably for little else. After John Thomas Becher's death in 1848, George was, and continued to be until his death in 1865, the dominant figure in the Minster. In fact, as John Murray Wilkins's obituary notes, an Order in Council in 1843 had declared that 'on the next avoidance of the living of Southwell [the newly created rectory], the then Archdeacon of Nottingham was to become *ipso facto* rector of Southwell.'[1] This may explain why previous writers have assumed that George became rector of Southwell following the dissolution of the college of canons. Nevertheless George was effectively the rector, and would have determined how his son exercised a ministry virtually as his curate.

George's dominant position is confirmed by the 1851 census return for Southwell. It records George and his family living at the Residence, 21 Church Street. John Murray Wilkins and is family lived at 23 Church Street, in what, in the 1855 visitation return and entries in Crockford's *Clerical Directory*, he described as 'The Rectory House'. Only on his father's death did John Murray Wilkins move into the Residence. He

---

[1] *Nottingham Journal*, 15 Jan. 1881.

then became (or at least he styled himself, as the post ceased to exist with the death of its last holder) prebendary of Normanton in Southwell collegiate church, the benefice that his father had held from 1823 until his death. This may further explain why it has been assumed that he had succeeded his father as rector. In 1855 John Murray Wilkins returned his benefice income as rector of Southwell as £450, the same income that he had received at least fifteen years earlier. At his death the income of the rectory, of which the patron was then the bishop of Lincoln, was said to be £850.[1]

John Murray Wilkins was rural dean of the newly formed rural deanery of Southwell from 1854 to 1874. In 1854 he was also appointed the 'Official' or principal officer of his father as archdeacon of Nottingham. The Official was the archdeacon's surrogate and had authority to undertake all his administrative functions. This included the swearing in of churchwardens, granting licences, exercising discipline and judging legal cases. He might also conduct visitations on the archdeacon's behalf. In 1859 he was made prebendary of Bedford Major in Lincoln Cathedral. The writer of his obituary suggests that this appointment was a reward for his services to the diocese of Lincoln. His 'success in school management' was such that 'on the new education code coming into operation, the rev. gentleman was selected by the Bishop of Lincoln to draw up a scheme of directions for the future guidance of school managers in the diocese ... '

J.M. Wilkins was genuinely committed to furthering the education of the poor. As one example he promoted 'Harvest Meetings' of church school teachers, that is, meetings held during what later became the summer holidays but were then seasonal holidays to allow children to help with the harvest. In late August and early September 1858 the third of these meetings was held in Southwell. The *Nottingham Review* reported that it was attended by 23 schoolmasters, 13 school mistresses, and 10 students and pupil teachers from 17 parishes in Nottinghamshire and 13 in Lincolnshire. This in-service training took two weeks of, so it was reported, seven hours hard study a day. In fact the days started at 7.30 a.m. and finished at 9 p.m. as this timetable shows:

---

[1]   Obituary, loc. cit.

7.30	Morning Prayer in the Collegiate Church.[1]
9–10	Holy Scripture [a study of the early chapters of *St Luke*]
10–10.45	Arithmetic
10.45–11.15	Drill
11.15–11.45	Church Catechism and Liturgy (alternately)
11.45–12.30	Dictation: including Writing and Spellings, Parsing and Paraphrasing – on paper.
2–3	Reading and Grammar
3–3.30	Arithmetic and Algebra
3.30–4	Vocal Music
7.30–9	Conversation Discussions, Criticisms on Lessons etc.

Despite the length of these days the *Review* said that 'we may add that [the teachers'] earnestness was such that they seldom left off after the time prescribed.'[2] J.M. Wilkins superintended the training but J. Richardson, of the National Society, was the 'organising master'.

Wilkins was also active in promoting the Church's choral tradition. He founded the Nottinghamshire Church Choral Union, and, so his obituary noted, was its 'manager' for many years. He organised an annual festival for parish church choirs in Southwell. For example, in March 1858 no fewer than 300 choristers and 100 clergy representing 30 choirs attended the festival. This was held in the quire of the Minster. They were taught Gregorian chants for psalms and canticles, a Palestrina anthem, ancient Easter hymns, and Merbecke's setting for the holy communion.[3]

In 1876 a number of influential Southwell residents wrote to the Ecclesiastical Commissioners complaining of the 'dismantled and forlorn condition' of the Minster and that Wilkins, they said, was too 'physically and mentally incapacitated to provide for our present urgent necessity'.[4] His obituary noted that for several years before his death Wilkins had not

[1]   Note that Southwell St Mary was still known as 'the Collegiate Church', evidently at least until the last surviving prebendary died. Its local designation 'The Minster' seems not to have been in official use.

[2]   *Nottingham Review*, 20 Aug. 1858.

[3]   Ibid., 25 March 1858.

[4]   Letter in Harold Brooke, *Closed for Business: Ewan Christian's Restoration of Southwell Minster 1848–1888* (Southwell, 1997), 65–7. The letter was signed by, among others, the Revds Arthur Tatham (senior curate), R.R. Smith (minor canon) and F. Williamson, and four MPs. John Henry Becher, John Thomas Becher's grandson, also signed.

lived in Southwell 'on account of his impaired health' and curates had been 'entrusted with the duties' of the rector. James John Trebeck, assistant curate of Southwell, succeeded Wilkins as rector in 1881 and was to become sub-dean of Southwell when the Minster become the cathedral of the newly created diocese in 1884.[1] George Ridding, the first bishop, was *de jure* dean but delegated his cathedral functions to Trebeck. The 1843 Order in Council which stipulated that the archdeacon of Nottingham should be the rector of Southwell was either forgotten or ignored in light of the impending creation of the new diocese.

A more rounded view of John Murray Wilkins was provided by Samuel Reynolds Hole who knew Wilkins throughout the forty years that he was rector of Southwell. In his *Memories*,[2] Hole tells of meetings of the Royal Sherwood Archers:

> Our meetings were held in a fair ground overlooking the valley of the Trent and Southwell, half garden and half town, with its grand old church. The latter was largely indebted to Archdeacon Wilkins, who occupied 'The Residence', for the restoration and maintenance of the fabric. Murray, his son, was rector, a man of much humour, and of practical energy in his work, for he was the first to introduce into the Midlands Counties the harvest and choral festivals which are now universal; and I remember, as a specimen of his wit, the remark which he made upon our archers, 'that, though the gentlemen shot with yew bows, the ladies shot better with *beaux yeux*.' And, apropos to his musical instincts, as we were walking down the main street of Southwell, he stopped opposite a bank, which was then kept by Messrs Wild and Sons, and sang *sotto voce*, 'I know a bank, wherein the Wilds' time goes.'
>
> One day the Roman Bishop of Nottingham, Roskell,[3] came to inspect the minster. He was of portly and imposing aspect, and, when he was gone, the rector inquired of the chief mason what he thought of the visitor. 'Well, sir', wad the reply, 'I saw nothing very particular about him. He seemed to me *the kind of man as 'ud be pretty reg'lar 'ome at meal times'*.[4]

[1] James John Trebeck 1838–1905. In 1874 he married Mary, daughter of Christopher Wordsworth, bishop of Lincoln.

[2] S.R. Hole, *Memories of Dean Hole* (1893).

[3] Richard Roskell (1817–83), Roman Catholic bishop of Nottingham 1853–74.

[4] Hole, *Memories*, 5.

Unlike his father, John Murray Wilkins published comparatively little: *Unity and love essential to the 'making increase of the body of Christ'* (a sermon on Eph. 4:15-16); *How shall we sing the Lord's Song in a strange Land? A missionary sermon* (on Ps. 137:4), published in 1853; *Early Church History: A lecture* (1855); *Church Music: a Lecture* (1856) and *The Worship of Christ's Church a shadow of heavenly things. A Sermon* (on Heb: 8:5) ... *with an appendix* (1860).

The condition of the churches

In 1855 John Murray Wilkins did nothing to conceal his opinion of the poor state of the parish churches in his rural deanery. Of only nine of the 23 churches he visited could he say that they were 'neat and in good order'. Of a further eight he reported that they were 'in tolerable repair', though some of these were either 'small, old and poor' (Halloughton) or the roof wanted repair (Calverton) or had 'the floor blocked up with old rickety pews of all shapes, heights and sizes - W Gallery hardly safe' (Upton) or were 'blocked up with Pews, about which there are many disputes' (North Muskham). At Upton, the font was 'a depository for snuffers, candlesticks etc.' and the communion table in Farnsfield parish church was 'a mere shelf'. Thus, in Wilkins opinion half the churches deemed in reasonable repair were scarcely fit for use. The remaining six churches (over 25 per cent of the total) were almost dilapidated. Of Caunton parish church Wilkins reported that 'the whole building [is] in wretched condition – the Architect says it will not bear repair'. Farnsfield (where Wilkins's father had been incumbent and whose cousin now held the benefice) possessed 'a most wretched church – a new one grievously wanted', with a font described as 'a chimney pot sort of thing by the altar'. Maplebeck church was 'in very bad repair – hardly safe – bad roof.' Of North Muskham parish church which Wilkins had initially believed was in 'pretty good repair', though blocked up with pews, he subsequently noted that the 'Tower and roof found to be bad.' Norwell church was 'in a most wretched state – just weather tight – the Floor is uneven as if there has been an earthquake'. Woodborough church Wilkins found to be 'in bad repair within & without – not weather tight – roof bad. Dreary and neglected look.'

  Wilkins's evidence of the font in Upton parish church being used as 'a depository for snuffers, candlesticks etc.' and of its 'shabby' communion table, of Woodborough church's 'dreary and neglected look', and, not least, of Caunton church's 'wretched look', was confirmed by S. Reynolds Hole's memory of the state of village churches when he was vicar of Caunton in the 1850s. Writing in 1894 of their condition fifty years earlier he said:

> Shall we look into the church, of all buildings in the parish the dirtiest and most desolate? The walls, once a gay gamboge, have acquired from the damp and the drip a green and yellow melancholy. The bats, which dwell in the rotten timbers of the roof, float silently to and fro; the impudent sparrow twitters his distain; the corpulent spider darts up his lift to his lair; and the church mouse, and the earwig, and the beetle, the moth, and all manners of flies, scared by our strange intrusion, are agitated by a sudden conviction that there is no place like home.
>
> The font, never used for its sacred purpose, the babes being baptized at home in a yellow basin, generally associated with the porridge or the pudding, is filled with the broad ropes, by which coffins are let down into the grave, with an assortment of candle-ends, and a tin box containing the only instruments of ignition then in common use, the flint and the steel, which produced by quick attrition the spark, which smouldering in the timber, set aflame the brimstone on the wooden match.
>
> The altar was scantily draped with an ancient baize, patched and faded. I remember distinctly the only ornaments, the overcoat, hat, and whip of the curate, who had ridden five miles to his work.
>
> The ground floor was covered with pews of all shapes and sizes, except where in damp and distant corners a few of the old oak benches still remained, and the poor, like the publican, worshipped afar off. Diotrephes, the squire, loved to have the pre-eminence, and maintained it in a huge, high quadrilateral, which occupied half the chancel, with table, carpets, and fireplace, and soft seats and comfortable corners, suggesting and inducing
> 'that repose,
> Which stamps the caste of Vere de Vere' … [1]

John Murray Wilkins was outspoken about the general condition of the churches in his rural deanery, yet when he undertook his visitation the church of which he was the rector was also in poor repair. John Thomas Becher had left Southwell collegiate church in a sad physical

---

[1] Quoting Alfred Lord Tennyson: S.R. Hole, *More Memories: being thoughts about England spoken in America* (1894), 16ff. Notwithstanding the poor state of Caunton parish church when he became incumbent in 1850, Hole did not undertake a major restoration until 1869.

condition.[1] Quite apart from widespread and relatively superficial decay,
it was reported in April 1853 by James Nicholson, clerk of the fabric,
that on removing the coats of whitewash from the interior of the nave
'which has accumulated for centuries' it had been revealed that 'the
defective portions of the fabric had been repaired with plaster and
cement instead of stone.' This was said to 'fully account for the fissures
and the giving way of the central tower.'[2] Clergy and churchwardens
may well have felt that if the chapter of the collegiate church, patrons of
so many of their benefices, could allow the Minster to decay to the point
where its great tower was in danger of collapse, why should they be too
concerned about the state of their own churches.

Some forty years later James John Trebeck, now rural dean, conducted his two much more detailed surveys preparatory to the bishop of
Southwell's visitations in 1892 and 1896.[3] He found that, with several
exceptions, the condition of the fabric of the churches had hardly
improved. In 1892 he noted that the internal and external walls of Oxton
St Peter and St Paul were 'in places defective' or 'slightly defective'. Of
Edingley St Giles Trebeck wrote 'As bad as possible' across the
questions about the state of the nave and chancel. Maplebeck St
Radegund was, he reported, 'Thoroughly dilapidated.' The walls of the
nave of Rolleston Holy Trinity were 'bad' as were the church's roof
timbers, floor and joists. This church had been described as virtually
dilapidated twelve months earlier. It was reported in 1891 that its nave
and aisles were in 'an advanced state of dilapidation', that the south wall
was 'several feet out of perpendicular', that the roof was 'unsound and
very unsightly', and that the nave was 'disfigured with box pews and
benches of all shapes and periods.' The church was in no better state
three years later, with its 'naves and aisles ... in a deplorable condition.'[4] Other parish churches in the deanery were, or had recently been,
in poor condition. We have noted the state of Winkburn St John of
Jerusalem. A painting of the interior of Upton St Peter shows its poor
condition prior to its restoration in the 1860s. The external walls of
Morton St Denis (held with Rolleston) had been 'defective' in 1892
though the church had been 'wonderfully transformed' before it was

[1] For its condition and subsequent restoration see Brooke, *Closed for Business.*
[2] Quoted, ibid., 10–11.
[3] SMHL, 699.
[4] *Southwell Diocesan Magazine,* iv (no. 43), Sept. 1891, 143; vii (no. 81), Nov. 1894, 185.

THE VISITATION

reopened for worship on Ascension Day 1895.[1]

Despite this evidence of continuing neglect, in the years between the visitations of the deanery churches in 1855 and 1892 much had been spent on restoration and rebuilding. The 1860s and 1870s were the high years of what came, disparagingly, to be called 'churchwardens restorations'. In August 1875 a return to the House of Lords, dated 22 June 1874, showed the number of churches (including cathedrals) in every diocese in England (except Peterborough, Gloucester and Bristol whose returns were published separately) which had been built or restored at a cost exceeding £500 since 1840.[2]

The returns for the rural deanery of Southwell as it was in 1855 are given in the table opposite. The table is by no means complete. It omits the substantial restoration of Norwell St Laurence in 1857–9 and 1872–5 at a total cost of over £3,000, and also the building of Southwell Holy Trinity in 1846 and of Carlton-on-Trent St Mary,[3] consecrated in 1851, as well as the desultory and piecemeal restorations of Southwell St Mary since 1848. The cost of building Southwell Holy Trinity (excluding the endowment of the vicarage, and the building of the parsonage house and the school) was, as we have seen, about £3,000. The cost of the work on Southwell St Mary in the years covered by the House of Lords returns is much more difficult to estimate. A rough calculation of the cost of capital works and contracted repairs after 1848, based on figures given by Harold Brooke,[4] produces a minimum cost of at least £2,000 up to 1874. This figure excludes professional fees and the wages of the one or two craftsmen based more or less permanently at the Minster.[5] Even so, the building was in very poor condition when the new diocese of Southwell was created in 1884, and for the first four years of the life of the new diocese it could not be used as its cathedral. If these additional costs, with, say, £2,500 as a figure for Carlton-on-Trent St Mary, and £3,000 for the restoration of Norwell St Laurence are included the total spent on restorations and new building in the rural deanery, this amounts to a minimum of £23,000 incurred between 1840 and 1875.

[1]   Further to this, and on the general state of the churches in the new diocese in the 1890s, see M.R. Austin, '"The Many High Proude Ones"', in Stanley Chapman and Derek Walker (eds), *Southwell: The Town and its People, Part II* (Southwell, 2006), 181–3.

[2]   *House of Lords Accounts and Papers*, volume XIV.X.

[3]   Built by public subscription, principally from 'J. Vere & friends' as the 1855 visitation return records. No cost is given.

[4]   Brooke, *Closed for Business*.

[5]   In the 1850s the wages of the Minster's stonemason averaged 7s. or 8s. a week. By the early 1870s two craftsmen were together earning 30s. a week.

Church Restoration
in Southwell Rural Deanery

Church		Cost	Date
Bilsthorpe	Restored	£900	1870
Bleasby	Restored	£871	1867
Blidworth		£1,305	
Caunton	Restored	£2,000	1870
Farnsfield	Rebuilt	£2,762	1860
Kirklington	Restored	£600	1874
Norwell	Restored	£2,000	1874
Upton	Restored	£1,356	1860–67
Total expenditure		£11,794	

Church services: frequency and attendance

In the 1850s, despite the poor condition of many of the deanery churches worship was conducted at least once every Sunday in each of them. One service was conducted in eight parish churches; in two parishes services alternated between two on one Sunday and one on the next; ten parishes had two services each Sunday; and in three parishes (Southwell St Mary, Caunton and Calverton) there were three services each Sunday. Daily services were conducted in the collegiate church, and also in the 'wretched' parish church in Caunton where the moderate high churchman, S. Reynolds Hole, was the incumbent. The number of services of holy communion varied between four a year in seven parishes, six a year in seven parishes, seven or eight times a year in three parishes, and once a month (and on the greater festivals) in four parishes. These last were Southwell collegiate church, Southwell Holy Trinity, Caunton and North Muskham. The number of communicants was on average about 17 per cent of the Sunday attendance, suggesting that generally less than a fifth of the congregation remained after Morning Prayer for the celebration of holy communion that followed it.

Both the census of religious worship in 1851 and the rural dean's articles of enquiry in 1855 required the clergy to provide statistics of church attendance. In 1851 the clergy were asked to record actual attendances on 30 March and to note the average attendance for the previous twelve months. In 1855 the rural dean asked them to provide 'the average number of persons present in Sundays'. In both cases the difficulty of distinguishing the number of separate individuals attending one or more times on a Sunday from attendances at each service makes a reliable comparison impossible. In addition, insufficient information was given for four deanery parishes to enable any comparison between them to be made, but, given these caveats, of the remaining 19, the numbers returned in 11 cases were much the same in 1851 and 1855. In two parishes, Bilsthorpe and Edingley, attendance was lower in 1855 than in 1851. Numbers attending services in two parishes, Caunton and Kirklington, appear to have been considerably higher in 1855 than in 1851, though, again, these supposed differences may merely indicate that total attendances have been confused with separate persons attending more than once on a Sunday. Nevertheless the Caunton and Kirklington statistics are startling at first sight. At Caunton in 1851 the 'usual number of attendants' at the parish church at the two services totalled 185, including 75 'Sunday Scholars'. Using Michael Watts's formula the 110 adult attendances probably represents 85 separate individuals. In 1855 Samuel Reynolds Hole confidently returned 250 as the 'average number of persons attending.' At Kirklington where Thomas Coats Cane was the non-resident incumbent there were 60 adult attendances at its one service, though, in signing the return his note that he 'declines answering voluntary questions' places his figures in further doubt. In 1855 Cane told the rural dean that his church was 'full in the afternoons' but provided no figures.

The uncertainty of the attendance statistics suggests that little value can be attached to them individually. However, taken as a whole and measured against parish populations, they indicate that although only four parishes had populations exceeding 1,000, with only one, Southwell St Mary, in excess of 2,000, nevertheless the larger the parish the lower the percentage of the population that worshipped in the Church of England. This confirms the national picture. If we can trust S. Reynolds Hole's estimate that 250 people regularly attended Caunton parish church, some 41 per cent of a population of 611 worshipped with him, though only 11 per cent of his average Sunday congregation attended the monthly service of holy communion. Sixty-five regularly attended Hockerton parish church from a population of 114 (50.6 per cent) and at Carlton-on-Trent it was claimed that 250 attended the parish church from a population of 231 (65 per cent). Of Morton's population of 140, 75 attendances were recorded (54 per cent). On these figures Carlton-on-Trent had the highest percentage of its population attending the parish church in the rural deanery, and Woodborough, with 4.7 per cent of its population attending had the lowest. However, the larger the parish the more likely it was to contain at least one nonconformist chapel.

Of greater significance is the relationship of attendance to the number of houses in the parish (information required by the 1855 visitation). On this measurement Carlton-on-Trent again heads the list with 150 attendances from 47 houses, and Woodborough at the bottom with 40 attending from 185 houses. To repeat, there is no certain way of assessing how many of these attendances represented individuals attending at one service only, these statistics providing evidence only of general trends.

The parish clerks

The services were conducted by the clergyman, with responses by the congregation led by the parish clerk occupying the lowest seat of a three-decker pulpit. Parish clerks had to be over the age of twenty and be able to read and write, as they had to know the liturgy and, on occasion, to sign marriage registers as witnesses. Of the clerks in the Southwell rural deanery that can reliably be traced, with the exception of one, a farm labourer, most were skilled craftsmen: five cordwainers, two framework knitters, a master tailor, a lace-maker, a blacksmith, a carpenter, and a shoe-mender. They also included two farmers, a cottager, and a schoolmaster. Remarkably, the parish clerk of Kirklington was the squire's son-in-law, though he 'officiates by Deputy' who was the local shoemaker. The only full-time parish clerk, Peter Coxon of the collegiate church, also served as the chapter verger. The wages that clerks were paid varied from the payment only of fees arising from baptisms, marriages and funerals to a fixed wage of between £2. 11s and £6 together with fees. In several parishes 'Xmas boxes' formed part of the clerk's wage. In Farnsfield the wages of the clerk and his deputy was raised by a parish levy, with farmers paying 1s a year, and cottagers 2d. In 1848, of the eight parish clerks in Nottingham only three had supplementary employment, none of them in a skilled trade – one as a sheriff's officer, one as a house agent and one as a schoolmaster.[1]

---

[1] Knight, *Nineteenth-century Society*, 189.

9

The Visitation Answers

A transcript of John Murray Wilkins's visitation of the Southwell deanery parishes is given below. The customary headings of *pro forma* articles were copied by him into a plain notebook.[1]

Amendments to the original text made by crossings-out (as, for example, when there had been a change of incumbent or following a further visitation) have been incorporated into this edition except where they are corrections of obvious errors. Crossings-out are indicated by *cr*, and substituted material by *sub*. Spellings have generally not been changed, but, where necessary, punctuation has been added for clarity. Wilkins's abbreviations (e.g. 'marrs' for 'marriages') have usually been avoided, particularly where they include final superscripts. As the manuscript is somewhat haphazard, and to save space, I have attempted to bring some order to this transcription while retaining, so far as possible, the idiosyncratic character of the original text. In general editorial material is within square brackets. For clarity most headings are in bold type. It may be helpful for readers to have beside them the relevant parish returns to the national census of religious worship for Nottinghamshire conducted in 1851 and published in Michael Watts (ed.), *Religion in Victorian Nottinghamshire: The Religious Census of 1851* (Nottingham, 1988). Where they can be traced career details of the clergy are given for the period before, and a few years after, 1855. Further information is available in editions of *Crockford's Clerical Directory*. Details of parish clerks, where traceable, have been taken from census returns. The 24 parishes in Wilkin's list (including the donative of Winkbourne or Winkburn) were:

Bilsthorpe	Maplebeck
Bleasby[2]	Morton

---

[1] Southwell Minster Historic Library, 699.

[2] In 1831 the parishes of Bleasby (a vicarage) and neighbouring Morton (a perpetual curacy) were held by different incumbents, but in 1841 they were held by the same incumbent, Robert Henry Wylde, though not, it seems, united. They had been united by 1855. The incumbent was then John William Marsh.

Blidworth
Calverton
Carlton on Trent[1]
Caunton
Edingley
Farnsfield
Hallam
Halloughton
Hockerton
Kirklington

Muskham, North
Muskham, South
Norwell
Oxton
Southwell Collegiate Church
Southwell Trinity Church
Upton
Winkbourne
Woodborough
Rolleston[2]

Bilsthorpe, Rectory

Visited: May 11 1855 [also] Nov. 1860
Population: 217 **Value returned:** £360 **Acreage**: 1480 [*cr* 1572 *sub*]
Houses: 44
Patron: Earl of Scarborough [*cr* Capt Saville[3] *sub*]
Incumbent: Rev. Frederick Lumley BA[4] [*cr* Robt Sutton *sub*] **Insti-tuted:** 1847 [*cr* 1859 *sub*] **Resides:** in the Glebe House.
Church: Dedicated to S. Margaret. small – Nave 40 by 18, Chancel 18 by 15 and West Gallery. Gallery all pewed and part of Nave. Repair good. Roof good. Spouting is to be put up. **Chancel:** good – pew to be thrown open. **Room:** 108. Free: 33, in Nave [*cr* 145 Appropriated - 70, Free 55, Children 20 *sub*] **Number of Pews:** 18 – all allotted to houses. **Faculty Pews:**[5] none **Communion Table, Rails, Kneeling Hassocks, Cover, Linen:** [all] good. **Communion Plate:** Alms Dish, Flagon, Chalice, Patin [sic]: [all] good – plated. **Font:** near West door. **Reading**

---

[1] By 1831 the parish of Carlton-on-Trent had been united with neighbouring Norwell with the incumbent living in Norwell.

[2] The return for Rolleston is listed by Wilkins out of alphabetical order but in this edition it is placed following Oxton for ease of reference.

[3] This should be Savile.

[4] Frederick Savile Lumley (1819–59), the illegitimate son of John Lumley, 8th earl of Scarborough. Corpus Christ College, Oxford, BA, 1846.

[5] Faculty pews were those installed by individuals for their own use having first obtained a faculty to do so. Appropriated pews could either be possessed by owners of houses in the parish to which they were attached by limited freehold, or bought, owned and sold by individuals as freehold property, or maintained by clergy and churchwardens and leased to individuals. Free pews were provided by the parish for the use of the poor. Where they existed they were invariably placed in the least convenient areas in churches. The law relating to pews at this time is set out in A. Heales, *The History and Law of Church Seats or Pews* (1872).

Pew: good **Pulpit:** good. **Surplices:** Two – good[1] **Ten Commandments:** yes.**Table of Degrees:** no **Alms Chest:** yes. **Books:** good. **Registers:** in iron chest in Rectory, Earliest Date AD 1654.**Bells:** Two. Chamber and Ladders good. **Ringers** – Parish Clerk **Keys:** under custody of Rector.

Church Services: One every Sunday, mornings and afternoons alternately. **Communions:** Four [*cr* 8 *sub*] times a year. **Average number of Communicants:** 14 or 15 [*cr* 24 *sub*]. **Baptisms:** in Church – after service. **Catechising in Church:** no. **Average number of persons present on Sundays:** 45 to 50.

Churchyard: Sufficient – well kept & fenced [*additional notes illegible*].

Parish Clerk: Thomas Rouse. **Appointed:** [*blank*] **Salary:** [*blank*] **Efficient:** yes.

Churchwardens: Two. **Properly Elected, sworn in, accounts kept, attend Services, keep order etc:** [all] yes.

Church Rate: yes. **Funds for Church Repair:** none. **Charities:** [*blank*]

Glebe House: A new good one lately built by Lord Scarboro'.

Terrier: Lands 78 acres. **Tithes:** commuted at £360. **Q.A.B:**[2] none.

Fees: Marriages: 10s/6s. **Churchings** 6d. **Burials:** 1 penny. **Average number of:** baptisms: 5 Marriages: 3 Burials: 6.

School: One promised by Lord Scarboro'.**Sunday:** Average attendance of Boys 14. Girls 26. **Day:** Boys and Girls about 25.**Under Government Inspection:** No **How supported:** Rector & childrens pence. **Expenditure:** [*blank*] **Master:** [*blank*] **Mistress:** yes.

Bleasby, Vicarage

Visited: May 18 1855 [also] Dec 1860

Population: 358 [*cr* 332 *sub*] **Value Returned:** £107 **Acreage** 1550 [*cr* 1461 *sub*] **Houses:** 73.

Patron: Chapter of Southwell.

---

[1]   In every parish surplices were (or should have been) provided at the expense of the churchwardens.

[2]   i.e. Queen Anne's Bounty augmentations.

Incumbent: Rev John William Marsh BA.[1] **Instituted:** 1848. **Resides:** In the Vicarage House.

Church: Dedicated to St Mary.**Chancel:** 21 by 10 . **Nave:** 45 by 16. **North Transcept:** 24 by 16 – used as a Sunday School with Gallery above – Tower opened from Nave – all neat and good order. Chancel – Ecclesiastical Commissioners. **Room:** 160 + Free 24 (in Gallery). Faculty Pews: [blank] Pews 32 – all allotted by award or Faculty in 1816 to Houses. **Communion Table:** good **Communion Rails:** good **Communion Cover:** good **Kneeling Hassocks:** good **Linen:** good **Communion Plate:** Alms Dish: Pewter - old. Flagon: Pewter - bad. Chalice: silver, good. Patin [*sic*]: silver – good. **Font:** New and good – at W End. **Reading Pew:** good **Pulpit:** good **Surplices:** one good. **Ten Commandments:** yes **Table of Degrees:** no **Alms Chest:** no **Books:** good **Registers:** In Wooden Chest in Church – Earliest Date 1640. **Bells:** Two. **Chamber & Ladders & Ropes:** good **Ringers:** Clerk [*cr* and others?]. **Keys:** Clerk.

Church Services: Once every Sunday, Two every alternate Sunday. **Communions:** 6 times a year. **Average no. of Communicants:** 20. **Baptisms:** after 2nd lesson. **Catechising:** in Church - sometimes. **Average no. present on Sundays:** about 120.

Churchyard: Sufficient – in good order. Two footpaths awarded by Enclosure Commissioners?

Parish Clerk: John Corden.[2] **Efficient:** yes. **Appointed:** More than 20 years ago. **Salary:** £4 & fees.

Churchwardens: Two. **Properly elected:** yes. **Sworn in:** yes. **Accounts kept:** yes. **Attend services:** yes. **Keep order etc:** yes.

Church Rate: yes – sufficient. **Funds for Church Repair:** none. **Charities:** £1 per ann.

Glebe House: New and good, built by the late vicar about 10 or 12 years ago - £500 borrowed from Q.A.B. Sum paid by Q.A.B in 1855 - £31 6s 3d.

Terrier: Lands, Tithes, Great Tithes, Q.A.B: [*all blank*].

Fees: Marriages, Churchings, Burials [*all blank*]. **Average no.** marriages: 2 or 3. Baptisms: 4.Burials: 9.

---

[1]   John William Marsh (1821–82), son of Edward Garrard Marsh of Hampstead, prebendary of Woodborough; Wadham College, Oxford, BA 1845, MA 1856; d. 1845, p. 1846; vicar of Bleasby with Morton 1848–74, rector of Winchester St Michael 1874–82. In 1867, with Waite Hockin Stirling, he published *The Story of Commander Allen Gardiner RN, with Sketches of Missionary Work in South America*. Gardiner's second wife was Marsh's sister Elizabeth, the eldest daughter of Edward Garrard Marsh and Lydia Marsh.
[2]   Aged 55, a smith.

School: Sunday: Boys 24.Girls 24. **Day:** Boys [*blank*]. Girls [*blank*]. **Under Government Inspection:** [*blank*]. **How supported:** Subscription. **Expenditure:** about £5. **Master:** yes – pretty good. **Mistress:** [*blank*]

Blidworth, Vicarage

Visited: May 10 1855
Population: 1376 **Value Returned:** £188 **Acreage:** 5303 **Homes:** 280
Patron: Canon of Oxton in Southwell Coll: Ch:
Incumbent: Revd Collingwood Foster Fenwick LL.B[1] **Instituted:** 1824. **Resides:** at Ryde in the Isle of Wight. **Curate:** Revd John Porter MA. Licensed 1850. Stipend £100, Fees and Glebe House. Resides in the Glebe House.
Church: Dedicated to S. Mary – rebuilt and enlarged in 1839. **Nave & aisle:** 60ft by 30. **Chancel:** – a mere recess. **Room:** 300. Free, 70 [*cr* 139 *sub*]. **Faculty Pews:** none. Pews allotted to Houses, 46. **Communion Table:** Good. **Communion Rails:** Good. **Communion Cover:** Good. **Hassocks:** Good. **Linen:** Good. **Plate:** Alms Dish, Chalice, Flagon, all Good. Patin [*sic*] : silver. **Font:** Good. **Reading Pew:** good. **Pulpit:** good. **Surplices:** Two – good. **Ten Commandments:** yes. **Table of Degrees:** no. **Alms Chest:** no. **Books:** not very good – some new ones promised. **Registers:** Well kept – in iron safe in vestry, Earliest Date AD 1566. **Bells:** Three. **Chamber, Ladders etc.** good. **Ringers:** Parish Clerk. **Keys:** kept by Curate.
Church Services: Two full each Sunday. **Communions:** Seven in a year. **Average no. of Communicants:** 20. **Baptisms:** in Church. **Catechising in Church:** no. **Average no. present on Sundays:** 200.
Churchyard: In tolerable order – more ground will soon be wanted.
Parish Clerk: John Hodgkinson.[2] **Appointed:** 1850 **Salary:** 0 - Fees. **Efficient:** yes.
Churchwardens: Two – The Parish Churchwarden an active Wes-

---

[1] Collingwood Forster Fenwick (1796–1858); Trinity Hall, Cambridge 1812, from Brasenose College, Oxford; formerly lieutenant, Grenadier Guards; LL.B. 1817; p. (bp Gloucester); rector of Street, Somerset, with chapel of Walton annexed, 1820 (vacant, 1823); vicar of Blidworth and Oxton, 1824–58; rector of Brook, Isle of Wight, 1836–58; married Eliza, 2nd daughter of Admiral Christie, of Baberton; died at Ryde. At the time of the 1841 census Fenwick (then aged 45) was living at the parsonage in Brook in Hampshire with his wife Elizabeth (45) seven children, a William Smith (15) and three servants. He has not been traced in the 1851 census.

[2] Aged 42, a farmer of 42 acres.

leyan. **Properly Appointed:** yes. **Sworn in:** yes. **Accounts kept:** yes.
Attend Services: yes. **Keep order etc:** yes
 Church Rate: yes. **Fund for Church Repair:** no. **Charities:** none.
Glebe House: Bad, small and inconvenient.
 Terrier: Land [and] Tithes 143 acres of poor land. Q.A.B: none
Great Tithes – Ecclesiastical Commissioners.
 Fees: Marriages 5s & 2s/6. **Churchings:** 0. **Burials:** 1s/6. **Fees for
Baptisms:** 1s/6. **Average:** marriages: 11. baptisms: 45. burials: 30.
 School: Good & large buildings erected thro' the exertions of the late
Curate, Rev. M. Roe, at an expense of £1600. Boys school (large), Girls
ditto; Infant ditto & Two Class Rooms. **Sunday [school]:** Boys 35. Girls
35 . **Day (mixed)** Boys 20. Girls 15. Infants 36. **Under Government
Inspection:** yes. **How supported:** Subscription & sermon. **Expenditure:**
about £100. **Master:** Good – not certificated **Mistress:** Good – not
certificated.

Calverton, Vicarage

 Visited: May 10 1855 March [?] [18]56
 Population: 1450 **Value Returned:** £127 **Acreage:** 3320.**Houses:**
302
 Patron: Canon of Oxton in Southwell Coll: Ch:
 Incumbent: Rev. Samuel Oliver **Instituted:** 1827 **Resides:** in the
Glebe House
 Church: dedicated to S. Wilfred - A Nave nearly square (45 by 36
ft) entirely filled up by high pews, a Chancel 24 by 18, ditto, & West
Gallery – in tolerably good repair. [*pencilled note illegible*] **Chancel:** Mr
Hardcastle[1] [*pencilled note illegible*] – roof wants repair. 1 Pew allotted
to Great Tithe House. **Room:** 350. Free 100 (the Gallery) **Pews:** 50.
Faculty Pews: none. Pews allotted to persons 49. **Communion Table:
Rails:** good **Cover:** New one promised. **Hassocks:** good. **Linen:** <u>none</u>
Plate: Alms Dish: silver and pewter. Flagon: pewter. Chalice: silver
Patin [*sic*] silver patched. **Font:** in the Chancel **Reading Pew:** good.
Pulpit: good. **Surplice:** one, good. **Ten Commandments:** no. **Table of
Degrees:** no. **Alms Chest:** no. **Books:** good. **Registers:** kept in iron
chest in Vicarage House Earliest Date 1568 **Bells:** Two **Chamber,
Ladders, Ropes etc:** good **Ringers:** Parish Clerk **Keys:** Vicar.
 Church Services: Three full each Sunday. **Communions:** 4 times in

---

[1] Possibly Jonathan Hardcastle of Blidworth, a banker.

a year. **Average No. of Communicants:** 25. **Baptisms:** in the Church
– not during service. **Catechising:** Twice or thrice a year. **Average no.
present on Sundays:** 200 & 200 children

Churchyard: Sufficient – in good order. **Parish Clerk:** W. Bell.
Appointed: before 1835. **Salary:** Fees. **Efficient:** yes.

Churchwardens: Two. **Properly elected:** yes. **Sworn in:** yes.
Accounts kept: yes. **Attend services:** yes. **Keep order etc:** yes [*against
the entry for Churchwardens the following pencilled note:* 'Difficulties
anticipated from the parish chwarden not [*following words obscure,
probably* 'finding rate etc'].

Church Rate: Till this year – not refused. **Fund for Church Repair:**
none. **Charities:** £11 pr annum.

Glebe House: Small – old – not good - rather tumble down.

Terrier: Land [and] Tithes: about 200 acres – very poor land. **Great
Tithes:** Mr Hardcastle – under Ecclesiastical Commissioners. **Q.A.B:**
[*blank*] **Ecclesiastical Commissioners:** £18.

Fees: Marriages: 5s & 2/6. **Churchings:** 7d.**Burials:** 1/- **Average:**
Marriages: 8. Baptisms : 32. Burials: 20.

School: pretty good buildings – cost £300/subscr. Boys – Girls - &
2 Class Rooms. Vicar refused Government grants disliking the conditions
[*pencil additions illegible*]. **Sunday:** Boys 84. [*pencil note:* 90]. Girls 72
[*pencil note:* 130] **Day:** none [*cr in pencil* 47 Girls *sub*] [*Additional
pencil note:* 'School mistress £25 [*following words illegible*] & 2/3 of
hour' broken floor [*following word illegible*] fit school furniture (?).
Under Government Inspection: soon. **How supported:** Subscription &
sermon. **Expenditure:** about £8. **Master, Mistress:** Voluntary Teachers.
An Endowed School in the Village – Mr H. Smith, Banker of Nottingham – Trustee - & Manager. A Wesleyan Preacher the Master.

Carlton on Trent, a chapelry of Norwell

Visited May 15 1855

Population: 231 **Value Returned:** [*blank*] **Acreage:** in Norwell.
Houses: 47

Patron: see Norwell **Incumbent:** [*blank*] **Resides:** [*blank*]

Church:[1] A very handsome new church – built by subscription –
chiefly of J. Vere & friends – stained glass windows & organ etc - Nave
of N. & S. Aisles 54 by 33 & Chancel 33 by 13 – all open seats –

---

[1]   St Mary, consecrated in 1851.

chiefly allotted. **Chancel:** Stalls 48 – Sittings allotted to Houses 145 – Free 45. **Room:** 280 - Free 50 & 70 [*cr*] in chancel for children and servants – about 60. **Faculty pews:** none. **Communion Table, Rails, Cover, Hassocks, Linen:** all handsome. **Plate:** Alms Dish Chalice Flagon Patin [*sic*] silver – new handsome. **Font:** S.W. good new. **Reading Pew:** ditto. **Pulpit:** ditto. **Surplices:** new good. **Ten Commandments:** no. **Table of Degrees:** no **Alms Chest:** no **Books:** good. **Registers:** at Norwell. **Earliest Date:** [*blank*] **Bells:** one. **Chamber, Ladder, Ropes etc:** good **Ringers:** Clerk **Keys:** ditto.

Church Services: Once on Sundays M & Aft. alternately Fridays in Lent - & on Grt. Festivals **Communions:** 6 times a year. **Average no. of Communicants:** 25. **Baptisms:** in Church after Service. **Catechising in Church:** no. **Average present on Sundays:** about 150.

Churchyard: Good and large — A little fencing to be done. **Parish Clerk:** — Sudbury.[1] **Appointed:** 1852. **Salary:** £5 & Fees. **Efficient:** tolerable.

Churchwardens: Two. **Properly elected, sworn in, accounts kept, attend services, keep order etc:** [*all*] yes.

Church Rate: yes - sufficient. **Fund for Church Repairs:** no. **Charities:** none.

Glebe House: see Norwell.

Terrier: Land, Tithes, Grt. Tithes, Q.A.B: see Norwell.

Fees: Marriages, Churchings, Burials [*all blank*]. **Average:** Marriages, Churchings, Burials [*all blank*].

School: good. built and supported by Mr Vere. **Sunday:** Boys 25. Girls 35. **Day:** Boys 30 . Girls 35 . **How Supported:** Mr Vere. **Expenditure:** Mr Vere. **Master:** [*blank*] **Mistress:** yes.

Caunton, Vicarage

Visited: May 15 1855 [? May] 21 1856

Population: 611 **Value Returned:** £171 **Acreage:** 2900 [*cr* 3130 *sub*] **Houses:** 132

Patron: Bishops of Ripon and Manchester alternately (Bp of Ripon last turn).

---

[1] Possibly Thomas Sudbury, 37, a farm labourer.

Incumbent: Rev. Samuel Reynolds Hole BA[1] **Instituted:** 1850 **Resides:** in the Manor House

Church: Dedicated to S. Andrew. Nave & N. and S. Aisles 51 by 42, Chancel 35 by 15, & West Gallery. The whole building in wretched condition – The architect says it will not bear repair – New Church much wanted. **Chancel:** Lord Middleton (Lessee under Ecclesiastical Commissioners.

Room: 280 besides children. **Free:** about 150 & 80 children. **Pews:** 18 allotted to Houses. **Faculty Pews:** none. 1 open seat allotted to a House. **Communion Table, Rails, Cover, Hassocks, Linen** [all] very good. **Plate:** Alms Dish: brass (new) Flagon: pewter (old) Chalice: 1 old – silver, 1 new - ditto , the new [word illegible] Plate very handsome Patin [sic]: silver new. **Font:** W. S. W. Door – old. **Reading Pew:** good. **Pulpit:** good. **Surplices:** Two – one good. Two good belonging to the Vicar. **Ten Commandments:** yes – old. **Table of Degrees:** no. **Alms Chest:** no. **Books:** good. **Registers:** in Iron Chest in Church. **Earliest Date:** 1709. **Bells:** Three. **Chamber, Ladders, Ropes etc:** good. **Ringers:** Clerk. **Keys:** Clerk.

Church Services: Daily 8 A M. – Weds. Frids & Holy days 8 & 10A M.Sundays 9 AM Morning Prayer - 11 AM Litany and Communion 3 PM evening Prayer. **Communions:** Monthly & Greater Festivals. **Average no. of Communicants:** 28. **Baptisms:** In the Church after 2nd Lesson. **Catechising in Church:** in School. **Average present on**

---

[1]   Samuel Reynolds Hole (1819–1904). Only son of Samuel Hole (1778–1868) of Caunton Manor, Notts. Brasenose College, Oxford, 1840, BA 1844, MA 1878. Deacon 1844, priest 1845. Assistant curate, Caunton 1844, vicar of Caunton 1850–87. Rural dean of Southwell 1875, prebendary of Lincoln 1875, chaplain to Edward White Benson in 1883, proctor in Convocation in 1884. See *Oxford ODNB*: 'At Caunton he instituted daily services and never omitted a daily visit to the village school; but [these] clerical duties were varied by hunting, shooting, and other rural sports, and he was an enthusiastic gardener'. Hole's regard for his pastoral ministry seems not to have caused him to rebuild the parish church. When his father died in 1868, Hole became also squire of Caunton as well as incumbent. In 1887 he was made dean of Rochester. It is said of him that he was 'a moderate high-churchman who had been influenced at Oxford by E.B. Pusey'. On Hole's literary, sporting and rose-growing interests see the entry in *Oxford DNB* by G. Le G. Norgate, revised by M.C. Curthoys. John Tinkler, who was vicar of Caunton for 35 years until his death aged 91 in 1924, continued the high church tradition at Caunton. At his death it was said of him that he was 'a staunch adherent of the Oxford Movement' (*Southwell Diocesan Magazine*, vol. XXXVII, no. 435, June 1924, 62). A possible indication of the attitude of Samuel Hole's father to the poor is shown in the case of John Hunt of Caunton, 'a decrepid-looking man ... not having any visible means of subsistence' who was charged at Newark petty sessions on 6 August 1857 with sleeping in an outhouse 'belonging to Mr Hole of Caunton'. It was reported that 'the prisoner was in the habit of frequently sleeping in different outhouses, and smoking therein, much to the danger of the premises'. Hunt was sentenced to 21 days hard labour (*Nottingham Review*, 14 Aug. 1857).

Sundays: about 250.

Churchyard: Too small – crowded to excess. A Rate has been granted for enlargement – Land not yet obtained. Fencing not good – Footpaths all to be stopped up [*added in pencil:* 'a good piece of land obtained – to be added to the chyard (*following word illegible*)'].

Parish Clerk: George Elvidge **Appointed:** 1847 **Salary:** £5 & Fees **Efficient:** yes

Churchwardens: Two. **properly elected, sworn in, accounts kept, attend services, keep order etc:** [*all*] yes.

Church Rate: yes – sufficient **Charities:** none. **Fund for Church Repairs:** none. **Glebe House:** none.

Terrier: Lands/Tithes: commuted for 124 acres – poor land. **Great Tithes:** Lord Middleton – lessee under Eccl Comm.

Fees: Marriages: 10s and 5s. **Churchings:** offering made. **Burials:** 2s 6d

School: Two – good **Sunday:** Boys 40 Girls 40. **Day:** Boys 30 Girls 40. **Under Government Inspection:** no **Expenditure:** about £30 **Master:** Parish Clerk **Mistress:** His wife.[1]

Caunton includes the Hamlets of Knapthorpe, Beesthorpe, & Dean Hall.

Edingley, Perp[etual] Cur[acy]

Visited: May 11 1855 May 8 1858

Population: 380 **Value Returned:** £51 **Acreage:** 2000 [*cr* 1800 *sub*] **Houses:** 87

Patron: Chapter of Southwell.

Incumbent: Rev. Richard Bethell Earle (a Literate)[2] **Instituted:** 1854 **Resides:** at Southwell, being Master of the Grammar School.

Church: S. Giles. Small and miserable – though in tolerable repair – a Nave 54 by 16 ft – with West Gallery. Walls and Roof want attention in a few places. **Chancel:** none. **Room:** 119. Free: 4 at the back of the Gallery. No room for School children. **Faculty Pews:** none. **Communion Table, Rails, Cover, Hassocks, Linen:** all good and new. **Plate:** Alms Dish: Pewter. Flagon: Pewter. Chalice: Silver, pretty good. Patin [sic] none **Font & cover:** good, by West Door. **Reading Pew:**

---

[1]   George Elvidge, 25, and Ann Elvidge, 23.

[2]   i.e. a man admitted to Anglican holy orders without a university degree. That a non-graduate was Master of the Collegiate Grammar School is noteworthy.

good. **Pulpit:** good. **Surplices:** one ragged. **Ten Commandments:** yes. **Table of Degrees:** no. **Alms Chest:** no. **Books:** tolerably good. **Registers:** Earliest Date: [blank] **Bells:** Two **Chamber, Ladders & Ropes:** pretty good. **Ringers:** Clerk.**Keys:** kept by the Clerk.

Church Services: one each Sunday – alternately Mornings [and] Afternoons. **Communions:** Four times in a year. **Average no. of Communicants:** about 8. **Baptisms:** in the Church, after Service. **Catechising in Church:** no. **Average no. in Church on Sundays:** 40 to 50.

Churchyard: sufficient. A footpath – a bad fence [cr] – a bad gate [added in pencil: 'a style'] – a wet ditch that might easily be drained off. **Parish Clerk:** David Copeland.[1] **Appointed:** 1820. **Salary:** £2 11s & Fees. **Efficient:** yes.

Churchwardens: two. **properly elected, sworn in, accounts kept, attend services, keep order etc:** [all] yes.

Church Rate: none – not refused. **Funds for Church Repair:** [against both entries:] Clerk's Salary & other necessary payments made from money derived from the parish letting out the village lanes. **Charities:** about £11 pr. ann.

Glebe House: none. A small Farm house and homestead contiguous to the Churchyard recently enfranchised by Ecclesiastical Commissioners on very easy terms – [next word obscure] ought to have been made a Glebe House.

Terrier: Lands: about 15 acres. Tithes: none. Great Tithes: Ecclesiastical Commissioners. Q.A.B: pr. an. 19£ 10. Ecclesiastical Commissioners: £20 pr. ann. formerly paid.

Fees: Marriages: 10s & 5s. **Churchings:** 6d. **Burials:** 1s. **Average:** marriages: 1 in 1853. Baptisms. 10. Burials: 4 or 5.

School: a small Endowed School. **Sunday [school]:** Boys, 12. Girls, 12 – besides the Day Scholars. **Day [school]:** Boys, 15. Girls, 15. **Under Government Inspection:** no. **How Supported:** Endowment, House and 5½ acres of land. **Master:** yes – Harvey. **Mistress:** [blank].

Farnsfield, Vicarage

Visited May 11 1855 [also] May 8 1856
Population: 1149 **Value Returned:** £165 **Acreage:** 3920 **Houses:** 119 [cr 282 sub]

---

[1] Aged 56, a framework knitter.

Patron: The Chapter of Southwell.
Incumbent: The Rev. Henry Robert Wilkins BA.[1] **Instituted:** 1849.
Resides: In a hired house in the Village.
Church: dedicated to S. Michael. A most wretched Church – a new
one grievously wanted. [*added:* 'new consecrated Oct 4/60']² A squarish
nave, 53 by 36, A small Chancel 15 by 18 at one corner, and Two
Gallery
Galleries – The whole ground floor blocked up with Font
pews up to the altar. **Chancel:** Lessees under Eccles. Comm. – now
enfranchised.
Room: 279 [*cr* 400 *sub*]. Free: 70 in North Gallery.
Fac[ulty] Pews: none. No. of Pews: 55 – all claimed by
Houses. [*added later:* Appropriated: 230, 96 Free,
75 children, [*total*] 400 [*sic*].

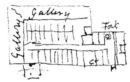

Communion Table: a mere shelf. **Rails:** tolerable. **Hassocks:** good.
Cover: good. **Linen:** good.
Plate: Alms Dish, Flagon, Chalice, and Patin [*sic*]: [all] Silver –
handsome – a present from Miss Milward in 1848. **Font:** The old one
built up under the W. Gallery – The font used a chimney pot sort of
thing by the altar. **Reading Pew:** pretty fair. **Pulpit:** ditto. **Surplices:**
good – three. **Ten Commandments:** no. **Organ:** yes. **Table of Degrees:**
no. **Alms Chest:** no. **Books:** good. **Registers:** in Iron Chest in Vicar's
house. Earliest Date: 1572. **Bells:** 5 and a clock**. Chamber, Ladders,
Ropes etc**: good. **Ringers:** <u>not</u> under Vicar's control.[3] **Keys:** Clerk.

---

1   Christ's College Cambridge, d. 1845, p. 1846, vicar of Farnsfield 1849. Henry Robert
Wilkins was George Wilkins's nephew and conducted his funeral in 1865.

2   This note added later in ink. In October 1858 the archdeacon of Nottingham chaired
a meeting in Farnsfield of 'influential gentlemen' who accepted a 'beautiful design' of a
church to replace the existing church which was said to be 'extremely incommodious, and
one of the worst specimens of the "Conglomerated" style of architecture in the neighbourhood. 'In the new design accommodation was to be 'amply provided for those to whom the
gospel is especially to be preached, viz., to the poor'. The new church was estimated to
cost £2,500, of which £1,750 had already been contributed (including a single donation of
£1,000).

3   The fact that the ringers were not under the vicar's control may explain a report in the
Nottingham Review for 28 Nov. 1856 under the headline 'Church Poverty at Farnsfield'.
The report ran: 'The church bellringers have not been able to practice this season for want
of funds. Donations, we are told, would be thankfully received to enable them to buy a

Church Services: Two every Sunday. **Communions:** once in six weeks. **Average no. of communicants:** 30. **Baptisms:** in Church – during service sometimes. **Catechising in Church:** no. **Average no. present on Sundays:** about 140, besides children.

Churchyard: small & full. More ground much wanted – good walls all round – no footpaths.

Parish Clerk: Mr. Curtis.[1] Deputy: C. Dixon.[2] **Appointed:** 1850. **Salary:** Fees and 1s from each Farmer, 2d from each cottager. **Efficient:** yes.

Churchwardens: Two. **Properly elected, sworn in, accounts kept, attend services, keep order etc:** [all] yes.

Church Rate: not refused. **Fund for Church Repair:** none. **Charities:** a few pounds a year.[3]

Glebe House: none.

Terrier: Land [and] Tithes: 180 acres. **Great Tithes:** Eccles. Com. **Q.A.B:** £4. 15 pr ann.

Fees: Marriages: 10s and 5s. **Churchings:** 6d. **Burials:** 1s. **Average:** Marriages: 4. Baptisms: 30. Burials: 18.

School: An Endowed School- greatly altered – Trustees were lately appointed, & will not dismiss the Master who is totally unfit for his office. The children that were at the School have been taken away & sent to the Dissenting School. The Vicar, not being put into the Trust Deed, is powerless. **Sunday [school]:** Boys: — . Girls: very few. **Day:** Boys: — . Girls: not half a score. **Under Government Inspection:** no. **How supported:** Endowment of a good House, garden, orchard and homestead. **Expenditure:** Two acres of valuable land bringing in £10 pr. annum, & also £14 pr. ann. Left by Mr Houldsworth. **Master:** Very bad. **Mistress:** [blank]. [pencil notes added subsequently: 'May 21. Schoolmaster dismissed' and 'New schools nearly finished May 9 1856.']

few candles, etc. Several weddings have taken place lately without the customary bell-ringing. The correspondent adds:- Where does all the money go to, [sic] they get as the parish pay for bell-ropes. The parishioners are without either bell-ringers or accounts.'

[1] Probably Francis Curtis, 63, a farmer of 93½ acres employing two labourers.

[2] Probably Charles Dixon, 38, a cordwainer employing two men.

[3] The paucity of charities was remedied in part by Henry Robert Wilkins and his wife. The *Nottingham Review* for 12 Dec. 1856 reported that at Farnsfield there had been the first distribution of soup for the season. Poor families were given tickets and given a pint of 'good soup' for a penny. 'Praise is due to the worthy vicar and his lady for their persevering efforts.'

Halam, Perpetual Curacy

Visited: May 7 1855
Population: 391. **Value Returned:** £85 **Acreage:** 1600 [*cr* 1310 *sub*]
Houses: 87
Patron: Chapter of Southwell
Incumbent: Rev. Alfred Tatham MA **Instituted:** 1854.**Resides:** at
Southwell, being a Minor Canon of the Coll[egiate] Ch[urch].
Church: a nave and chancel & West Gallery – in tolerable repair
except for Chancel. The whole of the ground floor blocked up with high
square pews - no room for School children. **Chancel:** Roof and walls
much out of order – Belongs to Eccles Comm. to whom application has
been made by the Incumbent, but no reply received. **Room:** 146. **Free:**
36. The W. Gallery. **Faculty Pew:** one, in Gallery. **Pews:** 21, allotted to
Houses. **Communion Table, Rails, Cover, Hassocks, Linen:** [*all*] good.
Plate: Alms Dish & Flagon: Pewter – shabby. Chalice & Patin [*sic*]:
Silver - pretty good. **Font:** near West Door blocked up by pews – totally
inaccessible. **Reading Pew:** good. **Pulpit:** good. **Surplices:** one – old.
Ten Commandments: yes. **Table of Degrees:** no. **Alms Chest:** no.
Books: pretty good. **Registers:** In Iron Chest at the Churchwardens.
Earliest Date: 1560. **Bells:** Two – one cracked. **Chamber, Ladders,
Ropes etc:** ladder bad. **Ringers:** Clerk. **Keys:** [*blank*].
Church Services: one full every Sunday. Two ditto every alternate
Sunday. **Communions:** 6 in a year. **Average no. of Communicants:** 20.
Baptisms: private. **Catechising in Church:** no. **Average Church-goers
on Sundays:** about 100.
Churchyard: small – more room wanted. Two footpaths to be
stopped up.
Parish Clerk: John Hallam. **Appointed:** 1840. **Salary:** £4 & fees.
Efficient: yes.
Churchwardens: Two. **Properly elected, sworn in, accounts kept,
attend services, keep order etc:** [*all*] yes.
Church Rate: Sufficient. **Fund for Church Repairs:** Interest of a
Legacy of £100. **Charities:** [*blank*]
Glebe House: none.
Terrier: Land – 40 acres in Morton, 1½ in Halam. **Tithes:** no. **Great
Tithes:** Eccles. Com.**Q.A.B:** £1. 10s pr. ann. **Eccles. Com.** £3 pr. ann.
Augmentation Grant.
Fees: Marriages: 5s & 2s/6 **Churchings:** 6d. **Burials:** 1s. **Average:**
Marriages: 2. Baptisms: 8. Burials: 7½.
School: A barn belonging to Sir R. Sutton fitted up by Incumbent at
an expense of £100 – 27 by 15 ft. **Sunday:** Boys: 30. Girls: 40. **Day:**

not yet. **Under Govt. Inspection** [*blank*]. **How supported:** By Incumbent. **Mistress:** not yet appointed. Some children go to school at Southwell.

Halloughton, Perpetual Curacy

Visited: May 9 1855
Population: 79 **Value Returned:** £46. **Acreage:** 977 **Houses:** 16
Patron: Bishops of Ripon and Manchester alternately.
Incumbent: The Rev. Thomas Coats Cane MA.[1] **Instituted:** 1840.
Resides: In Southwell parish, ½ mile from H[alloughton] Church.
Church: S. James – a small, old, and poor, building – in tolerable repair – nave 33 by 20, & chancel 25 by 15. **Chancel:** Sir R. Sutton – Lessee under Eccles. Com. **Room:** 85. **Free:** 25. **Communion Table, Rails, Cover, Hassocks, Linen:** [*all*] good. **Plate:** Alms Dish: Pewter, old. Flagon: Pewter, old. Chalice: Silver, pretty good. Patin [*sic*]: Pewter, old. **Font:** West end – not good. **Reading Pew:** rickety. **Pulpit:** rickety and shabby. **Surplices:** one, good. **Ten Commandments:** no. **Table of Degrees:** no. **Alms Chest:** no. **Books:** new Bible wanted. **Registers:** In iron chest at Mr Cane's house. **Earliest Date:** 1622. **Bells:** one. **Chamber, Ladder, Ropes etc:** good. **Ringers:** Clerk. **Keys:** Clerk.

Church Services: one every Sunday – morning & afternoon alternately. **Communions:** 6 times in a year. **Average no. of communicants:** about 10. **Baptisms:** in Church – in service. **Catechising in Church:** no. **Average Churchgoers on Sundays:** about 40.

Churchyard: Large & in pretty good order – claimed by Lessee & leased out again.

Parish Clerk: Churchwarden acts. **Appointed:** [*blank*]. **Salary:** [*blank*]. **Efficient:** [*blank*]

Churchwardens: Two. **Properly elected, sworn in, accounts kept, attend services, keep order etc:** [*all*] yes.

Church Rate: yes – sufficient. **Funds for Church Repair:** none. **Charities:** none.

Glebe House: none.

Terrier: Lands: 10 acres. Tithes: [*blank*]. Great Tithes: Sir R. Sutton – Lessee under Eccles. Com. Q.A.B. £10 pr. ann – formerly paid by

---

[1] Thomas Coats Cane (1801–87); St John's College, Cambridge, BA 1823, MA 1828, d. (bishop of Chester) 1824, p. (archbishop of York) 1824; vicar of Kirklington 1837–67; perpetual curate of Halloughton 1840–67; married Mary Brittle (or Brettle) of Thurgarton in 1826.

Lessee.

Fees: Marriages: 10s & 5s. **Churchings:** 6d. **Burials:** 1s. **Average:** Marriages: one since 1852. Baptisms: one or two. Burials: one or two.

School: none. There being very few children who go to school (week days) at Southwell.

Hockerton, Rectory

Visited: May 11 1855
Population: 114 **Value Returned:** £244 **Acreage:** 1373 **Houses:** 22
Patron: Mrs Whetham, Kirklington Hall[1]
Incumbent: Rev. John P. Mills[2] **Instituted:** 1852 **Resides:** in the Rectory
Church: Dedicated to S. Nicholas. A Nave 36 by 18, Chancel 20 by 14, West Gallery, & Tower in good repair. Chancel ditto [in good repair]. **Room:** 81, & in Gallery for 40 children. **Free:** 7. **Pews:** 20. **Pews allotted or claimed:** 14 to Houses, 6 to domestics from any House. **Communion Table, Rails, Cover:** [all] very good. **Hassocks, Linen:** [all] good. **Plate:** Alms Dish, Chalice, Flagon, Patin [sic]: [all] silver – good. **Font:** West end – good. **Reading Pew:** good. **Surplices:** Two – good. **Pulpit:** good. **Ten Commandments:** yes. **Table of Degrees:** no. **Alms Chest:** yes. **Books:** very good – new. **Registers:** Kept in Iron Chest in Rectory. Earliest Date: 1562. **Bells:** Three. **Chambers, Ladders, Ropes etc:** good. **Ringers:** Clerk. **Keys:** Clerk & Rector.

Church Services: Two every Sunday. **Communions:** Six times a year. **Average no. of Communicants:** 9. **Baptisms:** during service. **Catechising in Church:** no. **Average Churchgoers on Sundays:** 60 or 70.

Churchyard: Sufficient & pretty good order. No boundary between the North side of the Church and the Rector's garden. An old pathway to the Ch[urch] alongside the Rector's garden now taken into the garden – steps to a path made equally convenient to the parishioners.

Parish Clerk: Thomas Rickett. **Appointed:** 1845. **Salary:** £4 & Fees.

[1]   Susanna Whetham.

[2]   John Pritchard Mills, son of John Mills of Hereford, gent.; St Edmund Hall, Oxford, BA 1829; d. 1830, p. 1831; curate, Chapel Hill, Monmouth, 1830; curate, Portbury, Somerset, 1833; rector of Hockerton 1852 until his death in December 1855, father of John Fuller Humfrys Mills, St Edmund Hall, Oxford, BA 1843; d.1853; p. 1854; assistant curate, Nottingham St Peter 1854–5, rector of Hockerton 1856–82.

Efficient: [blank].

Churchwardens: Two. **Properly elected, sworn in, accounts kept, attend services, keep order etc:** [*all*] yes.

Church Rate: yes – sufficient – when wanted. **Fund for Church Repair:** none. **Charities:** 6s & 1d pr. ann.

Glebe House: New and good – built by the Rector, who got no money for Dilapidations – Debt on House to Q.A.B. £657. **Terrier:** Lands: 40 acres. Tithes: commuted at £230.

Fees: Marriages: 10s & 5s. **Churchings:** 7d. **Burials**: 6d. **Average:** Marriages: ½. Baptisms: 2. Burials 1½.

School: None - the children go some to Southwell, some to Winkbourne, & some to Kirklington. Sunday: about 14 Boys and Girls.

Kirklington, Perpetual Curacy

Visited: May 9 1855
Population: 276 **Value Returned:** £49 **Acreage:** 1976 **Houses:** 43
Patron: The Chapter of Southwell.
Incumbent: Rev. Thomas Coats Cane.[1] **Instituted:** 1838. **Resides:** at Southwell (by licence).[2]
Church: Dedicated to S. Swithin. Nave 45 by 24 & Chancel 36 by 25, & West Gallery. In tolerably good repair, and good order.Chancel: Mrs Whetham (Lessee?). **Room:** 260. **Free:** 70, 40 in the Gallery. **Faculty Pews:** none. **No. of Pews:** [blank] **Communion Table, rails, Cover, Hassocks, Linen:** [all] good. **Plate:** Alms Dish: pewter. Flagon: pewter. Chalice: silver. Patin [*sic*]: silver. **Font:** Curious old Norman Font in good condition – W. end. **Reading Desk:** good. **Pulpit:** good **Surplices:** one good. **Ten Commandments:** yes. **Table of Degrees:** no. **Alms Chest:** missing. **Books:** good – new **Registers:** kept in iron chest at the Churchwardens. Earliest Date: 1650 **Bells:** Three **Chamber & Ladders & Ropes etc:** good **Ringers:** Clerk **Keys:** ditto.

Church Services: Once every Sunday – alternately mornings and afternoons. **Communions:** 6 times a year. **Average no. of Communicants:** 40. **Baptisms:** during Service. **Catechising in Church:** no. **Average no. of Churchgoers on Sundays:** Ch[urch] full in afternoons.

Churchyard: large – leased to Mrs Whetham. Footpaths to be

---

[1] See under Halloughton.

[2] Brackenhurst Hall, the 'modern seat' of Thomas Coats Cane (*White's Directory of Nottinghamshire*, 1853).

stopped up – Fences to be made good.

Parish Clerk: Major Boddam,[1] who officiates by Deputy (Simpson).[2] **Appointed:** 1853. **Salary:** [*blank*]. **Efficient:** [*yes*].

Churchwardens: Two. **Properly elected, sworn in, accounts kept, attend services, keep order etc:** [*all*] yes.

Church Rate: if wanted. Current Expenses generally paid by Vol: Subscription. **Funds for Church Repair:** none. **Charities:** Int[erest] of £30 – for the poor.

Glebe House: none.

Terrier: Land: 5 acres at Curtlingstock[3] – 5½ at Halam. **Tithes:** none. **Great Tithes:** Mrs Whetham (lessee under Eccles. Com). **Q.A.B.:** £10 2s pr. ann. (grant £400). **Eccles. Commissioners:** £20 – formerly paid by Chapter of Southwell.

Fees: Marriages: 10s & 5s. **Churchings:** 6d. **Burials:** 1s. **Average no:** Marriages: 2. Baptisms: 7. Burials: 3½.

School: Good School House is [?] built and supported entirely by Mrs Whetham. **Sunday [school]:** Boys: 25. Girls: 25. **Day:** Boys and Girls about 21. **How supported:** Mrs Whetham. **Mistress:** yes.

Maplebeck, Vicarage?[4]

Visited: May 14 1855

Population: 162 **Value Returned:** £68 **Acreage:** 1136 **Houses:** 34

Patron: The Duke of Newcastle.

Incumbent: Rev. William Parsons Turton MA.[5] **Instituted:** 1849. **Resides:** in the Glebe House (?).

Church: nave and N. Aisle 42 by 25, Chancel 24 by 16. In very bad repair – hardly safe – bad roof. Walls and floor (brick). Restoration promised by the Duke of Newcastle. **Chancel:** Duke of Newcastle. **Room:** 93. **Free:** sufficient. **Pews:** 21. Seven allotted to six houses. **Communion Table:** shabby. **Rails:** shabby. **Cover:** new. **Hassocks:** not very good. **Linen:** good. **Plate: Alms Dish:** Pewter. **Flagon:** Pewter. **Chalice:** Silver. **Patin [sic]:** Pewter. **Font:** West End – Whitewashed –

---

[1]   Possibly Alexander Boddam, Susanna Whetham's son-in-law.

[2]   Possibly William Simpson, aged 35, a cordwainer.

[3]   Cortlingstock or Costock, Nottinghamshire, near Loughborough.

[4]   Maplebeck was a vicarage.

[5]   William Parsons Turton (1819–96), Jesus College, Cambridge BA 1841, MA 1846; d. (Lincoln) 1842, p. 1843; minor canon, Southwell collegiate church, 1842; perpetual curate Edingley 1844–9, vicar of Maplebeck 1849–96, also donative curate of Winkbourne.

old – pretty good. **Reading Pew:** rickety. **Pulpit:** rickety. **Surplices:** one pretty good. **Ten Commandments:** yes. **Table of Degrees:** no. **Alms Chest:** no. **Books:** pretty good – Prayer Book very bad – new one wanted. **Registers:** in iron chest in Church. Earliest Date: 1562. **Bells:** Three – one cracked. **Chamber, Ladder and Ropes etc:** [*blank*]. **Ringers:** Clerk. **Keys:** Clerk.

Church Services: Once on Sundays, Mornings and Afternoons alternately. **Communions:** 4 times (sometimes 6) in a year. **Average no. of Communicants:** 10. **Baptisms:** in Church – not during Service. **Catechising in Church:** no. **Average no. of Churchgoers on Sundays:** about 60.

Churchyard: Sufficient – in pretty good order.

Parish Clerk: Charles Blyton.[1] **Appointed:** 1820. **Salary:** £2 & Fees. **Efficient:** yes.

Churchwardens: Two. **Properly elected, sworn in, accounts kept, attend services, keep order etc.:** [*all*] yes.

Church Rate: yes **Funds for Ch[urch] Repair:** none. **Charities:** £3 pr. ann. For the poor – under Trustees (not Ch[urch]wardens).

Glebe House: A new House built for the Clergyman in a field adjacent to the Ch:yard – at 5s rent. House not made over to the living – the land being entailed.[2]

Terrier: Land: none. **Tithes:** £4 pr. ann. **Great Tithes:** Duke of Newcastle. **Q.A.B.:** Int[erest] on a grant of £400 – also of a Parl[iamentary] gr[ant] of £200. Duke of Newcastle. £20 pr. ann. With £19 additional wh[ich] is optional – For what not known.

Fees: Marriages: 10s & 5s. **Churchings:** 7d. **Burials:** 1s. **Average no.:** Marriages: 1. Baptisms: 4. Burials: 3.

School: Sunday [school]: In the chancel – Boys, 13, Girls, 8. **Master:** the Parish Clerk – pretty good. **How paid:** £2 from the Duke of Newcastle. The children go to Winkbourne School.

Morton, Perpetual Curacy united to Bleasby

Visited: May 18 1855
Population: 140 **Value Returned:** £81 **Acreage:** 498 **Houses:** 38
Patron: The Chapter of Southwell.

---

[1]   Aged 65, a 'Cottager and Parish Clark'.

[2]   'a handsome brick building, erected by the noble Duke about 3 years ago' (*White's Directory of Nottinghamshire*, 1853).

Incumbent: Rev. J. W. Marsh.**Instituted:** see Bleasby. **Resides:** see Bleasby.

Church: St Denis. A small brick building, erected about 100 years ago – A nave 35 by 19 & a Chancel which is a mere recess. All neat & in good order. **Room:** 100. **Free:** 14. **Pews:** 14 allotted to houses by alleged Faculties or award. **Communion Table:** a shelf. **Rails, Cover, Hassocks, Linen:** [*all*] good. **Plate:** Alms Dish: Pewter – old. Flagon: Pewter – old. Chalice: Silver – good. Patin [sic]: Silver, good. **Font:** Inside Altar rails - There has been none till lately – No room elsewhere. **Reading Pew:** good. **Pulpit:** good. **Surplices:** Two – one good. **Commandments:** yes. **Table of Degrees:** no. **Alms Chest:** no. **Books:** good. **Registers:** kept by the Vicar at Bleasby. Earliest Date: 1640. **Bells:** 2. **Chamber, Ladder, Ropes etc:** good. **Ringers:** Clerk. **Keys:** Clerk and Churchwarden.

Church Services: Once every Sunday, morning and afternoon alternately. **Communions:** 6 or 8 in a year. **Average no. of Communicants:** 9 or 10. **Baptisms:** After 2nd Lesson. **Catechising in Church:** yes. **Average no. of Churchgoers on Sundays:** 70 or 80 – some from Fiskerton & Bleasby.

Churchyard: large & good & well kept.

Parish Clerk: The Clerk from Bleasby. **Appointed:** 1849. **Salary:** £3 & Fees. **Efficient:** yes.

Churchwardens: one appointed by the Vicar. **Properly elected, sworn in, accounts kept, attend services, keep order etc:** [*all*] yes.

Church Rate: Yes – sufficient. **Charities:** none.

Glebe House: see Bleasby.

Terrier: Land: [*blank*]. **Tithes:** [*blank*]. **Q.A.B.:** [*blank*].

Fees: Marriages: [*blank*]. **Churchings:** [*blank*]. **Burials:** [*blank*]. **Average:** Marriages: 1 or 2. Baptisms: 4 or 5. Burials: 4 or 5.

School: Yes. Lately built by subscription – cost about £40. **Sunday [school]** Boys & Girls: 35. **Day:** Boys & Girls: 25. **How Supported:** Subscription. **Expenditure:** about £16. **Mistress:** Yes – pretty good.

Muskham, North, Vicarage

Visited: May 15 1855

Population: 877 **Value Returned:** £230 **Acreage:** 2180. **Houses:** 186.

Patron: Bishops of Ripon and Manchester alternately – Bishop of Manchester last turn.

Incumbent: Rev. John Winstanley Hull MA.[1] **Instituted:** 1853.
Resides: In hired house in the village.[2] **Curate:** none.

Church: Dedicated to S. Wilfrid. Chancel 30 by 15. Nave & N. & S.
Aisles 39 by 42. West Gallery. Blocked up with Pews, about which there
are many disputes. Pretty good repair. [*Added in pencil:* 'Tower and roof
found to be bad and has been thoroughly repaired and re-timbered and
leaded.'] **Chancel:** Eccles. Commissioners & Duke of Newcastle. **Room:**
224. **Free:** 30 in Nave. **Pews:** 40 – all allotted to Houses – one allotted
to <u>six</u> Houses. **Communion Table, Rails, Cover, Hassocks, Linen:** [*all*]
good. **Plate:** Alms Dish: silver. Flagon: silver. Chalice: plated – good,
but not Ecclesiastical – a Tankard & 2 Salvers. Patin [sic]: silver. **Font:**
Good, by S.W. Door. **Reading Pew:** pretty good. **Pulpit:** ricketty &
small. **Surplices:** 2 – one good. **Ten Commandments:** no. **Table of
Degrees:** no. **Alms Chest:** none. **Books:** pretty good. **Registers:** In Iron
Chest in Church. Earliest Date: 1704/5. **Bells:** Three – one cracked.
Chamber, ladders, Ropes etc: pretty good. **Ringers:** Clerk. **Key:** Clerk.

Church Services: Twice on Sundays. **Communions:** Monthly – just
increased in frequency. **Average no. of Communicants:** about 20
(before alteration). **Baptisms:** In Church – after Service. **Catechising in
Church:** no. **Average no. of Churchgoers on Sundays:** under 100 –
increasing 'to see the new parson'.

Churchyard: pretty good. Fence to be made good. Dropping from
spouts <u>to be attended to</u> - [added note in pencil: 'promised piece of land
adjacent – wd. do for Parsonage House [*word illegible*] and fence
belonging to the G.C. [?] very bad and [*following words illegible*].

Parish Clerk: Samuel Thompson.[3] **Appointed:** 1847. **Salary:** £5 &
Fees. **Efficient:** yes.

Churchwardens: Two. **Properly elected:** The week <u>before</u> Easter.
Sworn in, accounts kept, attend services, keep order: [*all*] yes.

Church Rate: yes – sufficient. **Fund for Church Repairs:** none.
Charities: [*blank*].

Glebe House: A cottage – let to the parish Clerk.

---

[1]   John Winstanley Hull (1825–1902) was the son of William Winstanley Hull, barrister,
of London and grandson of Dr John Hull. Educated at Charterhouse and Brasenose College,
Oxford, BA 1847, MA 1850; d. 1848, p. 1850 (bishop of Manchester); curate of St
Michael's on Wyre; perpetual curate, Grimsargh, 1849; translator of *Gieseler's Ecclesiastical History*, vols. III, IV and V for *Clark's Theological Library*, 1853–4.

[2]   In 1861 Hull, aged 36, lived in Norwell Lane with his wife Charlotte Augusta (43), and
their children Mary Beatrice (7), William Winstanley (6), twin daughters: Charlotte Frances
and Charlotte Joanna (4), an as yet unbaptised son (subsequently named Henry), and five
servants. By the time of the 1871 census the number of servants had been reduced to two.

[3]   Aged 26, a master tailor.

Terrier: Land/Tithes: 113 acres – including 20 acres in Holme & <u>claimed</u> for that Church, but the claim is disputed. **Great Tithes:** allotted – D[uke] of Newcastle, Eccl. Com. & others. **Q.A.B.:** Int[erest] of £200. **Eccles. Commissioners:** £20 pr. ann.

Fees: Marriages: 10s & 5s. **Churchings:** 1s. **Burials:** 1s. **Average:** Marriages: 6. Baptisms: 25. Burials: 14.

School: [*blank*]

Muskham, South, Vicarage

Visited: May 17 1855
Population: 263 **Houses:** 51 **Acreage:** 2631 **Value Returned:** £139
Patron: Bishops of Ripon and Manchester alternately.
Incumbent: Rev. John Drake Becher MA.[1] **Instituted:** 1838. **Resides:** at Southwell.

Church: Dedicated to S. Wilfrid. Chancel 36 by 15, Nave & N. & S. aisles 45 by 39. West Gallery. In good order & repair throughout – fine old tower.**Chancel:** Lord Middleton (Lessee under Eccl. Com.) **Room:** 206. **Free:** 60 – 30 of them in Gallery. **Pews:** 20 – allotted to Houses. **Communion Table, Rails, Cover, Hassocks, Linen:** [all] good. **Plate:** Alms Dish, Flagon, Chalice, Patin [sic]: [all] silver, good. **Font:** Handsome – at S. W. Door. **Reading Pew:** good. **Pulpit:** good. **Ten Commandments:** yes. **Table of Degrees:** yes. **Alms Chest:** yes. **Books:** good. **Registers:** In Iron chest in Church. Earliest Date: 1559 – some old ones missing. **Bells:** Three. **Chamber, Ladders, Ropes etc:** good. **Ringers:** clerk. **Keys:** Clerk.

Church Services: Twice on Sundays – mornings and afternoons except during the winter months. **Communions:** 4 – Xmas, Easter, Whitsuntide, Michaelmas. **Average no. of Communicant:** 20. **Baptisms:** After 2nd Lesson. **Catechising in Church:** in School – sometimes in Church. **Average Churchgoers on Sundays:** about 110 besides children.

Churchyard: Sufficient & in good order.

Parish Clerk: John Fletcher. **Appointed:** 1838. **Salary:** £4. 4s & Fees. **Efficient:** yes.

Churchwardens: Two. **Properly elected, sworn in, attend service, keep order:** [all] yes. [*the heading* 'accounts kept' *missing*].

Church rate: yes – sufficient.**Funds for Church Repairs:** none.

[1] John Drake Becher (1806–64), son of John Thomas Becher; St John's College, Cambridge, BA 1828, MA 1831; d. (Rochester) 1829, p. (London) 1830; vicar of South Muskham 1835–64. He lived at Hill House, Southwell.

Charities: Int[erest] of £100 – Vicar & Ch:wardens Trustees.

Glebe House: A cottage let to the Schoolmaster.

Terrier: Land: 3 acres. **Tithes:** Commuted at £139. 10s. **Great Tithes:** Lord Middleton (Lessee under Eccles. Com.) **Q.A.B.:** Int[erest] of £200. **Easter Dues:** average about £2.

Fees: Marriages: 10s. 6d. and 5s. **Churchings:** 1s. **Burials:** 1s. **Average:** Marriages: 3.Baptisms: 6. Burials: 7.

School: In the Church. **Sunday [school]:** Boys 14 - Girls 11. **Day:** none. **How Supported:** Subscription. **Expenditure:** about £10. **Master:** yes – pretty good.

Norwell, Vicarage. (see Carlton on Trent)

Visited: May 15 1855

Population: 726 **Houses:** 162 **Acres:** 3720 **Value Returned:** £336 [*added in pencil:* E.C.[1] (1856) £26 pr. ann. to be [*following words illegible*].

Patron: Bishops of Ripon & Manchester alternately – Bishop of Ripon last turn.

Incumbent: Rev. James Morris Maxfield (a literate). **Instituted:** 1854. **Resides:** in the Glebe House.

Church: Dedicated to S. Lawrence – a very fine old Church – In a most wretched state – just weather tight – the Floor is uneven as if there had been an earthquake – old high square pews, large enough to hold 8 or 10 in each, average occupants 2 or 3 – The whole Church , without and within, wants a thoro' restoration & at large expense.[2] **Chancel:** Eccles. Com. – Wants a thoro' restoration – roof not weather tight. **Room:** 234 [*cr* 240 *sub*]. **Free:** <u>NONE</u> - Gallery for 50 children. **Pews:** 46 – Sittings allotted 164. Farm Servants etc 70. **Communion Table, Rails, Cover:** [*all*] pretty good. **Hassocks, Linen:** [*all*] good. **Plate:** Alms Dish, Flagon, Chalice & Patin: [all] Silver – very handsome especially the Flagon. **Font:** good – N[ear] N. W. Door. **Reading Pew:** good. **Pulpit:** good. **Surplices:** Two – one good. **Alms Chest:** yes. **Ten Commandments:** not legible. **Table of Degrees:** yes. **Books:** pretty good. **Registers:** In Iron Chest in Church. Earliest Date: 1685. Complete

---

[1]   i.e. the Ecclesiastical Commissioners.

[2]   For a comprehensive account of the subsequent restoration of the church at the initiative of James Morris Maxfield see Norwell St Laurence, Southwell, on the website *churches. Nottingham.ac.ukn12/hincumb.html*.

to 1855. **Bells:** Three. Chamber, Ladders & Ropes: pretty good. **Ringers:** Clerk. **Keys:** Vicar & Clerk.

Church Services: Once on Sundays - Mornings and Afternoons alternately. From May to Sept. Evening Service additional once a fortnight. **Communions:** 6 in a year. **Average Communicants:** 12. **Baptisms:** in Church – after Service. **Catechising in Church:** in School. **Average present on Sundays:** about 150.

Churchyard: Five roods – a fence and some tomb stones to be attended to. [*added in pencil:* 'a brickwall 110 ft long promised [*next word illegible*] on behalf of Eccles. Commrs. 50 yards built 1857 [*next words illegible*].

Parish Clerk: John Chappell.[1] **Appointed:** 1845. **Salary:** Fees & Xmas boxes. **Efficient:** yes.

Churchwardens: Two. **Properly elected, sworn in, accounts kept, attend services, keep order etc:** [*all*] yes.

Church Rate: Sufficient for current expenses. **Funds for Ch[urch] Repairs:** none. **Charities:** [*blank*].

Glebe House: Small – Present Vicar spent nearly £100 on it out of his own pocket.

Terrier: Lands [and] Tithes: 200 acres - not very good land. **Great Tithes:** [blank], **Q.A.B.:** £6. 10s pr. ann. **Corn Rent:** nearly £40 pr. ann. **Railway:** Money invested from land bought by [?] — £13 pr. ann.

Fees: Marriages: 10s & 5s. **Churchings:** 1s. **Burials:** 1s. **Average:** Marriages: 2 or 3. Baptisms: 31. Burials: 13.

School: Two – not very good. **Sunday:** Boys 25, Girls 28. **Day:** Boys & Girls about 70. **Government Inspection:** no. **How supported** [and] **Expenditure:** An Endowment producing £42, with good house & homestead – under Trustees – Vicar elected a Trustee. **Master:** inefficient. **Mistress:** his wife – Inefficient.

[*Added note in pencil across lower left hand corner of page:* 'N. Aisle of nave. Roof new lead [*next word illegible*] roofed. Window restored – East window and others put in good order'].

Oxton, Vicarage

Visited: May 10 1855 May 16 [18]56
Population: 850 **Houses:** 185 **Acres:** 3580 **Value Returned:** £195
Patron: Canon of Oxton in Southwell Coll[egiate] Ch[urch].

---

[1] Aged 52, a master cordwainer.

Incumbent: Rev. Collingwood Foster Fenwick LL.B. **Instituted:** 1824. **Resides:** at Ryde – in the Isle of Wight. **Curate:** Rev. Henry Wall Tibbs[1] (T.C.D.). **Licensed:** 1851. **Stipend:** £95, fees & House. **Resides:** in the Vicarage House.

Church: Dedicated to SS. Peter and Paul – neat and in good order. Chancel: 30 by 15, Nave & N. & S. Aisles 40 by 48. West Gallery (for Singers). **Chancel:** Messrs [?] Sherbrook & J. D. Becher – Wants repair – especially E. Window. [added in pencil: 'N. window unsafe – filled with loose items']. **Room:** 364. **Free:** 214. **Pews:** allotted to families and houses. **Communion Table, Hassocks, Rails, Cover:** [all] good. **Linen:** new is to be bought. **Plate:** Alms Dish, Flagon, Chalice, Patin: [all] plated – good. 1 silver Chalice. **Font:** good – In the Chancel. **Reading Pew:** good. **Pulpit:** good. [added in pencil: 'improved by removal of sounding board']. **Surplices:** all good – [added in pencil: 'another purchased']. **Ten Commandments:** yes. **Table of Degrees:** no. **Alms Chest:** none. **Books:** New Bible wanted – many misprints. **Registers:** kept at the Vicarage. Earliest Date: 1562. **Bells:** 4 – one broken. **Chamber, Ladders, Ropes etc:** good. **Ringers:** under controul. **Keys:** Curate.

Church Services: Twice every Sunday. **Communions:** Once every six weeks – and Festivals. **Average no. of Communicants:** 30. **Baptisms:** during service. **Catechising in Church:** no. **Average no. of Churchgoers on Sundays:** [blank].

Churchyard: Pretty good – more ground wanted.

Parish Clerk: William Wain.[2] **Appointed:** 1850. **Salary:** £3 & Fees. **Efficient:** yes.

Churchwardens: Two. **Properly elected, sworn in, keep accounts, attend services etc:** [all] yes.

Church Rate: yes. **Funds for Church Repair:** none. **Charities:**

[1] Durham University 1835, BA 1839, University College, Durham 1840, L.Th., 1841, Durham MA 1842, Oxford MA, 1860; d. 1841, p. 1842. Assistant curate, Oxton 1850–9; Shelford 1859–62; perpetual curate, Bobbington (dio. Hereford) from 1862. Member of learned societies including the Royal Irish Academy, the Society of Antiquaries of Scotland and the Syro-Egyptian Society. During his curacies in Oxton and Shelford Tibbs published numerous pamphlets and sermons including *What the Bible says of Unity and Dissensions in Religion* (1857), *Uniformity in Matters of Faith* (1854), *Lectures on the Four Ages of Human Life* (1857), *The Poor Exalted in Christ* (1858) and *The Poor Man's Daily Companion, a Rule of Life, with Short Prayers and other Devotions for Poor Persons* (1860, 2nd edn 1863), and, in 1857 *Vita dell B.V.M. Madre del Nostro Signore Gesú Cristo estatta dal Nuovo Testamento e raccontata nelle medesime parole dela Sacra Scrittura, con unã breve Introduzione* (compiled for the Anglo-Continental Association 1857, and translated into Portuguese in 1859).

[2] Aged 42, a lacemaker.

[*blank*].

Glebe House: In tolerable [*cr* bad *sub*] repair [*added note in pencil:* 'repairs sh[ould] be made. Mr Tibbs wants £5 or £10 pr ann. for repairs'].

Terrier: only an incorrect one of 1781 to be found. **Great Tithes:** Messrs [?] Sherbrook and J.D. Becher etc.

[*entry for fees omitted*]

Schools: Two – Endowed – in a house of Mr Sherbrooke's, who is a Trustee – entirely under his controul. **Sunday:** Boys, 33 – Girls, 40. **Day:** Boys, 40 – Girls, 40. **Under Government Inspection:** no. **How supported:** Endowment & Pence. A House for the Master. **Expenditure:** Boys £34. **Master:** not very efficient. **Mistress:** very fair.

[*added note in pencil:* '[*word illegible*] for Visit [ation?] Chwarden – Keys – Degrees [?]

Rolleston, Vicarage

Visited: May 31 1855

Population: (with Fiskerton, Hamlet) [*blank*]. **Houses:** [*blank*] **Acres:** [*blank*].

Value Returned: £246.

Patron: The Chapter of Southwell.

Incumbent: The Revd. Robert Hodgson Fowler MA.[1] **Instituted:** 1841. **Resides:** In the Vicarage House.

Church: A nice old Church, in tolerable repair. Chancel 36 X 15, Nave & N. & S. Aisles 54 X 33. W. Gallery – Organ – fine tower – in pretty good order – might be made a very nice Church.[2] **Chancel:** Messrs. Manners Sutton & Plumtre – lately well repaired. **Room:** 238. **Free:** 130 & School children in Chancel. **Pews:** 21 – claimed by Houses. **Communion Table, Rails & Hassocks:** [*all*] good. **Cover:** good & new – given by Parish. **Linen:** ditto, given by Vicar. **Plate:** Alms Dish: none. Flagon: old – Pewter – curiously carved. Chalice & Patin [*sic*]: silver – good. **Font:** nr. S. W. Door – Shabby. **Reading Pew & Pulpit:** pretty good. **Surplices:** Two old – a new one to be ordered. **Ten Commandments:** yes. **Table of Degrees & Alms Chest:** none. **Books:** Pr[ayer]

[1] Son of the Revd Charles Fowler, of Southwell; Exeter College, Oxford, BA 1819, MA 1825; vicar choral, Southwell collegiate church; vicar of Rolleston 1841 to his death in 1858.
[2] When James John Trebeck, the rural dean, visited in 1892 the church was in a very dilapidated condition.

Bk. Very bad – new one much wanted. **Registers:** In iron chest in Vicarage House. Earliest Date: 1559 – Some very curious old registers the [*following word or words illegible*]. **Bells:** 4 – and a Clock. **Chamber, Ladders, Ropes etc:** good. **Ringers:** Clerk. **Keys:** Vicar.

Church Services: Two full – every Sunday. **Communions:** 4 times a year. **Average no. of Communicants:** About 20. **Baptisms:** In Church – after Service. **Catechising in Church:** no. **Average no. of Church-goers on Sundays:** About 120, besides children.

Churchyard: Sufficient - & in good order.

Parish Clerk: John Pettener. **Appointed:** 1851. **Salary:** Commuted rent charge – average about £6 or £7. **Efficient:** yes.

Churchwardens: Two. **Properly elected, sworn in, keep accounts, attend services etc:** [*all*] yes.

Church Rate: yes – sufficient. **Charities:** Interest of about £130 – properly administered by Vic[ar] & Ch[urch] wds.

Glebe House: New & good – built by present Incumbent, money borrowed from Q.A.B. in 1844 –£793. Payment to Q. A. B. last year - £45. 19. 3. Additional cost to the Incumbent (much unexpected between £500 & £600).

Terrier: Land: 25 acres. **Tithes:** commuted (Rolleston £188. 15s Fiskerton £76) corn rent charge. **Great Tithes:** Messrs Manners Sutton & Plumtre.**Easter Offerings:** average about £3.

Fees: Marriages: 10s & 5s. **Churchings:** 7d. **Burials:** 1s. **Average no:** Marriages: 2 or 3. Baptisms: 12. Burials: 8.

School: Sunday: (in Chancel) Boys & Girls – 30. **How supported:** Subscription. **Expenditure:** about £5 5s. **Master:** yes – pretty good. Children go to School in Morton – which has been built partly for the convenience of both parishes – Rolleston parish contribute[s] to its support.

Southwell, Coll. Ch. [*cr & Rectory sub*]

Visited: May 18 1855

Population: 2471 less 145 in H[ouse] of Correction. **Houses:** 545. **Acres:** 4550. **Value Returned:** £450.

Patron: Canon of Normanton in Southwell Coll. Ch.

Incumbent: Revd. John Murray Wilkins M.A. **Instituted:** December 1840. **Resides:** In the Rectory House. **Curate:** Rev. Oldfield Kelsall

Prescot.[1] **Licensed:** 1853. **Stipend:** £50. **Resides:** in the Parish.

Church: The Collegiate Church which is the Parish Church also. **Communion Table, Rails, Hassocks, Cover, Linen, Plate:** all good and handsome. **Church Room:** 654 & 120 children. Free: 135. Pews: 116 – Let to Families, not to Houses. **Font:** good – In the Nave at W. Door. **Reading Pew & Pulpit:** good. **Surplices:** Four, good. **Commandments:** no. **Table of Degrees:** no. **Alms Chest:** yes.**Books:** good. **Registers:** In Iron Chest in Vestry. Earliest Date: 1559.

Church Services: Daily Mornings and Afternoons (Minor Canons). Thrice every Sunday. Mornings – canon residentiary[2] & Rector. Afternoons: Min[or] Canons. Evenings: Rector. **Communions:** Monthly & Greater Festivals. Early Communions (additional) at Xmas, Easter, & Whitsunday. **Average Communicants:** 60. **Baptisms:** In Church – Not during Service – Font being in the Nave.[3] **Catechising in Church:** no. **Average Churchgoers on Sundays:** 600 or 700, besides Children.

Churchyard: Large & good – The Churchyard belongs to the Chapter.

Parish Clerk: Peter Coxon – who is also Verger to the Chapter.[4] **Appointed:** 1848. **Salary:** Fees & Xmas boxes etc etc. **Efficient: yes**

Churchwardens: Four – Two for the parish, and Two by the Rector. **Properly elected, sworn in, keep accounts, attend services etc:** [*all*] yes.

Church Rate: not required. **Fund for Church Repair:** yes. The Eccles. Commissrs. pay all expenses. **Charities:** [blank].

Glebe House: Old, but pretty good. Debt on – still due to Q.A.B. - £47. 13s – Payment/[18]55 - £9. 10. 7.

Terrier: Land: About 40 acres (40 at Woodboro). **Houses:** Small House in Southwell – Public House in Woodboro'. **Tithes:** commuted at 3 shillings & six pence pr. ann. **Grt. Tithes:** Lessees under Eccles: Com: **Q.A.B:** £13. 11. 6. **Easter Dues:** Average £9. **Railway:** Land bought by, & money invested, producing £17 pr. ann. Eccles. Commissrs: £301 pr. ann.

Fees: Marriages: 10s & 5s. **Churchings:** 6d. **Burials:** 1s. **Average:** Marriages: 19. Baptisms: 62. Burials: 42.

---

[1]   Brasenose College, Oxford, d. 1853, p. 1854, assistant curate, Southwell 1853–6, perpetual curate Dukinfield St John, Cheshire 1856–60, assistant curate North Wraxall in 1861.

[2]   George Wilkins.

[3]   This suggests that the principal Sunday services were held in the Quire.

[4]   In 1851 Coxon lived with his 19-year-old wife and their small baby in a cottage in Moor Lane in Southwell.

Schools: Two good, & Master's House – built by subscription in 1840. **Sunday:** (in addition to Day scholars) Boys, 33 – Girls, 29. **Day:** Boys, 80 – Girls, 70. **Under Government Inspection:** yes. **How supported:** Subscription & [*children's*] Pence & Government Grants. **Expenditure:** About £100 pr. ann – exclusive of Govt. allowances. **Master:** Good, Certificated – (House, ½ the Pence, £45 - & Govt. allowance. **Mistress:** Good – certificated - ½ the Pence, £35 - & Govt. allowance.[1]

Southwell, Trinity Church

Visited: May 19 1855
Population: 900. **Houses:** 216. **Value Returned:** £100.
Patron: Trustees.[2]
Incumbent: Rev. John Conington. **Instituted:** 1846.[3] **Resides:** in the Glebe House.
Church: Built by subscription & consecrated in 1846.[4] Church, 24

---

[1] These were the National Schools. No reference is made here to Southwell Collegiate Grammar School.

[2] The first trustees were the Revd Edward Garrard Marsh (Aylesford, Kent) and prebendary of Woodborough in Southwell collegiate church, Colonel Whetham (Kirklington Hall), the Revd John Dixon Hales (Richmond, Surrey), the Revd Charles Wasteneys Eyre (Carlton in Lindrick), and the Revd Henry Western Plumptre (Eastwood).

[3] John Conington (1794–1878), son of James Conington of Horncastle; Queens' College, Cambridge, migrated to Jesus College, BA 1822; d. (Bristol) 1821, p. 1822; curate of Ancaster 1821-5; curate of Navenby, Lincs., 1825-46; perpetual curate of Holy Trinity Church, Southwell, 1845-78; married Sophia Christiana, daughter of John Lucas Calcraft.

[4] The parish return for the Census of Religious Worship in 1851 recorded that 'Trinity Church', Southwell was 'Conse[crated] 31 March 1851 as an additional Church. Erected by private subscription except a grant from the Nottinghamshire Church Building Soc. of £500. Cost £4000 or thereabouts'. However, the church was undoubtedly consecrated on 31 March 1846, by John Kaye, bishop of Lincoln. The *Nottingham Mercury* (3 April 1846) reported that the bishop signed the deed of consecration and ordered it to be registered, yet the Bishop's Register only notes the presentation of a perpetual curate to the new benefice on that date, the church itself being 'lately erected and consecrated' (LAO, DIOC/REG/40, 511). A second consecration register (LAO, DIOC/CONSEC REG/2, 134) seems merely to note details of a conveyance, endowment, appointment of trustees and a declaration of patronage for the church and burial ground, dated 31 March 1846. The date of consecration given in the 1851 return is therefore unexplained, although John Conington, the first incumbent, signed the return. The census of religious worship took place the day before, on 30 March 1851. The 1851 return also states that the church was endowed thus: 'land church yard £0. 10. 0; permanent endowment: £32. 9. 8; pew rents £111. 10. 10.' This gave a total of some £145 a year. The cost of the new church was £2,500 made up of two subscriptions of £2,000 and £500 respectively, together with an further £500 in a grant from the Nottinghamshire Church Building Society (1851 census return). An additional

X 18, Nave & N. & S. Aisles, 81 X 48. & W. Gallery – all very neat & in good order. **Chancel:** Good. **Room:** 633. **Free:** 230.[1] **Pews:** 98 – for letting. **Communion Table, Rails, Hassocks, Cover, Linen, Plate:** [all] good. **Font:** Good and handsome – at W. end. **Reading Pew & Pulpit:** Stone – handsome. **Surplices:** Three – good. **Ten Commandments:** yes. **Table of Degrees:** no. **Books:** good. **Alms Chest:** no. **Registers:** Complete from 1846 – In Iron Chest in Glebe [house]. **Bells:** one. **Chamber, Ladders, Ropes etc:** good. **Ringers:** Sexton. **Keys:** Incumbent, Clerk & Ch:wardens.

Church Services: Two every Sunday, Mornings and afternoons. Thursday Evens. [evenings] – generally. **Communions:** monthly and Grt. Festivals. **Average Communicants:** 37. **Baptisms:** After 2nd Lesson. **Catechising in Church:** In School. **Average Churchgoers on Sundays:** about 250.

Churchyard: Sufficient & in good order.

Parish Clerk: Thomas Marshall.[2] **Appointed:** 1846. **Efficient:** yes. **Salary:** Fees etc.

Churchwardens: Two. **Properly appointed, sworn in, accounts kept, attend services etc:** [*all*] yes.

Church Rate: no. **Fund for Church Repair etc:** yes – sufficient. **Charities:** none.

Glebe House: yes. 1 acre of grounds. Built by subscription – good.

Terrier: none. Endowment: Int[erest] of £1000 on Govt. Securities & Pew Rents.

Fees: Marriages: no Marriages at this Church. **Churchings:** 6d. **Burials:** 1s. **Average:** Baptisms: 20. Burials: 6.

Schools: Good and large – built by Subscription.[3] Two rooms that may be thrown into one. **Sunday:** Boys, 30. Girls, 50. **Day:** Infants: 100. **Government Inspection:** yes. **How supported:** Subscription & Pence.

£1,000 was raised to endow the incumbent. The *Nottingham Mercury* (3 April 1846) gave the actual cost of the building of the church (by N. Parkin of Southwell) as £3,005 against an estimate of £2,562. The land purchased was some 2,110 acres and cost about £800. See M. Huthwayte and P. Young, *Holy Trinity Southwell 1846–1996* (Southwell 1996), 7.

[1] The accommodation was variously calculated. Newspaper reports of the consecration of the church in 1846 give total sittings as 600, of which 200 were free or let at low rates as the bishop of the diocese should decide. The 1851 census of religious worship gives a total of 600, with 203 free and 397 'other'.

[2] Possibly a shoemaker, aged 69.

[3] The cost was £520 (Huthwayte and Young, *Holy Trinity*, 8). The 1851 census return made by John Conington noted that the cost of the erection of the church and school together with the endowment capital approximates to '£4,000 or thereabouts'.

Expenditure: about £40 pr. ann. **Mistress:** yes – good – not certificated.

Upton, Vicarage

Visited: May 12 1855
Population: (less Union Workhouse 132) 497 **Houses:** 118 **Acres:** 1860 **Value Returned:** £91
Patron: Chapter of Southwell.
Incumbent: Revd Frederick William Naylor BA.[1] **Instituted:** 1840.
Resides: in the Vicarage House.
Church: Dedicated to S. Peter. Chancel: 36 X 15, Nave & N. Aisle 52 X 25, Chantry Chapel N. of Aisle. W. Gallery. The floor blocked up with old rickety pews all shapes, heights and sizes – W. Gallery hardly safe – a 2nd Gallery W. end of Aisle for 30 children. Building in tolerable repair. **Chancel:** Lessees under Eccl. Com – floor bad. **Room:** 180. **Free:** 20. **Pews:** [blank]. **Communion Table, Rails, & Hassocks:** shabby. **Cover & Linen:** tolerably good. **Plate:** Alms Dish & Flagon: Pewter – shabby. Chalice and Patin [sic]: silver – good. [*A note written obliquely across the return at this point:* 'Church Restored 1867. Cost £1000 & opened Nov 21/67'] **Font:** W. end – a depository for snuffers, candlesticks, etc. **Reading Pew & Pulpit:** pretty good. **Surplices:** Two – one good. **Ten Commandments:** no. **Table of Degrees**: no. **Alms Chest:** no. **Books:** good. **Registers:** In iron Chest in Vicarage. Earliest Date: 1580. **Bells:** Four – one cracked. **Chamber, Ladders, Ropes etc.:** good. **Ringers:** [*blank*]. **Keys:** Vicar & Clerk.
Church Services: Twice each Sunday. **Communions:** 4 times a year. **Average no. of Communicants:** 52 different persons in a year.[2] **Baptisms:** sometimes private – in Church "when they bring them." **Catechising in Church:** no. **Average Churchgoers on Sundays:** About 100 besides children.

[1] 1810–58; St John's College, Cambridge, BA 1832. Ord. deacon (Chester, *Litt. dim.* from York) 13 Jan. 1833; priest 1834. Vicar of Upton 1840–58. Married (1) 1842, Elizabeth Milnes, dau. of John Wright; (2), 1845 Maria Ann Barton. In the 1851 census F.W. Naylor was living in the vicarage with his wife, Maria Ann (then aged 34) and their children Frederick Burton Naylor (3) and Ellen Maria Naylor (2), two pupils (William Broughton Smith, 18, and Thomas Walter Huthwaite, 15), and three servants (Ann Gill, 27, Mary Ann Hubbard, 24, and Eliza Linker, 16).
[2] Naylor published two sermons on Confirmation in 1853: *Confirmation realized, or the Vow earnestly made and faithfully performed* (a sermon on Ps. lvi, 12), and *Confirmation abused: or Better not to vow unto God than to vow and not pay* (a sermon on Eccl. v, 4–5).

Churchyard: Large but not well kept. Fences pretty good – improving. Some graves left in a very unseemly state.

Parish Clerk: – Whitworth.[1] **Appointed:** More than 20 years ago. **Efficient:** not in Churchyard. **Salary:** £6 & Fees.

Churchwardens: Two. **Properly appointed & sworn in, accounts kept, attend services etc:** [*all*] yes.

Church Rate: not required. **Fund for Church Repairs [and] Charities:** Almost £40 pr. ann. spent on Church, School, & Poor.

Glebe House: New & good. Built by Subscription – grant of £200 from Q.A.B.

Terrier: Land [and] Tithes: 41 acres. **Great Tithes:** Eccles. Commissrs. **Q.A.B.:** no. **Eccles: Commissrs:** £20 pr. ann. paid formerly by Ch[apter] of Southwell.

Fees: Marriages: 10s & 5s. **Churchings:** 6d. **Burials:** 1s. **Average:** Marriages: 2½. Baptisms: 14. Burials: 11.

School: Endowed – In unsatisfactory condition. **Sunday:** Boys 25 Girls 25. **Day:** Boys 8. Girls [blank].**How Supported:** Endowment & Pence. **Expenditure:** £5 pr. ann., house & Garden. **Master [and] Mistress:** old & inefficient.

Winkbourne

This was claimed as a donative chapel and, though listed by John Murray Wilkins, was not visited by him. However, he left two pages blank in his notebook evidently in case he was required to complete a return. That Winkbourne was a donative and outside episcopal jurisdiction had been disputed for at least one hundred years. In 1777 Mary Burnell, patron of the donative, claimed that Winkbourne was a donative against the counterclaim of the archbishop of York that it was a perpetual curacy and therefore within his jurisdiction (NAO, DD/CW/7/40). In 1853 the church was said to be 'a small ancient structure, and the tower, in which are three bells, is completely covered with ivy. It has just been new roofed, and thoroughly cleaned and repaired at the expense of E.V. Pegge Burnell, Esq., who is patron of the curacy, of which the Rev. P. Turton [sic] is incumbent. The living is a donative'.[2] The return for the parish for the 1851 religious census was completed by W. Parsons Turton, the officiating minister. He noted that

---

[1] Possibly Abraham Whitworth, aged 49, a carpenter.

[2] *White's Directory of Nottinghamshire* (1853).

'The Church of Winkbourn adjoins the hall and is entirely at the discretion of E.P. Burwell [sic]. There is only an officiating minister who is not licensed or inducted. It is now held with Maplebeck the adjoining Parish.' J.M. Wilkins's successor as rural dean, James John Trebeck, seems not to have included the donative in his two visitations in the 1890s. In 1911 J.C. Cox found the church 'smothered in trees, and so hidden away behind the Hall that it is difficult to find ... Tower in bad condition and emcumbered with ivy ... The squire of Winkburn [Col. E. S. Pegge Burnell] keeps [the] register in his own hands and refuses access to it'.[1] Winkbourne (or Winkburn) St John of Jerusalem appears in the *Southwell Diocesan Church Calendar* as a donative until 1913. Thereafter it is listed as a perpetual curacy, held with Maplebeck.

Woodborough, Perpetual curacy

Visited: May 10 1855
Population: 852. **Houses:** 185. **Acres:** 1940. **Value Returned:** £93.
Patron: Chapter of Southwell.
Incumbent: Revd. Samuel Lealand Oldacres BA.[2] **Instituted:** 1840.
Resides: In the Parish – In the School House.
Church: A fine old Church – dedicated to S. Swithin – Chancel 39 X 18 (very fine). Nave and Aisles 39 X 36 – W. gallery. In bad repair within & without - not weather tight – roof bad. Dreary and neglected look. [*added in pencil:* 'nothing done'] **Chancel:** Mr. Matthews (?) Enfranchised from Eccles. Com: **Room:** 200. **Free:** About 80 – Gallery for Free School – 50. **Pews:** 12 – allotted – 32 open seats about ½ allotted & ½ free. **Communion Table, Rails, & Linen:** pretty good. **Hassocks & Cover:** none. **Plate:** Alms Dish, Flagon, Chalice & Patin [sic] – all silver & good. **Font:** In the Chancel – curious old Norman. **Reading Pew & Pulpit:** good. **Surplices:** one good. **Ten Command-ments:** no. **Table of Degrees:** no. **Alms Chest:** no. **Books:** Very bad – new ones much wanted. [*added note in pencil:* 'presented by Mrs M. Parkyns']. **Registers:** In iron chest at Mr Oldacre's. **Earliest date:** 1547. **Bells:** Four – one cracked – A new clock. **Chamber, Ladder & Ropes:** new rope [*cr* wanted]. **Ringers:** Clerk. **Keys:** Mr. O & Clerk.

[1]   J.C. Cox, *The Churches of Nottinghamshire* (1912), 235–6.
[2]   Samuel Lealand Oldacres (1809–76); born in Woodborough, the son of the Revd Samuel Oldacres; Emmanuel College, Cambridge, BA 1831; d. (York) 1832, p. 1833; curate of Gonalston, Notts., 1831–4; curate of Lowdham, 1834–7; master of Woodborough Free School 1837–54; vicar of Woodborough 1840–76.

Church Services: Two every Sunday. **Communions:** 4 times a year. **Average Communicants:** 10. **Baptisms:** private. **Catechising in Church:** no. **Average Churchgoers on Sundays:** about 40.

Churchyard: Pretty good – new wall built. <u>Claimed by Mr Matthews.</u>[1]

Parish Clerk: Joseph Flinders.[2] **Efficient:** [*blank*]. **Appointed:** 1852. **Salary:** £4 & Fees.

Churchwardens: Two. [*the following crossed out:*] one has absconded with some of the [Church] Rate that was granted for paying for the Clock, subscription having proved insufficient. **Properly appointed, sworn in, accounts kept, attend services, keep order etc:** [*all blank*].

Church Rate: yes. **Fund for Church Repairs:** no. **Charities:** [*blank*]. **Glebe House:** none.

Terrier: Land: 55½ acres. **Tithes:** none. **Great Tithes:** Eccles Com. **Q.A.B.:** £4. 8. 9 pr. ann. **Eccles Com (?)** £12 pr. ann. out of Prebendal Estates.

Fees: Marriages: 5s & 2s. 6d. **Churchings:** 7d. **Burials:** 6d. **Average:** Marriages: 5. Baptisms. 22. Burials: 17.

School: Free endowed School & good Master's House. The Master is appointed by the Incumbents of Woodboro, Lambley, & Epperstone. **Sunday:** Boys 30 [*cr* 40 *sub*]. Girls 20 [*cr* 12 *sub*]. **Day:** Boys 36 Girls 9. **How supported:** Endowment House - & 65 acres of land. **Master:** Rev. S. Oldacres, Incumbent.

[The following is written in pencil on the rear flyleaf of the notebook: 'Oh! says the Gardener, as he [?] down the walks, who removed that plant?, who gathered that flower? His [?] says, 'The Master,' & the Gardener holds his peace. (Woodboro')]

---

[1] Possibly Samuel Matthews, a farmer.

[2] Possibly a framework knitter, aged 49.

Index